Breakthrough Language Series

ARABIC

Nadira Auty
Rachael Harris
Clive Holes
Faculty of Oriental Studies, Cambridge University

General editor Brian Hill
Professor of Modern Languages, The University of Brighton

Series advisers
Janet Jenkins Director of Programmes, The Open Learning Foundation
Duncan Sidwell Principal Modern Languages Adviser, Leicestershire LEA

MACMILL...

First published 1992 by
THE MACMILLAN PRESS LTD
Houndmills, Basingstoke, Hampshire RG21 2XS
and London
Companies and representatives
throughout the world

Audio producer: Gerald Ramshaw, MAX II

ISBN 0–333–51611–7 paperback
ISBN 0–333–56693–9 cassettes
ISBN 0–333–56692–0 book and cassette pack

A catalogue record for this book is available
from the British Library.

Printed in Hong Kong

10 9 8 7 6 5 4 3 2
01 00 99 98 97 96 95 94

Contents

Acknowledgements

The authors owe a debt of gratitude to a number of people who gave their time freely at various stages in the production of this course. In Amman, we would like to thank Munir Awwad and his family, relatives and friends for their kind hospitality, their help in making arrangements for some of the location recordings and for their participation in the dialogues. Equally, we are indebted to the British Council staff in Amman, especially the Director Miles Roddis and his secretary Hind Samman, for allowing us to use the Council's facilities and to record some of its staff and students. The Jordanian staff at the Marriott Hotel, Amman, were also extremely co-operative and feature in some of the recordings – our thanks to them. In Britain, thanks are due to our editors at Macmillan, Kathryn Walker and Jane Wightwick, for their patience in coping with a complex manuscript and for the many useful comments they made on both its content and organisation. We also appreciated the patience and professionalism of Gerald Ramshaw who organised all aspects of the production of the recordings.

The authors and publishers wish to thank the following for permission to use copyright material: Konica Corporation for advertisement for print film; Marriott Hotels, Resorts for material from a menu and advertising publications; Picturepoint Ltd for illustrations on pages 27, 151 and 195. Al Fanoos Video for front and back video covers.

Illustrations drawn by Mahmoud Gaafar.

Every effort has been made to trace all the copyright holders, but if any have been inadvertently overlooked the publishers will be pleased to make the necessary arrangement at the first opportunity.

HOW TO USE THIS COURSE

This course has been designed to be used in self-directed study, although it can also be used as the basis for work in the conventional classroom. Take your time to read through the next few pages before you start this course. If you understand how the course works and what is expected of you, you will get that much more benefit from it.

Breakthrough Arabic has been written for anyone who wishes to understand the Arabic which is spoken in the street, the restaurant, the hotel, at work in government or company offices and on social occasions of various kinds. But the course is not merely a 'passive', listening type of course. You will learn how to respond to what you hear appropriately, and to initiate Arabic conversation yourself. The Arabic dialogues which form the core of this course were recorded on location in Amman, Jordan with native speakers talking completely naturally without any kind of script or direction in workplaces, stores, restaurants, taxis and in their homes. The variety of spoken Arabic these speakers use in the dialogues, and which is practised in the accompanying exercises, is that of Jordan. Of course, even in a relatively small country like Jordan there is a variety of accents to contend with; but since the course reflects the usage of educated people, it avoids extreme localisms and will be fully comprehensible in other parts of the Arab world. Some of the voices which you will hear in the studio-recorded exercises originate from places outside the immediate area – Jerusalem and Beirut for example – as well as Jordan. This was deliberate on our part, since you are bound to hear different Arabic accents wherever you go in the Arab world, and it is as well to get used to this early on. However, the Arabic spoken by Lebanese, Syrians and Palestinians is very similar to that of Jordanians.
    Since this course teaches spoken not written Arabic (although there is a short writing section in each unit for those who wish to become acquainted with the Arabic script), we have chosen to use a transliteration system which is a modified form of the Roman alphabet. This will take a little getting used to, since there are a number of sounds in Arabic which have no equivalent in European languages and cannot be represented conventionally. However, using a transliteration system has the advantage of allowing us to distinguish the sounds of the spoken language more consistently than using the Arabic script would, and also massively speeds up learning.

General hints to help you use the course

- Have confidence in us! Real language is complex and you will find certain things in every unit which are not explained in detail. Don't worry about this. We will build up your knowledge slowly, selecting only what is most important to know at each stage.
- Try to study regularly, but in short periods. 20–30 minutes each day is usually better than 3 1/2 hours once a week.
- To help you learn to speak, say the words and phrases out loud whenever possible.
- If you don't understand something, leave it for a while. Learning a language is a bit like doing a jigsaw or a crossword: there are many ways to tackle it and it falls into place eventually.
- Don't be afraid to write in the book and add your own notes.
- Do revise frequently. It helps to get somebody to test you – and they don't need to know Arabic.
- If you can possibly learn with somebody else you will be able to help each other and practise the language together.
- Learning Arabic may take more time than you thought. Just be patient and above all don't get angry with yourself.

Suggested study pattern

Each unit of the course consists of approximately fourteen pages in the book and ten minutes of recording. The first page of each unit will tell you what you are going to learn and suggests what we think is the best method for going about it. As you progress with the course you may find that you evolve a method of study which suits you better – that's fine, but we suggest you keep to our pattern at least for the first two or three units or you may find you are not taking full advantage of all the possibilities offered by the material.

The book contains step-by-step instructions for working through the course: when to use the book on its own, when to use the recording on its own, when to use them both together, and how to use them. On the recording our presenter Nadira will guide you through the various sections. Here is an outline of the study pattern proposed.

Study guide

At the beginning of each unit you will find a summary of what it contains. Use this as a check list and mark off the tasks as you complete them.

Dialogues and *Practise what you have learned*

In this course, the book is an accompaniment to the recordings, rather than vice versa. The presenter on the recordings, Nadira Auty (one of the authors), will guide you through the material and give advice and instructions on how to do the exercises, when to move on to the next dialogue, and so on.

Start with the first dialogue in each unit and then do the (usually three) exercises which go with it in the *Practise what you have learned* section. Then go on to the next dialogue and its exercises, and so on until you have worked through all the dialogues and *Practise what you have learned* exercises.

You will need to listen to each dialogue several times over, and look carefully at the notes and glossary provided before beginning the exercises. Try this as a method of tackling each dialogue:

● Listen without the book to get some idea of what the dialogue sounds like.
● Then study the written version carefully line by line with the notes, but without listening to the recording, in order to get a rough idea of the meaning.
● Next, listen for a second time, this time following the written version in the book at the same time as you listen.
● Finally, go back and listen again without the book.

Follow this procedure two or three times for each dialogue, until you are familiar with what it sounds like and understand the gist of what is being said, if not every single word.

Then try the two listening exercises based on the main language points of the dialogue, which follow next on the recording. Nadira will explain what you have to do before each exercise. Again, repeat each listening exercise two, three, or more times before checking your answer in the *Answer key*. The third of the three exercises after each dialogue is a speaking exercise. Usually, this involves you in taking part in a short Arabic conversation similar to the ones in the dialogues. Nadira will prompt you in English when it is your turn to speak. Pause the recording after her prompt, and try your Arabic. Release the pause button, and you will hear a correct version. Remember that practice makes perfect, and that speaking is the most difficult skill of all, so repeat, repeat and repeat again!

Key words and phrases

When you have worked through the dialogues and *Practise what you have learned* exercises in the way described, try to learn the words and expressions in the *Key words and phrases* section by heart. The words in these sections will gradually build the core of the Arabic vocabulary which you will need to be able to use.

Grammar	Even if grammar is not your particular cup of tea, study the grammar section of each unit carefully, but not until you have worked through the stages above. Though far from being a phrase book, we emphasize that this is *not* a grammar course either. The coverage of grammatical points is clear, but does not contain unnecessary details. The grammar points dealt with relate to the dialogue material in each unit, and have been deliberately selected for their usefulness in helping you understand and communicate accurately and appropriately in spoken Arabic. The terminology is deliberately non-technical as far as possible. There are exercises in this section in which you can test your understanding of the grammatical explanations given. After completing the grammar section, you may like to go back over the dialogues once more, this time looking at their grammatical structure. This will help you develop better understanding of how people structure their speech, and eventually improve your ability to do likewise accurately.

Your turn to speak

After completing the grammar section, there is a chance to speak more naturally by creating your own sentences and, eventually, your own mini-speeches. Here Nadira will put you in the position of having to make small talk to an imaginary friend at a social gathering, chat on a bus, order a meal, reserve a room, explain to a receptionist who you are, and so on. This is the most open-ended, unguided, and so demanding kind of exercise in each unit. There is no 'correct' answer: try each exercise several times over, practising the vocabulary, phrases and grammar which you have learned up to that point. Vary what you say each time you try the exercise, as far as the demands of the exercise allow. Then listen to a possible version of what you might have said. The fact that one or all of your versions may be different does not mean that they are 'wrong'.

Did you know?

The *Did you know?* section provides a little light relief, usually in the form of practical information about the manners and customs of the Arab World which anyone visiting or living there should be aware of.

Writing

Finally, work through the writing section – or skip it entirely if you are not interested in learning to read signs on shops, traffic signs, names on business cards, etc. Each unit introduces two or three letters of the alphabet, shows how they are written, and gives examples of them in words which you are likely to encounter in their written form in everyday life. The objective is to get you to recognize what you see, not necessarily to be able to write yourself. Because the grammar and vocabulary of written Arabic is different from that of the spoken kanguage, sometimes there is not an exact correspondence between how a word is spelt in Arabic and how it is usually pronounced, or how something would be expressed in written Arabic and how it would normally be said. These discrepancies are pointed out where necessary.

At the back of the book

Glossary

A complete alphabetical list of all the Arabic words which occur in the course is provided together with an English translation. There is also a shorter English–Arabic glossary consisting of just those words and phrases which occur in the *Key words and phrases* section of each unit.

Grammar summary

At the end of the book you will also find a very brief summary of all the major grammatical points.

Symbols and abbreviations

If your cassette recorder or CD player has a counter, set it to zero at the start of each unit and then write the number in the recording symbol showing the beginning of each group of dialogues. This will help you find the right place on the tape quickly when you want to wind back.

m.	masculine	pl.	plural	♦	This arrow indicates the
f.	feminine	lit.	literally		most important words and
sing.	singular				phrases.

Hints on pronunciation

There is no denying that speakers of English and other European languages experience some initial difficulty in pronouncing Arabic words correctly, and in recognising what they hear. There are a number of sounds in Arabic which we do not have in European languages, and it takes practice to master them. So do not expect that you will get a perfect pronunciation immediately. The secret is to listen carefully and imitate what you hear – and practise, practise, practise! Arabs are extremely tolerant of foreigners' mispronunciations, and are usually flattered that a foreigner has tried to learn their language at all. In any case, the context in which you use Arabic means that an Arab will usually understand what you say even if you do not pronounce it perfectly every time.

Below, you will find a simple guide on how to pronounce the difficult sounds. The other sounds are more or less similar to English. In a short time you will be able to dispense with this guide, and in any case the best advice is to listen carefully to the native speakers on the tapes, and imitate the way they speak.

Consonants

j as in **dajaaj** chicken. The **j** is usually pronounced like the 's' in English 'leisure' and 'pleasure' or the 'j' in the French 'je'. Some speakers, however, pronounce it like the 'j' in English 'judge'. Either pronunciation is acceptable.

' as in **sa'al** he asked. This sound exists in English, but usually as a replacement for another letter in some accents. It is like the catch in the throat when words are pronounced with a cockney accent: 'butter' ('bu'er') or 'put it' ('pu'i''). In Arabic it can occur in any position in a word, for example **'aal** he said, **y'uul** he says, **wara'** paper.

r as in **rajul** man. This is a 'rolled r', made with the tip of the tongue vibrating against the back of the upper front teeth. It is heard in some European languages such as Italian ('ragazza'). In Arabic it occurs in all positions in a word, for example, **raas** head, **barra** outside, **'amr** command.

x as in **xuruuj** exit, **duxuul** entrance. This sound is similar to the Scottish pronunciation of 'ch' in 'Loch Ness', or the 'ch' in German 'Achtung' or in the composer's name 'Bach'.

gh as in **gharb** west, **lugha** language. This sound is similar to that made in the throat when gargling, or to the gutteral 'r' in the Parisian French pronunciation of 'grand'.

There are a number of so-called 'emphatic' consonants in Arabic: **S, T, D** and **Z** (or **DH**). In each case, the tip of the tongue is in the same place as for the corresponding unemphatic consonants **s, t, d** and **z** – touching the back of the upper front teeth – but the rest of the tongue is flattened and pressed against the roof of the mouth. This produces a much duller, heavier sound than in the case of the unemphatic consonants. It is difficult to illustrate the difference from English, but the somewhat heavier sounding

4

'ss' at the end of 'toss' compared to the lighter sounding 'ss' at the end of 'kiss' gives some idea of the difference between **S** and **s**, and that between the 't' in 'hot' and the 't' in 'bit' between **T** and **t** respectively. But this is only an approximation of the difference. Listen carefully to the speakers on the tape when words come up involving these consonants. It is important to get used to recognising and producing the so-called 'emphatics', as some words are distinguished in meaning only by the fact that they have emphatic versus unemphatic consonants.

9 as in **9arabi** Arab, Arabic. This is one of the most difficult consonants, represented by a figure 'nine' as there is nothing remotely like it in English. It is produced by constricting the top of the windpipe, and if you are pronouncing it correctly you should sound slightly as if you are being strangled! It is a common consonant in Arabic, and can occur anywhere in a word, for example, **9aalam** world, **si9ir** price, **baa9** he sold.

H is another difficult one, and is a kind of strong, hoarse-sounding version of **h** which is similar to the hoarse expulsion of breath which is sometimes made by people breathing on glass or spectacle lenses before cleaning them. Again, there is a feeling of constriction at the top of the throat when pronouncing **H**, just as there is with **9**, except that **H** is a voiceless sound in which your vocal chords do not vibrate. Examples: **Hammaam** bathroom, **baHr** sea, **milH** salt.

Variations

The above are the main consonant sounds in Arabic. However, there are one or two more which you will also hear, especially in the speech of educated people because of the influence on their speech of literary Arabic. Less educated people tend to use these sounds less:

q, as in **qur'aan** Koran, is a sound which is usually found in 'literary' words which have been borrowed into spoken Arabic. None the less it is quite common even in the speech of uneducated people. It is a little like the 'k' in English 'bulk' or the 'ck' in 'hock', but further back in the throat. In many very common everyday words, **q** or **'** occur as variants, for example, **funduq** or **fundu'** hotel, **suuq** or **suu'** market, **waqt** or **wa't** time. In these same words, you will hear some Jordanians, especially if they come from outside the main towns, use a **g** like English 'g' in 'go': **fundug, suug, wagt**.

th like the English 'th' in 'thin' or 'bath', as in **thalaatha** three. This is a more 'educated' (and, paradoxically, a more 'Bedouin') pronunciation which replaces **t** in some words, and **s** in others.

dh, as in **haadha** (this), is like the English 'th' in 'that' or 'bathe'. **dh**, which again is a 'literary' pronunciation is normally pronounced as a **d** in less educated or more relaxed speech in some words (**haada** this) and as a **z** in others (**haaza**).

Single and doubled consonants

Consonants in Arabic can occur singly or doubled, and it is very important to lengthen the pronunciation of a consonant which is doubled, as its meaning will be different from just a single consonant. So, for example, **mara** means 'woman' but **marra** (pronounced **mar-ra**) means 'time' in the sense of 'two times, three times'. So **hal-mara** means 'this woman', but **hal-marra** means 'this time'; **sabab** means 'reason, cause', but **sabbab** means 'he caused'.

Long vowels

The long vowels, like doubled consonants, are written double in the transliteration and should be pronounced approximately twice as long as single ones:

aa is something like the vowel sound in southern British pronunciation of 'wear', 'tear', 'care', for example **baab** door, **talaata** three. If emphatic consonants come before or after it, **aa** has a much heavier sound. So **Saab** (he hit[the target]) sounds like the British English pronunciation of the Swedish automobile manufacturers 'Saab'.

ii is like the vowel in English 'tea', except it is held longer.

uu is a vowel something like that in 'cool' or a longer version of the vowel in the English 'sue'.

ee is similar to the vowel in English 'bate' or 'nail'.

oo is something like the British English pronunciation of the vowel in 'bore', 'law', for example, **yoom** day.

aw is a diphthong like the vowel in 'cow', for example, **Hawl** about, around.

ay is a diphthong like the vowel in 'pay', for example, **rayyaH** he relieved, put at ease.

TALKING ABOUT YOURSELF

You will learn

- to greet people
- to talk about names, addresses and phone numbers
- to talk about where you're from
- the numbers 1-10

To keep track, mark the tasks below as you complete them.

Before you start, make sure you have read the Introduction, pages 1–6. It explains how *Breakthrough Arabic* works and gives some helpful tips on how to study.

Study guide

Dialogue 1 + Practise what you have learned
Dialogue 2 + Practise what you have learned
Dialogue 3 + Practise what you have learned
Dialogue 4 + Practise what you have learned
Dialogue 5 + Practise what you have learned
Key words and phrases
Grammar
Your turn to speak
Did you know?
Writing

Remember to listen to your recording before you look at each unit. Nadira will guide you through the unit.

Dialogues

1 *Munir meets Clive for the first time*

Munir	marHaba yaa ax.
Clive	marHaba.
Munir	tismaH lii?
Clive	tfaDDal...

- **marHaba** hello. This is one of many greeting phrases we will meet. It is informal.

- **yaa ax** (lit. O brother) is an informal but polite way of addressing a man who is approximately the same age as yourself. To a woman you would say **yaa uxt** (O sister).

- **tismaH lii?** (lit. do you permit me...?) This phrase is used to a man if you're asking him if he minds what you're about to do (e.g. sit at his table in a café, smoke a cigarette, come into a room). To a woman you would say **tismaHii lii?**

- **tfaDDal** (lit. be so kind) This is the reply meaning ' please do!' when someone asks your permission to do something. Or it can simply be used as an encouraging phrase when offering food, drink, a lift, a chair, etc. To a woman you would say **tfaDDali**.

2 *Has Clive been in Amman long?*

Munir	mbayyin HaDirtak mish min sukkaan 9ammaan... ajnabi...
Clive	ee... ajnabi... ingliizi.
Munir	ahlan wa sahlan fiik.
Clive	ahlan biik.
Munir	zamaan jiit 9ala 9ammaan?
Clive	ana jiit min yoomeen bas.

mbayyin	it seems	**zamaan**	a (long) time
mish	not	**ana**	I
min	of, from; **min** ... ... ago	**yoom**	day
sukkaan	inhabitants, population	**bas**	only
ingliizi	English(man)		

- **mbayyin HaDirtak mish min sukkaan 9ammaan** it seems you're not from Amman (lit. it seems your presence not from the inhabitants of Amman). **HaDirtak** (your presence) is a polite way of saying 'you' to a man.

- **ee** yes. More common expressions for 'yes' are **ah, na9am** and **aywa**. 'No' is **laa**.

- **ajnabi** foreign(er). This form of the word is used for a male. A woman foreigner is **ajnabiyya**. Similarly, an English woman is **ingliiziyya**; an American woman **amriikiyya**.

- **ahlan wa sahlan**. This is a common informal greeting or welcome, to which may be added **fiik** or **biik** (to you) for a man, **fiiki** or **biiki** for a woman. The usual reply is **ahlan biik** or **ahlan fiik**.

- **zamaan jiit 9ala 9ammaan?** have you been in Amman long? (lit. [long] time you came to Amman?). The verb **jiit** itself means 'you (or I) came' without it being necessary to specify **ana** (I) or **inta** (you).

- **min yoomeen bas** only two days ago (lit. from two days only). The **-een** ending added to **yoom** (day) means 'two', so we have **shahar** (month) and **shahreen** (two months). **jiit min shahreen** would thus mean 'I came two months ago'.

Practise what you have learned

1 Listen to the recording. Which of the speakers is talking to a man and which to a woman? (Answers p.18)

2 You will hear three short dialogues. Indicate which of the pictures matches each of them? (Answers p.18)

(a) **(b)** **(c)** **(d)**

3 Your turn to speak. Here are two short dialogues for you to take part in. In the first dialogue, listen to the first speaker, then press the pause button and give the appropriate answer. You will then hear the correct version. Then move on to the next part of the dialogue and do the same. In the second dialogue, Nadira will guide you. After she speaks, press the pause button and respond. Release the pause button and you will hear the correct version.

4 Sentences **(a)** to **(e)** below are things which might be said to you. Which of the replies numbered **1** to **6** is the appropriate reply to each? Write the numbers in the boxes, and when you have finished check your answers by listening to the recording.

    (a) *Man* ana min 9ammaan ☐

    (b) *Woman* marHaba ☐

    (c) *Woman* ahlan wa sahlan ☐

    (d) *Woman* tismaHii lii ☐

    (e) *Man* ahlan wa sahlan ☐

    1 marHaba   2 ahlan wa sahlan   3 ahlan wa sahlan fiik
    4 ahlan wa sahlan fiiki   5 tfaDDal   6 tfaDDali

5 Listen and mark off the box to indicate which country the speakers are from (Answers p.18)

	UK	USA	Saudi Arabia	Germany	France	Lebanon
1						
2						
3						
4						
5						

6 Your turn to speak. Nadira will guide you through your part in the conversation and give you a correct version.

Dialogues

3 *Names*

Munir	ana ismi muniir 9awwaad... Hadirtak shu l-ism il-kariim?
Clive	ismi Clive... Clive Holes.
Munir	il-baraka, ahlan wa sahlan fiik.
Clive	ahlan wa sahlan.

shu what
il- the
kariim noble
baraka blessing

> ◆ **ana ismi...** my name is... (lit. I, my name...). **isim** (name) becomes 'my name' by adding **-i** at the end. However, whenever **-i** is added to a word which ends with consonant-**i**-consonant (such as **isim**) the **i** is dropped. **isim + i** therefore become **ismi**. The same happens before a word beginning with a vowel, as in **il-ism il-kariim** (see next note).
>
> ◆ **HaDirtak shu l-ism il-kariim?** what is your name? (lit. your presence, what the name the noble?). A more informal way of saying the same thing would be simply **shu ismak?** (lit. what your name?) in which the **-ak** signifies 'your' when addressing a man. Add **-ik** instead of **-ak** if addressing a woman.
>
> ◆ **il-baraka** (lit. the [God's] blessing) a polite response to the fact that the other speaker had answered his question about his name.

Practise what you have learned

7 Complete the conversation between Nadya and Mahmoud using the words below. Words may be used more than once. (Answers p.18)

ismi   fiiki   ismik   ahlan wa sahlan

Mahmoud marHaba. ana _____ maHmuud. shu _____ ?

Nadya _____ naadya.

Mahmoud ahlan wa sahlan _____ .

Nadya _____ .

8 Names are hard enough to catch when you're introduced to someone from your own country. Try to write down the names of the people you will hear on the recording. It will help if you read the section on names in *Did you know?* Don't be discouraged if you find this hard. Check the answers on p.18 and then listen several times until you feel clear about the relation between what's on the paper and what you hear.

9 Your turn to speak. Take part in the conversation, playing the role of Peter or (if you are female) Rita Smith. There is no guidance in English, but after each of your turns you will hear a correct version.

Dialogues

4 *And what about children?*

Munir	mitzawwij batSawwar?
Clive	ee, mitzawwij u...
Munir	u 9indak iwlaad?
Clive	ee, waladeen.
Munir	kam walad maashaallah waladeen?
Clive	waladeen.
Munir	kbaar willa Sghaar?
Clive	Sghaar.
Munir	allah yixallii lak iyyaahum inshaallah.
Clive	allah yixalliik.

u and
9ind with, at
walad boy (pl) **iwlaad** boys; children
kbiir big, old (pl) **kbaar**
Sghiir small, young (pl) **Sghaar**
willa or

> **mitzawwij batSawwar** (you're) married, I imagine? The word for 'you' (**inta**) is omitted as it's obvious from the context who is being addressed.
>
> **9indak iwlaad** do you have any children? **9ind** literally means 'with, at' so this phrase says 'with you children?' This is the normal way of forming equivalent phrases to English sentences involving 'have' signifying possession or ownership: **9indi iwlaad** I have children (lit. with me children).
>
> **waladeen** two boys, see **yoomeen** 'two days' in Dialogue 2. The word for girl is **bint**.
>
> **kam walad?** how many children? (lit. how many boy?). **kam** (how many) is followed by a singular noun.
>
> **maashaallah** what God has willed. This is said when mentioning children or important possessions to protect them from 'the evil eye'.
>
> **kbaar willa Sghaar?** grown-up ones or small ones?
>
> **allah yixallii lak iyyaahum inshaallah** may God preserve them for you, if God wills. This phrase is another example of the polite conversational pleasantries so typical of Arabic conversation, and is a way of wishing a parent long life to support and enjoy his children. The answer **allah yixalliik** (God preserve you) is the standard polite response.

Practise what you have learned

10 Listen to the conversation between Salim and Suzanne and indicate if the following are true or false. (Answers p.18)

   (a) Salim is from Lebanon

   (b) Salim thinks Suzanne is from Amman

   (c) Suzanne is a foreigner

   (d) Suzanne is from America

   (e) Salim is a Jordanian

11 Your turn to speak. On the recording you will hear the same conversation again with Suzanne's part left out. Take her place, putting in the appropriate information about yourself. After each turn, you will hear Nadira give a possible answer.

Dialogues

5 *Iman is applying for a job*

Official shu l-ism il-kariim ballah?
Iman ismi iimaan maHmuud.
Official ahlan wa sahlan... shu l-9unwaan ballah, ween saakna?
Iman saakna fi jabal 9ammaan id-duwwaar is-saadis jaanib funduq
9amra.
Official Tayyib, 'addeesh il-9umur ballah?
Iman waaHad u talaatiin sana.

jabal 9ammaan a district in Amman
Tayyib OK

♦ **ballah** by God. This expression has little actual meaning, and is used as a way of making direct questions sound more polite.

♦ **shu l-9unwaan?** what's your address? (lit. what the address?). It is quite common in such questions to use 'the' instead of 'your' in Arabic, e.g. **shu l-isim?** what's your name? (lit. what the name?).

♦ **ween saakna?** where do you live? (lit. where living?). There is no need for the official to use the word 'you' (**inti** for a woman) as it is obvious from the context whom he's talking to. He would say **ween saakin?** to a man.

id-duwwaar is-saadis the Sixth Circle (lit. the circle the sixth). Most Amman residents use the seven traffic circles which form a semi-circular chain around downtown Amman as navigational points.

♦ **jaanib funduq 9amra** next to the Amra Hotel (lit. side [of] hotel [of] Amra). **jaanib** (by the side of) can also be pronounced **jamb**.

♦ **'addeesh il-9umur?** how old are you? (lit. how much the age?). Again, it is not necessary to say 'your' age in Arabic.

♦ **waaHad u talaatiin sana** thirty one (lit. one and thirty year)

Practise what you have learned

12 Listen to the recording. Can you fill in the blanks below, one for Farid and one for Hala? Look at the numbers in the list of key words. (Answers p.18)
Note: **shaari9 fu'aad** Fuad St   **Tarii' is-salaam** Peace Rd

(a) *Full name* Farid _____ (b) *Full name* Hala _____

No. & street _____   No. & street _____

City _____   City _____

Tel. no. _____   Tel. no. _____

13 Listen to Salwa talking about herself. Fill in the gaps in the shorter version below. (Answers p.18)
Note: **il-burSa** the stock market.

Salwa ana min _____ . _____ saakna fi _____ .

il-9unwaan _____ il-burSa. u ana _____ .

14 Your turn to speak. You're staying in the Palace Hotel (**funduq balaas**) in Prince Muhammad (**il-amiir mHammad**) Street. Explain to the taxi driver where you're staying, in response to his questions. Nadira will give a correct version.

Key words and phrases

To learn

marHaba	hello
tfaDDal(i)	please do
tismaH(ii) lii	do you mind if I...?
ingliizi (yya)	English
amriiki (yya)	American
ana	I
isim	name
ahlan wa sahlan	welcome, hello
ahlan fiik(i) or biik(i)	hello (reply)
na9am/aywa (or ee)	yes
laa	no
inshaallah	God willing
u	and
willa	or
mniiH	nice, good
fi	in
hoon	here
waaHad	one
itneen	two
talaata	three
arba9a	four
xamsa	five
sitta	six
sab9a	seven
tamaanya	eight
tis9a	nine
9ashra	ten

To understand

HaDirtak (HaDirtik)	you, polite (to a woman)
shu l-ism il-kariim?	what's your name? (polite)
ween saakin? (sakna)	where do you live? (to a woman)
shu l-9unwaan?	what's your address?

Grammar

'Is'/'are' sentences   In Arabic the verb 'to be' is not generally used when talking about a situation in the present. So we have **ana ingliizi** I am English, **ana min 9ammaan** I am from Amman, **ana hoon** I am here and **inta ingliizi** you are English etc.

mish before a word makes it negative, e.g. **ana mish ingliizi** I'm not English. To ask a question, change the intonation of the sentence by raising your voice at the end, e.g. **inta ingliizi?** Are you English?, **inta min 9ammaan?** Are you from Amman?

15   Listen to the recording. Is Nadira asking a question or making a statement? Underline the one you think. (Answers p.18)

(a) statement/question	**(b)** statement/question
(c) statement/question	**(d)** statement/question
(e) statement/question	**(f)** statement/question

'The' and 'a'   **il-** means 'the'. It is used both with nouns, e.g. **il-isim** the name, **il-9unwaan** the address, and with adjectives, e.g. **il-kariim** the noble (one), **il-ajnabi** the foreign (one). If a noun has **il-** (i.e. if it is *definite*) any adjective that goes with it must have **il-** too, e.g. **il-ism il-kariim** the noble name, **il-9unwaan il-9arabi** the Arabic address.

The **i** of **il-** drops if it is after a vowel (a, i, u), as in **shu l-isim?** What's (your) name? The **l** of **il-** also changes if the word that follows it begins with one of the following letters:

t, T, d, D, s, S, z, Z, sh, l, n, r, th, dh, DH

When **il-** comes before one of these letters, the **l** of **il-** becomes the same as that letter, as in **id-duwwaar** the roundabout, **is-saadis** the sixth. Don't try to learn this list of letters now, but you may like to refer back to it as you learn new words. It may help you to remember which letters affect **il-** in this way if you know that they are pronounced with the tongue on or just behind the teeth.

There is no word for 'a' or 'an' in Arabic so we have, for example, **isim** a name, and **walad** a boy. Adjectives follow the noun, e.g. **isim 9arabi** an Arab name, **walad Sghiir** a little boy.

16   Fill in the gaps below with the right form of **il-** (or nothing!) to give the Arabic phrase the same meaning as the English. (Answers p.18)

(a) _____ isim _____ amriiki   the American name

(b) _____ isim _____ ajnabi   a foreign name

(c) _____ sana _____ saadisa   the sixth year

(d) _____ walad _____ Sghiir   the small boy

(e) _____ iwlaad _____ Sghaar   small children

(f) _____ iwlaad _____ kbaar   the big children

Your turn to speak

In this section it's your turn to speak again but the exercises here are open-ended, i.e. you can adapt them to suit your own situation. On the recording there is a model version of what you could say, but this is just a suggestion.

17 Give a short speech about yourself including all the information you can in Arabic: your name, nationality, where you live, etc. Compare it with the one Nadira gives. If you are unsure, listen to Nadira first.

18 Take part in the conversation which starts with you saying hello and then asking a man if you can sit at his table in a café. How you reply to the rest is up to you. This time a model version will come after you have finished your conversation. Start with **marHaba** hello.

Answers

Practise what you have learned

Exercise 1 (a) to a woman (b) to a man (c) to a woman (d) to a man

Exercise 2 Conversation 1: (d) 2: (a) 3: (c)

Exercise 4 (a): 2 (b):1 (c): 4 (d): 6 (e): 3

Exercise 5 1. USA 2. Lebanon 3. Saudi Arabia 4. France 5. UK

Exercise 7 - marHaba ana ismi maHmuud. shu ismik?
- ismi naadya.
- ahlan wa sahlan fiiki!
- ahlan wa sahlan!

Exercise 8 (a) sahar 9ali il-Halabi (b) suheer (c) 9awaD muHammad 9aaTif (d) umm saalim and ra'fat

Exercise 10 (a) true (b) false (c) true (d) false (e) false

Exercise 12 Farid Salama Mursi   Hala Mustafa Nijim
4 Fuad St   5 Peace Rd
Irbid   Amman
Tel: 789312   Tel: 653824

Exercise 13 Salwa: ana min il-urdun u saakna fi 9amman. il-9unwaan shaari9 il-burSa, u ana sikirteera.

Grammar

Exercise 15 (a) statement (b) question (c) question (d) statement (e) question (f) question

Exercise 16 (a) il-ism il-amriiki (b) isim ajnabi (c) is-sana s-saadisa (d) il-walad iS-Sghiir (e) iwlaad Sghaar (f) il-iwlaad il-kbaar

Did you know?

Arabic names

Full formal personal names, male and female, consist of three parts: given name, father's name and grandfather's name. e.g. **aHmad 9ali SaaliH** Ahmed Ali Saleh, **maryam 9iisa xaalid** Maryam Isa Khaled. In addition, tribal names are still used in the conservative countries of the Arabian peninsula, and in the desert and rural areas of Syria, Jordan and Iraq, but not usually elsewhere in the Arab World.

Egyptians commonly use just their first two names (given name and father's name) and the third (grandfather's) is used only when thay are asked for their full name (on government forms, etc.). In Syria, Jordan, Palestine, and Lebanon, on the other hand, most people use a family name (usually designating place of origin or occupation) after the first given name, in exactly the same way as we do, e.g. **naadira xuuri** Nadira Khoury, where **naadira** is the given name and **xuuri** (meaning 'priest') the family name, **9umar najjaar** Omar Najjar (**najjaar** means 'carpenter'), **aHmad Tarabulsi** Ahmed Tarabulsi (**Tarabulsi** means 'from Tripoli').

It is common practice in Jordan, Syria and Palestine to call a parent 'Father/Mother of X' where X is the eldest son in the family, e.g. **abu Hasan** Hasan's father, to a man whose eldest son is called **Hasan**, whatever his own given name. His wife would be called **umm Hasan** Hasan's mother. This practice is a sign of respect, rather than of familiarity.

Writing

It is not necessary to be able to read Arabic in order to speak it. In fact, learning to read Arabic involves a lot more than just learning a new alphabet and writing system, because the grammar and vocabulary of the written language differ considerably from the spoken. Therefore, because this is essentially a spoken course, the basics of the writing system are introduced simply to enable you to read such written Arabic as you are likely to encounter and need to be able to read in everyday life in any Arab city: store, traffic and street signs, names and numbers on business cards, entries in telephone directories, restaurant menus, etc.

Let's start with some basic facts about the Arabic alphabet and script:

- the Arabic script goes from right to left;
- written Arabic words consist of consonants and long vowels (if they occur) only. Short vowels are not written (although of course they are pronounced!);
- Arabic words are written cursively (i.e. the consonants which form them are joined up) even in printing;
- the shape of each consonant changes slightly, depending on whether it (a) stands on its own, (b) comes at the beginning of a word, (c) comes in the middle of a word, (d) comes at the end of a word.

We will start our introduction to individual letters of the alphabet in Unit 2.

Transcription		Letter		Transcription		Letter	
'	=	أ	(1)	D	=	ض	(15)
b	=	ب	(2)	T	=	ط	(16)
t	=	ت	(3)	DH or Z	=	ظ	(17)
th	=	ث	(4)	9	=	ع	(18)
j	=	ج	(5)	gh	=	غ	(19)
H	=	ح	(6)	f	=	ف	(20)
x	=	خ	(7)	q	=	ق	(21)
d	=	د	(8)	k	=	ك	(22)
dh	=	ذ	(9)	l	=	ل	(23)
r	=	ر	(10)	m	=	م	(24)
z	=	ز	(11)	n	=	ن	(25)
s	=	س	(12)	h	=	ه	(26)
sh	=	ش	(13)	w	=	و	(27)
S	=	ص	(14)	y	=	ي	(28)

You will learn

- to introduce yourself
- to ask and reply to simple introductions
- to ask and reply to simple questions about places
- the numbers 10 - 20

Study guide

Dialogue 1 + Practise what you have learned
Dialogue 2 + Practise what you have learned
Dialogue 3 + Practise what you have learned
Dialogue 4 + Practise what you have learned
Key words and phrases
Grammar
Your turn to speak
Did you know?
Writing

A street in downtown Amman

Dialogues

1 *John meets Yousif in a café in the middle of Amman*

Yousif	marHaba.
John	marHabteen.
Yousif	il-ax ajnabi?
John	wallaahi ingliizi.
Yousif	ingliizi... min briiTaanya?
John	min briiTaanya.
Yousif	kam Saar lak hoon bi l-urdun...? kam yoom?
John	wallaahi ana Saar lii bas thalaatht iyyaam.
Yousif	thalaatht iyyaam.

briiTaanya Britain
Saar to become, happen
lak to you
lii to me
bi in (alternative to **fi**)
il-urdun Jordan
thalaatht iyyaam three days
bas only, just

---

marHabteen two welcomes! This is a common reply to **marHaba**. One can also say, with the same meaning, **ahleen**.

il-ax ajnabi? are you a foreigner? (lit. The brother [is] foreign?). The use of **il-ax** is polite, but a bit less formal than **HaDirtak**, which we met in Unit 1.

wallaahi by God. This is used to emphasize the truth of what one says. It is not a very strong oath.

kam Saar lak hoon... how long have you been here? (lit. how much has become to you here?) to which the answer is **ana Saar lii bas thalaatht iyyaam** I've been here just three days (lit. I has become to me only three days). So 'I've been...' is **Saar lii...** and 'you've been...' is **Saar lak...** when talking about time spent in a place.

thalaatht iyyaam three days. An alternative, slightly Bedouin-sounding, to the city-dweller's **talaat tiyyaam,** with the same meaning (see Grammar, Unit 3).

Practise what you have learned

1   Listen to the recording and mark off the correct answer. (Answers p.32)

     1   Where is the man from?
     (a)   Jordan
     (b)   Britain
     (c)   France

     2   How long has he been in Jordan?
     (a)   five days
     (b)   ten days
     (c)   two days

     3   He is
     (a)   married
     (b)   single
     (c)   don't know

     4   He has
     (a)   three children
     (b)   two children
     (c)   no children

2   You will have to learn the numbers 1 - 20 (They are in the 'Key words' section, p.30). Listen to the recording and cross out the numbers on your bingo card as the caller calls them out. What numbers are left? (Answer p.32)

6		10		
20		5		2
	4	13	19	
9	16	12	15	

3   Your turn to speak. In this exercise you will take part in a short conversation, consisting of a greeting, saying where you come from, and saying how long you have been in Jordan. You will be prompted. Listen and respond after the prompt. You will then hear the model.

Dialogues

2 *Names?*

John	ismak il-kariim?
Yousif	ismi yuusif.
John	yuusif... il-ism il-kaamil?
Yousif	yuusif al-majaali.
John	yuusif al-majaali.
Yousif	na9am u ismak iza mumkin?
John	ismi John.
Yousif	John... wi l-ism il kaamil?
John	John Brown.
Yousif	John Brown... ah, haadha isim jamiil.

iza mumkin please (lit. if possible)

> **ismak il-kariim?** your dear name? (lit. your name the dear?). A polite way of asking; an alternative to **il-ism il-kariim** which we met in Unit 1.
>
> **il-ism il kaamil?** your full name?
>
> **haadha isim jamiil** that's a nice name (lit. this [is a] name nice).

Practise what you have learned

4   Listen to the recording and mark off the correct answers. An official is asking a woman some questions. What does he want to know?

(a) the woman's name

(b) the woman's nationality

(c) the woman's address

(d) the woman's job

(Answers p.32)

5   Listen to the conversation. A Jordanian woman is speaking with another woman. Mark off the answers that the other woman gives.

marHaba   ahlan
aywa min il-urdun   laa, min suurya
min 9ashar tiyyaam   aywa zamaan

(Answers p.32)

6   Your turn to speak. You are going to take part in a conversation. Respond to the questions. Nadira will prompt you. Give your answers aloud in Arabic, then check by listening to the model version. Note **ziyaara** trip, visit; **ziyaarit 9amal** business trip.

Dialogues

3 *And what do you think of Jordan?*

Yousif	keef ra'ayt il-urdun? inshaallah kwaysa.
John	kwaysa, kwaysa, jamiila jiddan.
Yousif	ah, tamaam... wa n-naas huna? in-naas?
John	kwaysiin.
Yousif	kwaysiin... tikram!
John	inta min... aSlan min 9ammaan?
Yousif	laa, ana aSlan min ir-riif, min xaarij 9ammaan... ya9ni badawi.
John	badawi?
Yousif	na9am.

keef (or **kiif**) how
kwayyis nice (f. **kwaysa**)
jiddan very
tamaam excellent! great!
wa and (alternative to **u,** same meaning)
naas people
huna here (alternative to **hoon,** same meaning)
tikram thank you, you are too kind
inta you (m. sing.), **inti** you (f. sing.)
aSlan originally
riif countryside, country area
xaarij outside
badawi Bedouin (i.e. originally from the desert)

> ♦ **keef ra'ayt il-urdun?** what do you think of Jordan? (lit. how have you seen Jordan?). Note that, as he is talking to a foreigner here, Yousif tries to speak more 'correctly' than he normally would, and uses the very formal-sounding word **ra'ayt** for 'you think, see' rather than the more colloquial **shuft**. 'What do you think of...?' is normally **keef shuft...?** which is the verb you should use when asking someone's opinion about something. For example, meeting a man who has just returned from Britain you would say **keef shuft briiTaanya?** what did you think of Britain? To a woman you would say **keef shufti briiTaanya?** (the -i is for the feminine).

> ♦ **inshaallah kwaysa** nice, I hope (lit. if God wills, nice). Yousif answers his own question before John gets the chance to speak. **inshaallah** is used when you're talking about anything that's going to happen in the future (in this case, John giving his opinion of Jordan). **kwaysa** is the feminine of **kwayyis** (note the -a on the end which signifies the feminine) and is used here because Jordan, like most countries, is grammatically feminine in Arabic.

> **kwaysiin** nice. This is the plural of **kwayyis**, used because **naas** (people) is a plural.

> ♦ **ya9ni** literally this means 'it means'. It is used like the English 'I mean' or 'that is' in explaining something.

Practise what you have learned

7 Choose the correct question from the box to complete the dialogue. Then check with the recording for the model version.

> keef shufti l-urdun?
> inti min landan?
> u in-naas?

Samira _____ ?
Helen jamiila jiddan.

Samira _____ ?
Helen kwaysiin

Samira _____ ?
Helen laa, ana mish min landan, min liidz.

8 Your turn to speak. You are going to take part in a conversation. Respond to the questions. Nadira will guide you. Give your answers in Arabic, then listen to the correct version.

The Gilead Mountains, Northern Jordan

Dialogues

4 Where _exactly_ is Yousif from?

John	min ween bi DH-DHabT ya9ni?
Yousif	min sharq il-urdun.
John	min sharq il-urdun.
Yousif	na9am min sharq il-urdun.
John	u ism il-balad, law samaHt?
Yousif	ism il-balad al-muwaqqar.
John	al-muwaqqar.
Yousif	na9am, hiyya balad Saghiira.
John	balad Saghiira.
Yousif	laysat kabiira, na9am... haadha... wa inta, awwal marra fi l-urdun? awwal ziyaara ilak?
John	awwal ziyaara.

bi DH-DHabT exactly
balad town/village
law samaHt if you'd be so kind
al-muwaqqar al-Muwaqqar (name of a small town 10 miles east of Amman)
hiyya it, she
laysat it is not
awwal first
marra time

> **min ween bi DH-DHabT?** from where, exactly?
>
> ▸ **sharq il-urdun** east Jordan (lit. east [of] Jordan). Similarly, **shmaal il-urdun** north Jordan, **jnuub il-urdun** south Jordan. The West Bank is usually referred to as **iD-Diffa** the Bank or **iD-Diffa l-gharbiyya** the West Bank.
>
> ▸ **ism il-balad** the name of the town.
>
> ▸ **law SamaHt** (to a woman **law samaHti**) is used to show politeness when you ask someone to do something or answer a question.
>
> ▸ **hiyya balad Saghiira** it's a small town. **balad** 'town' is feminine, hence the use of **hiyya** 'she' and the **-a** feminine ending of **Saghiir** 'small'. Yousif pronounces the word **Saghiira** rather than the normal **Sghiira** because he is speaking carefully.
>
> **laysat** it is not. Again, this is a very 'correct' form of Arabic. In more relaxed circumstances, Yousif would simply have said **mish kbiira** for 'not big'.

Practise what you have learned

9 Listen to the recording first and then fill in the blanks using the words from the box.

> Sghiira, inta, marHabteen, kbiira, tfaDDal, briiTaanya

Ahmad marHaba.

John _____.

Ahmad tismaH lii?

John _____. HaDirtak min il-urdun?

Ahmad aywa, u _____.

John ana min briiTaanya.

Ahmad min ween bi DH-DHabt fi _____?

John min biirminghaam.

Ahmad biirminghaam balad _____?

John laa mish Sghiira, _____.

10 In this exercise you are going to practise numbers. Say the following numbers and then check with the recording.

(a)	2	(b)	5	(c)	10	(d)	15	(e)	17
(f)	20	(g)	11	(h)	3	(i)	19		

11 In this exercise you are meeting a foreigner. Find out:

(a) his name

(b) where exactly he is from

(c) if this is his first visit to Jordan

This time you will not be prompted. Listen for the responses to your questions. Then you will hear the whole dialogue. Start with the phrase **shu isim HaDirtak?** (Answers p.32)

Key words and phrases

To learn

min briiTaanya	from Britain
min amriika	from America
min il-urdun	from Jordan
yoom, (pl) iyyaam	day
yoomeen bas	only two days
kam	how much, how many
kwayyis, (f.) kwaysa, (pl) kwaysiin	nice, fine
jamiil	beautiful, pretty
jiddan	very
iHda9sh	eleven
itna9sh	twelve
talaatta9sh	thirteen
arba9ta9sh	fourteen
xamasta9sh	fifteen
sitta9sh	sixteen
saba9ta9sh	seventeen
tamaanta9sh	eighteen
tisa9ta9sh	nineteen
9ishriin	twenty
kbiir, (pl) kbaar	big, old
Sghiir, (pl) Sghaar	small, young
walad, (pl) iwlaad	boy, child
iza mumkin	if possible, please
awwal	first
taani	second; other

To understand

balad	town, village (sometimes country)
kam yoom Saar lak (lik) hoon?	how long have you been here?
min ween bi DH-DHabT?	where exactly (are you) from?
awwal ziyaara	first visit
kiif shuft il-urdun?	what do you think of Jordan?

Grammar

Adjectives

Adjectives in Arabic have three forms – masculine, feminine and plural. The feminine is formed from the masculine in most cases by adding **-a**. The plural of <u>some</u> adjectives is formed from the feminine (without the **-a**) by adding **-iin**. For example:

masculine	feminine	plural	
kwayyis	**kwaysa**	**kwaysiin**	nice, fine
saakin	**saakna**	**saakniin**	living
kaamil	**kaamla**	**kaamliin**	full, complete

Notice that in words like **kaamil** and **saakin**, in which the stressed part of the word is the **-aa-** vowel, the **i** drops out when the feminine or plural ending is added.

Noun-adjective phrases

The adjective in Arabic agrees with the noun in gender. If the noun is masculine, the adjective is masculine. If the noun is feminine, the adjective is feminine. Feminine nouns usually end in **-a**, or are feminine by meaning (e.g. **bint** girl). For example:

masculine	**isim** (m.) **jamiil** (m.)	a beautiful name
feminine	**ziyaara** (f.) **Tawiila** (f.)	a long visit

With nouns denoting plural human beings the adjective is plural. For example:

naas (pl) **kwaysiin** (pl)   nice people
in-naas il-kwaysiin   the nice people

12 Give the feminine and the plural of the following adjectives. (Answers p.32)

masculine	feminine	plural	
Hilw	_____	_____	nice, sweet
ta9baan	_____	_____	tired
9aTshaan	_____	_____	thirsty
za9laan	_____	_____	sad
ju9aan	_____	_____	hungry
mabsuuT	_____	_____	happy

The dual

Nouns in Arabic have three numbers – singular, dual and plural. The dual is formed by adding **-een** to the end of the noun. Nouns ending in **-a** (feminine) have the **-a** replaced by **-t** before adding the **-een** ending. For example:

walad	**waladeen**	two boys
yoom	**yoomeen**	two days
marHaba	**marHabteen**	two hellos
ziyaara	**ziyaarteen**	two visits

13 Form the dual of the following nouns. (Answers p.32)

singular	dual	
mudarris	_____	(male) teacher
mudarrisa	_____	(female) teacher
sayyaara	_____	car
usbuu9	_____	week
shahar	_____	month

Your turn to speak

14 You are on a bus in Jordan, sitting next to an Arab man. Greet him and introduce yourself. Say something about your family, your country and your city. Say something about Jordan and its people. You can hear on the recording a version of what you could have said.

15 This time you want him to introduce himself. Start by asking him some questions and listen to his response. Then you can listen to the whole model dialogue. Start with the phrase **shu il-isim min faDlak?** Then ask him if he's from Jordan; from where exactly; whether he has any children. He may then ask *you* a question!

Answers

Practise what you have learned

Exercise 1   1. (b) 2. (a) 3. (a) 4. (b)
Exercise 2   numbers left: 4
Exercise 4   (a), (d)
Exercise 5   marHaba; laa, min suurya; min 9ashar tiyyaam
Exercise 11 (a) Jabir Ahmad (b) Damascus, Syria (c) no, it is his second visit

Grammar

Exercise 12 Hilwa, Hilwiin; ta9baana, ta9baaniin; 9aTshaana, 9aTshaaniin; za9laana, za9laaniin; ju9aana, ju9aaniin; mabsuuTa, mabsuuTiin
Exercise 13 mudarriseen; mudarristeen; sayyaarteen; usbuu9een; shahreen

Writing

The word for 'door' is underlined: الرجاء اغلاق ال<u>باب</u> بهدوء

Did you know?

Greetings

Greetings and leave takings are indispensable ingredients in any Arabic conversation, wherever you are in the Arab World. They tend to be more elaborate than we are used to in the West. Even when addressing a person you have never met before (say at a reception desk when requesting information, or when getting into a taxi), it is customary to greet him/her and take your leave using standard polite expressions.

As in the West, greetings can be relatively formal or informal, depending on the occasion and the relationship between the speakers. Perhaps the most formal greeting, used throughout the Arabic-speaking (and indeed Islamic) world, is the traditional one of the desert Arab: **is-salaam 9aleekum** peace be upon you! The invariable response to this is **wa 9aleekum is-salaam** and on you be peace! While this is definitely formal-sounding, it is perfectly acceptable and 'safe' to use this on all occasions. It is always the person arriving, the 'newcomer' in the situation, who initiates the greeting.

In most circumstances in which you will find yourself, however, it is just as acceptable, and somewhat less 'stiff', to greet the other person with a more informal expression, such as **marHaba** Welcome! This can be said both by the person initiating the greeting and by the person replying. In reply to **marHaba**, it is also common to say **marHabteen** Two welcomes! Another common opening, especially when ushering someone into your house or office, letting them into your car, etc. is **ahlan wa sahlan** which roughly means 'Welcome among friends!' There are a number of possible replies to this: simply **ahlan** Welcome! or **ahlan biik** Welcome to you! or **ahleen** Two welcomes! or **yaa hala** Oh, welcome!

It is normal when meeting someone socially for the first time, and when meeting anyone you already know (even if you just bump into them in the street), to follow the initial expression of greeting by asking after their health. There are many expressions for this which vary from one Arab country to another, but the commonest and most widely used is **keef il-Haal** or **keef Haalak** (**Haalik** for a woman) How are you? (lit. how is the state/your state?). The commonest, most all-purpose reply is **il-Hamdulillaah** Praise be to God!, but many others are possible e.g. (in Jordan, Syria and Egypt) **kwayyis** Fine!

When taking their leave, the commonest expression people use is **ma9a s-salaama** (Go) in safety. This can also be used as a reply by the person staying. It is also possible for the person leaving to use the same phrase as is used in greeting i.e. **is-salaam 9aleekum**.

Writing

The first letter of the Arabic alphabet we are going to learn is ب
(called in Arabic **baa**) which is pronounced similarly to the English 'b'.
Remember that Arabic words, even when printed, have joined up letters.
In most cases, each letter has a slightly different shape depending on
whether it comes at the beginning, in the middle, or at the end of a word.

ب has the following shapes according to is position:

beginning a word ﺑ

in the middle ﺒ

at the end ﺐ

If we wrote an imaginary word consisting of three 'b's together, we would
therefore have:

ببب (Remember to read *right to left*)

The letter ا (called in Arabic **alif**), when written by itself, is a single
down stroke. Usually, it marks a long 'aa' vowel. When it follows **baa**, it
joins onto it: با

and is pronounced 'baa' (roughly the sound we make when imitating
sheep!). If we repeat these two letters again: بابا

we have written the word **baabaa**, which is the Arabic equivalent of
'Daddy'. Notice that ا never joins on to the letter which follows it.

If we now just put a ب after با we get باب

(pronounced '**baab**') and meaning 'door'. Look at the photograph of a door
sign below. The Arabic says 'Please close the door quietly'. Can you pick
out from the jumble of letter shapes the word for 'door'? (Answer p.32)

You will learn

- to ask what people would like to drink
- to say what you'd like to drink
- to order drinks and snacks
- to ask about and understand what's available
- to ask for the bill

Study guide

Dialogue 1 + Practise what you have learned
Dialogue 2 + Practise what you have learned
Dialogue 3 + Practise what you have learned
Dialogue 4 + Practise what you have learned
Dialogue 5 + Practise what you have learned
Key words and phrases
Grammar
Your turn to speak
Did you know?
Writing

Dialogues

1 *A tea party*

Ayda	eesh bitHibb tishrab?
Clive	shaay iza mumkin.
Ayda	shaay... eesh bitHibbi tishrabi?
Haifa	ay shii... ma9leesh, shaay OK.
Ayda	shaay Habbaab?
Habbab	il-kull batSawwar.
Zahra	shaay mniiH.
Ayda	shaay mniiH?.
Habbab	It's tea time!

shaay tea
ay shii anything
ma9leesh that's OK, no objection
il-kull everybody
batSawwar I imagine

> ◆ **eesh bitHibb tishrab?** What would you like to drink? (lit. what you like you drink?) This is how you would invite a man; to a woman you would say **eesh bitHibbi tishrabi?** (See Grammar, p.43)
>
> ◆ **ma9leesh** is often used when agreeing to a proposal, as here. It has other uses (see Dialogue 3).
>
> **il-kull batSawwar** [Tea for] everybody, I imagine?
>
> **shaay mniiH** Tea is nice (lit. tea [is] nice). In this kind of sentence, no word for 'is' is required in Arabic. Compare what we saw in Unit 1, **ana mish min 9ammaan** I'm not from Amman (lit. I not from Amman).

Practise what you have learned

1 On the recording you will hear three questions and a statement. Indicate which of the answers below fits which question by writing the letters of the questions in the appropriate boxes. Note **shukran** thanks. (Answers p.45)

Nadya	tikram.	☐
Ahmed	laa shukran.	☐
Nadya	shaay law samaHt.	☐
Ahmed	ay shii.	☐

2 Listen to Nadira making four offers of a drink. The first two are rather more casual than the second two. Repeat each line after Nadira until it comes quite fluently, then stop the recording and repeat all four again as if you were addressing a woman. Then listen to Nadira's correct version.

3 Your turn to speak. Nadira will guide you through two short conversations. In **(a)** you meet Samya in a café. In **(b)** you are sitting in a café when Mahmoud walks in.

Dialogues

2 *Clive orders breakfast*

Clive	shu 9indkum ya9ni?
Garsoon	fii 9indna il-yoom ... fii 9indna 'continental breakfast' ... fii 9indna fTuur amriiki, fii 9indna 'open buffet' ... bitHibb taaxud ... bitHibb tishrab 'ahwa willa shaay?
Clive	wallaahi ana baaxud il - 'Continental' u bashrab gahwa.
Garsoon	ahla wa sahla ... min ween inta?
Clive	wallaahi min briiTaanya.
Garsoon	ahla wa sahla fiik ... btiHki 9arabi kwayyis!
Clive	shukran.
Garsoon	shukran ilak.

fii	there is, are	**baaxud**	I take (e.g. a drink)
il-yoom	today	**bashrab**	I drink
taaxud	you (masc. sing.) take	**btiHki**	you (masc. sing.) speak
'ahwa or **gahwa**	coffee	**9arabi**	Arabic (language), Arab

♦ **shu 9indkum?** What do you have? (lit. what with you?)

♦ **fii 9indna...** We have... (lit. there is with us...)

fTuur amriiki American breakfast, i.e. sausages and eggs, coffee, etc.

♦ **bitHibb taaxud** Would you like to have...?

♦ **btiHki 9arabi kwayyis** You speak Arabic well.

---

3 *Clive queries the bill*

Clive	yaa Habiibi.. fii xaTa' fi l-iHsaab. ana maa axadtsh il-buufee.
Garsoon	haada 'Continental'.
Clive	haada 'Continental'?
Garsoon	'Ya', haada 'Continental'.
Clive	si9ruh 'addeesh ya9ni?
Garsoon	haada l-'Continental'.
Clive	kam ya9ni?
Garsoon	thalaat danaaniir urduni u byiiji 9aleeh, baDiif 9aleeh is-'service charge' u il-'government tax'.
Clive	ma9leesh.
Garsoon	OK?

Habiib	dear, 'mate', 'buddy'	**dinaar,** (pl) **danaaniir**	Dinar
xaTa'	mistake	**urduni**	Jordanian
iHsaab or **Hisaab**	bill, check	**byiiji 9aleeh**	on top of that
maa axadtsh	I didn't take	**baDiif**	I add
haada	this, that (alt. to **haadha**)	**9aleeh**	to it

♦ **yaa Habiibi** Hey, mate! (lit. oh, my dear). The **yaa** is used when calling someone by name e.g. **yaa 9ali** Hey, Ali! or by **Habiib, ax** (brother), **uxt** (sister), **9amm** (uncle), etc. when the person's name isn't known.

♦ **si9ruh 'addeesh** How much is it? (lit. its price how much?)

Practise what you have learned

4 For this exercise you will hear a list of drinks in Arabic. Can you guess which of the meanings below fits which of them? Write its number in the appropriate box. Note: **ma9a** with, **biduun** without. (Answers p.45)

tea with sugar ☐   mango juice ☐

tea without sugar ☐   apple juice ☐

Arab coffee (i.e. Turkish) ☐   Coca Cola ☐

instant coffee ☐   Pepsi ☐

orange juice ☐   Seven Up ☐

5 Listen to the waiter talking. Can you fill in the menu below *in English*, and say what kind of coffee the customer asks for? Turkish coffee comes **saada** without sugar or **Hilwa** sweet. Note: **SabaaH il-xeer** good morning.

```
                        MENU

        Breakfasts                        Drinks

   _____        _____

   _____        _____

   _____        _____

   _____

   The customer has _____ coffee.
```

(Answers p.45)

6 Your turn to speak. You will hear the dialogue again, with Clive's part missing. Can you fill it in for yourself? Try not to look at it in the book. You want the American breakfast and coffee, and you are from Canada (**kanada**). Pay particular attention to pronunciation here, especially that of **SabaaH il-xeer**. After each time you reply, you will hear a correct version.

7 Listen to the conversation, where Abdallah has just finished a meal in a café. Underline the correct statements below. (Answers p.45)

1	Abdallah is talking to	**2**	Abdallah wants
(a)	his friend	**(a)**	the bill
(b)	the waiter	**(b)**	some coffee
(c)	a stranger	**(c)**	some fruit juice
3	Abdallah queries an item on the bill and the waiter tells him it's	**4**	At the end Abdallah
(a)	the service charge	**(a)**	pays the bill
(b)	the price of the coffee	**(b)**	leaves without paying
(c)	a mistake	**(c)**	sends it back

8 Your turn to speak. Nadira will guide you as you go up to a woman in the street and ask her if she speaks English.

Dialogues

4 *Yousif orders a morning snack in a cheap restaurant in Amman. What do they have?*

Yousif   law samaHt shu fii 9indak?
Garsoon   9indna bi n-nisba la l-fTaar..;. fii fuul u HummuS u beeD u
           msabbaHa u fatta u maxluuTa.

bi n-nisba la ... as far as ... is concerned
fTaar (alternative to **fTuur**) breakfast
fuul beans
HummuS chick pea dip
beeD eggs
msabbaHa chick pea dip with spices and whole chick peas added
fatta dip with bread
maxluuTa a variety of dishes (lit. mixed)

5 *Yousif doesn't like spicy garnishes*

Yousif   Tayyib, iza samaHt haat waaHad mtabbal biduun tatbiila, ya9ni
           biduun filfil.
Garsoon   maashi.
Yousif   u haat waaHad... waaHad... ithneen shaay.
Garsoon   waaHad fuul?
Yousif   laa wallah! waaHad mtabbal 9aadi biduun ay shii... biddak tifTar
           yaa Clive?
Clive   laa.
Yousif   maa bidduh...

mtabbal purée of roasted eggplant pulp (popular dish)
biduun without
tatbiila spicy dressing
filfil hot pepper
9aadi ordinary, normal
bidd (+ pronoun ending) want, like, wish
tifTar you (masc. sing.) have breakfast

> ◆ **haat** (f. **haati**) bring! This is used only for commands.
>
> **waaHad mtabbal** one mtabbel, **ithneen shaay** two teas. Note that this
> is the usual way of ordering dishes in a restaurant i.e. the number
> followed by the thing you are ordering in the singular. Yousif, who is of
> Bedouin origin, often uses **th** instead of **t** in certain common words: here
> he says **ithneen** instead of **itneen**.
>
> **maashi** or **maashi l-Haal** is used like the English 'all right', 'OK', 'fine'
> when answering questions about how you are, or, as here, in agreeing to
> do something.
>
> ◆ **biddak tifTar?** Would you like to have breakfast? **bidd** means literally
> 'desire', so **biddak** means 'your (m.) desire' (you want) and **bidduh** 'his
> desire' (he wants). **maa biddak**, etc. means 'you don't want'.

Practise what you have learned

9 Here is a menu in English. Listen and mark off the items that the waiter mentions. (Answers p.45)

> ### MENU
>
> | Snacks | | Drinks | |
> |---|---|---|---|
> | Beans | ☐ | Tea | ☐ |
> | Cheese | ☐ | Coffee | ☐ |
> | Egg | ☐ | Orange juice | ☐ |
> | 'Fatta' | ☐ | Apple juice | ☐ |
> | Houmous | ☐ | Mango juice | ☐ |
> | | | Pepsi Cola | ☐ |

10 In this exercise you will hear three short conversations about the price of various things. For each one, fill in the table with the item or items talked about and their price. (Answers p.45)

	Item(s)	Price
(a)		
(b)		
(c)		

11 Your turn to speak – and understand. When faced with a waiter reeling off an incomprehensible list, it's useful to know how you can get him to slow down and explain. Here are some useful phrases:

(ana) mish faahim (**faahma** if you're a woman)	I don't understand
shu ya9ni x?	What does x mean?
na9am?	Pardon?
mumkin shwayy shwayy?	Can you say it slowly? (lit. possible little little?)

You will hear Nadira pronounce these for you. Practise saying them yourself. Now listen to the waiter. When he has finished his list, Nadira will guide you in getting him to slow down and in asking him what one of the items he mentions is. But begin by asking him what he has.

12 Your friends have sent you to order some snacks and drinks for all of you. Here's the list you have. Note: **Haliib** milk.

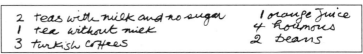

> 2 teas with milk and no sugar   1 orange juice
> 1 tea without milk   4 houmous
> 3 turkish coffees   2 beans

However you decide to let your friend Salwa order instead. Listen carefully to her giving the order on the tape and check it against your list. Where has she gone wrong? (Answers p.45)

13 Your turn to speak. You come into a café for a snack and sit down. Nadira will guide you as usual, as you order.

Key words and phrases

<table>
<tr><td>*To learn*</td><td>SabaaH il-xeer</td><td>good morning</td></tr>
<tr><td></td><td>shu 9indkum?</td><td>what do you have?</td></tr>
<tr><td></td><td>eesh bitHibb tishrab?</td><td>what would you like to drink?</td></tr>
<tr><td></td><td>fii shaay?</td><td>is there tea?</td></tr>
<tr><td></td><td>'ahwa?</td><td>coffee?</td></tr>
<tr><td></td><td>ma9a sukkar</td><td>with sugar</td></tr>
<tr><td></td><td>biduun sukkar</td><td>without sugar</td></tr>
<tr><td></td><td>Haliib</td><td>milk</td></tr>
<tr><td></td><td>baHibb Hummus</td><td>I'd like houmous</td></tr>
<tr><td></td><td>fuul</td><td>eggs</td></tr>
<tr><td></td><td>sandawitsh beeD</td><td>an egg sandwich</td></tr>
<tr><td></td><td>9aSiir burtu'aan</td><td>orange juice</td></tr>
<tr><td></td><td>9aSiir tuffaaH</td><td>apple juice</td></tr>
<tr><td></td><td>ay shii (or ay ishii)</td><td>anything</td></tr>
<tr><td></td><td>eesh (alternative to shu)</td><td>what?</td></tr>
<tr><td></td><td>byaaxud il-fTuur</td><td>he has breakfast</td></tr>
<tr><td></td><td>biddi l-Hisaab</td><td>I'd like the bill</td></tr>
<tr><td></td><td>law samaHt/samaHti</td><td>please, excuse me</td></tr>
<tr><td></td><td>(to a man/woman)</td><td></td></tr>
<tr><td></td><td>shukran</td><td>thank you</td></tr>
<tr><td></td><td>shukran ktiir</td><td>thank you very much</td></tr>
<tr><td></td><td>9afwan</td><td>you're welcome (after **shukran**)</td></tr>
<tr><td></td><td>'addeesh haada?</td><td>how much is this?</td></tr>
<tr><td></td><td>haada ktiir</td><td>that's a lot, too much</td></tr>
<tr><td></td><td>mish faahim/faahma</td><td>I don't understand</td></tr>
<tr><td></td><td>shu ya9ni x?</td><td>what does x mean?</td></tr>
<tr><td></td><td>na9am?</td><td>pardon?</td></tr>
<tr><td></td><td>mumkin shwayy shwayy?</td><td>can you say it slowly?</td></tr>
<tr><td></td><td>mit'assif (f. mit'asfa)</td><td>sorry</td></tr>
<tr><td></td><td>ma9leesh</td><td>never mind, OK</td></tr>
<tr><td>*To understand*</td><td>btiHki 9arabi?</td><td>do you speak Arabic?</td></tr>
<tr><td></td><td>biddak/biddik 'ahwa?</td><td>would you like coffee?</td></tr>
<tr><td></td><td>(to a man/woman)</td><td></td></tr>
</table>

Grammar

Pronoun endings   You already know many of these, in words like **ismi**, **ismak**, **ismik**, **9indna** (or **9idna**), **bidduh**. Make sure you know what they all mean. The pronoun endings are underlined. Here's the complete set, added to **isim** (name):

ismi	my name	**isimna**	our name
ismak	your name (to a man)	**isimkum**	your name (to more
ismik	your name (to a woman)		than one person)
ismuh	his/its name	**isimhun**	their name
isimha	her/its name	(or **isimhum**)	

If the word to which the pronouns are added ends in a vowel, that vowel becomes long. There are also some small differences in the endings, but only in the singular. Here's **fi** (in) with the endings:

fiiy	in me	**fiina**	in us
fiik	in you (m.)	**fiikum**	in you (pl)
fiiki	in you (f.)		
fiih	in him/it	**fiihun**	in them
fiiha	in her/it	(or **fiihum**)	

14   Translate into Arabic (Answers p.45)

(a) We want fruit juice.
(b) We have sandwiches.
(c) Is there sugar in it (the tea)?
(d) They want Turkish coffee.
(e) His name is John.
(f) Do you (f.) want breakfast?

Verbs   You also know quite a few of these: **tismaH** you allow, **tHibb** you like, **tishrab** you drink, **aaxud** I take, and **tiHki** you speak. These are all in what's called the 'non-past' tense, which is used to express present and future time. The only other tense in Arabic is the past. You've met **samaHt** lit. you allowed, **shuft** you saw, and **axadt** I took. Here we'll look at the forms of the non-past, leaving off the **b-** or **bi-** at the beginning – this will be explained in the next unit. Let's take **yHibb** he likes or loves.

aHibb	I like	**nHibb**	we like
tHibb	you (m.) like	**tHibbu**	you (pl) like
tHibbi	you (f.) like		
yHibb	he (or it) likes	**yHibbu**	they like
tHibb	she (or it) likes		

Almost all verbs go like this, so it's worth learning it. **yaaxud** (he takes) is slightly irregular. It drops the **u** if an ending is added: **taaxdi**, you (f.) take, **yaaxdu**, they take. Verbs agree with their subject like adjectives do, e.g. **il-bint btHibb shaay** The girl would like tea. Here both the noun **il-bint** and the verb **btHibb** are feminine.

15   Fill in the blanks with the correct form of the verb in brackets : (Answers p.45)

(a) ana _____ ashrab shaay, min faDlak.   (yHibb)
(b) _____ inglizi?   (yiHki)
(c) biddna _____ il-fTuur, law samaHt.   (yaaxud)
(d) eesh bitHibbi _____ ?   (yishrab)

Grammar

16 Complete the following conversation by filling in the right form of the verb to match the English translation. To check your answers, listen to the recording.

Iman joins her friends Basim and Salwa at a table in a café.

Iman	_____ **lii.**	Permit me.
Basim	_____. **ahlan.**	Please sit down. Hello.
Iman	**ahlan fiik.**	Hi.
Basim	_____ **shaay?**	Shall we drink tea?
Iman	**laa ma9leesh, b** _____ **'ahwa. b** _____ **shaay intu?**	No, never mind, I'll have coffee. Will <u>you</u> (pl) drink tea
Basim	**aywa. b** _____ **shaay.**	Yes, we'll have (take) tea.
Waiter	**shu b** _____ _____ ?	What would you (pl) like to drink?
Iman	**b** _____ **'ahwa Hilwa u**	I'll have sweet coffee and
	humma b _____ **shaay,**	they'll drink tea, please.
	law samaHt.	
Basim	**u il-uxt b** _____ **Haliib**	And she'll have milk please.
	iza mumkin.	
Iman	**maashi.**	OK.

Independent pronouns

You already know some of these: **ana** I, **inta** you (m.), **inti** you (f.). Here is the complete list:

ana	I	**niHna**	we
inta	you (m.)	**intu**	you (pl)
inti	you (f.)	**humma**	they
huwwa	he/it (masc. nouns)		
hiyya	she/it (fem. nouns)		

These are used for the subject of the sentence, e.g. **ana min briiTaanya** *I am from Britain*, **hiyya jamiila** *she is beautiful*. There is no separate pronoun corresponding to the English 'it'.

Numbers

Numbers from 3 - 10 lose their ending **-a** when they are used with a noun:

arba9a	four	**arba9 banaat**	four girls
sab9a	seven	**saba9 iwlaad**	seven children,
		saba9 tiyyaam	seven days

(**iyaam** becomes **tiyyaam** after the numbers 3 - 10)

When used with a noun, numbers from 11 - 19 add **-ar**, and the noun from 11 onwards takes the *singular* form. For example:

iHda9sh	eleven	**iHda9shar yoom**	eleven days
itna9sh	twelve	**itna9shar bint**	twelve girls
9ishriin	twenty	**9ishriin usbuu9**	twenty weeks
waaHad u xamsiin	fifty-one	**waaHad u xamsiin dinaar**	fifty-one dinars

Your turn to speak

17 Here's part of a menu from the Marriott Hotel in Amman. Imagine you're talking to the waiter. Ask him what a couple of the unfamiliar dishes are, then order what you like. Compare this with Nadira's questions and orders on the recording.

APPETIZERS & SOUPS	مقبلات وأنواع الشوربة
HOMMOS 0.500 MUTABEL 0.500 TABBOULEH 0.500 SAMBOUSEK (6) 1.400 KUBBEH (5) 1.200	حمص ٥٠٠, • متبل ٥٠٠, • تبولة ٥٠٠, • سمبوسك (٦) ٤٠٠,١ كبة (٥) ٢٠٠,١

18 Imagine you're visiting the same restaurant with a Jordanian couple. Ask them what they'd like to eat and drink, making some particular suggestions. Again, compare your questions with what Nadira says.

Answers

<table>
<tr><td>Practise what you
have learned</td><td colspan="2">Exercise 1   tikram (d); laa shukran (c); shaay law samaHt (a);
ay shii (b)</td></tr>
<tr><td></td><td colspan="2">Exercise 4
<table>
<tr><td>tea with sugar</td><td>5</td><td>mango juice</td><td>3</td></tr>
<tr><td>tea without sugar</td><td>7</td><td>apple juice</td><td>10</td></tr>
<tr><td>Arab coffee</td><td>4</td><td>Coca Cola</td><td>9</td></tr>
<tr><td>instant coffee</td><td>8</td><td>Pepsi</td><td>1</td></tr>
<tr><td>orange juice</td><td>6</td><td>Seven-Up</td><td>2</td></tr>
</table>
</td></tr>
<tr><td></td><td colspan="2">Exercise 5   Breakfasts: American, Jordanian, French, sandwiches
Drinks: tea, coffee (Arab and instant), juice
He has Arab coffee with a little sugar</td></tr>
<tr><td></td><td colspan="2">Exercise 7   1: (b) 2: (a) 3: (b) 4: (a)</td></tr>
<tr><td></td><td colspan="2">Exercise 9   The snacks and drinks on the menu which the waiter
mentions are: egg (sandwich), hummus, beans, tea, coffee,
orange juice, mango juice, Pepsi Cola</td></tr>
<tr><td></td><td colspan="2">Exercise 10   (a) American breakfast   2 Dinars
(b) Hummus sandwich   1 Dinar
(c) 3 Beans, 1 Fetta, 2 Eggs   4 Dinars</td></tr>
<tr><td></td><td colspan="2">Exercise 12   Mistakes:
- 2 teas with milk, one without sugar (instead of 2 teas with
  milk and no sugar)
- 4 Turkish coffees (instead of 3)
- 2 eggs (instead of 2 beans)
- she forgot the tea without milk</td></tr>
</table>

<table>
<tr><td>Grammar</td><td>Exercise 14   (a) biddna 9aSiir (b) 9indna sandwitshaat (c) fii sukkaar
fiih? (d) biddhum 'ahwa 9arabiyya (e) ismuh John
(f) biddik fTuur?

Exercise 15   (a) baHibb (b) btiHki (c) naaxud (d) tishrabi</td></tr>
</table>

<table>
<tr><td>Writing</td><td>Exercise 19   Bata (name of manufacturer); Bilal (man's name)</td></tr>
</table>

Did you know?

Food

The Arabs are justly famed for their generous hospitality. An invitation to dine at an Arab friend's house is likely to be a lavish affair, however humble his or her status. Honouring a guest by offering the very best that can be afforded is accepted by every Arab as an absolute duty.

In Arab homes, and in all but the most westernised Arab restaurants, food is traditionally served somewhat differently from the way it is served in Europe. In Lebanon, Syria, Jordan and Palestine, the meal may begin with an (often large) variety of hot and cold hors d'ouvres (called **mazza**) all served at the same time, from which the diners will take a little of each. After this, all the savoury or spicy main dishes, of which again there may be several, are put on the table at the same time, rather than in the form of separate courses. Often, the Arab host or hostess will insist on piling high the guest's plate with the best pieces of meat or fish or whatever else has been served, as a sign of hospitality. The serving of food in this way is often accompanied by repeated exhortations to have more (**tfaDDal, xud kamaan!**) even after the guest has said **shukran, ana shab9aan** Thank you, but I'm full. After the main courses, a sweet dessert is normally served, and then small cups of coffee. Traditionally it is quite normal, and not at all rude to leave immediately after the coffee, although usage varies with the degree of westernisation. At the end of a meal it is customary for the guest to say **daa'iman** (always) which indicates that he or she hopes that the host or hostess will always be in a position to entertain so well. In the westernised cities of the Arab World food is now universally eaten with knife, fork and spoon, although in villages and among less educated people (who are often the most insistent that you share with them what little they have) people still use their fingers or a piece of flat unleavened bread to scoop up the food. The right hand, not the left, is used for this purpose.

The sale and consumption of alcohol is strictly controlled, if not completely prohibited, in all Arab countries as it is specifically designated **Haraam** (prohibited) to all Muslims by the Koran. Pork is similarly prohibited.

Here are some typical main dishes in the Arab World:

shurba	soup, e.g. **shurbit 9adas** lentil soup, **shurbit samak** fish soup
kufta	spicy meatballs (or cubed meat loaf)
maHshi	stuffed vegetable, e.g. **wara' 9inab maHshi** stuffed vine leaves, **malfuuf maHshi** stuffed cabbage
kabaab	meatballs (usually cooked on a skewer)
marag	stew
mashwi	roasted meats in general, or individual, e.g. **dajaaj mashwi** roast chicken

And here are some typical sweet desserts:

maHlabiyya	sweet rice pudding
'aTaayif	pancakes
kunaafa	sticky pastry made of baked noodles and stuffed with nuts
umm 9ali	filo pastry filled with raisins and baked in milk

Writing

The next letter we will learn is called **lam**, and sounds like an English 'l'. Written on its own it looks like this:

ل

At the beginning of a word it joins on to a following letter. So **lam** followed by a **baa** looks like this:

لب

In the middle of a word it looks like this (**baa -lam -baa**):

بلب

And at the end like this (**baa -lam**):

بل

How would we pronounce this last combination of letters? Let's write in some short vowels. These are written above or below the letter which precedes them. So if we wish our **b*l** shape to say **bal**, we write in the **a** (written as a short diagonal line) above the **baa**:

بَل

If we wish **b*l** to say **bil** we write the **i** (written as a short diagonal) below the **baa**:

بِل

If we wish **b*l** to be pronounced **bul**, we write the **u** above the **baa** in the shape of a comma:

بُل

Now let's put the two **bul**'s together:

بُلْبُل

This says **bulbul** nightingale. We hope that if you follow this course, Arabs will say to you **tiHki 9arabi bulbul** You speak Arabic like a nightingale!

Writing

Remember that in any kind of Arabic writing you encounter on street signs, hoardings or billboards, business cards, etc. the short vowels are never normally marked. So the word nightingale (perhaps as the name of a restaurant) would appear as:

بلبل

When **lam** is followed by **alif**, the resulting shape looks like this:

لا

By itself, this is a complete word, pronounced **laa** and meaning 'no'.

The second letter in this Unit is ت, called **taa** and pronounced similarly to an English 't'. ت is exactly the same basic shape as ب **baa** which we have already met, the only difference being that ت has its two dots above, while ب has its one dot below. It is written in exactly the same way as ب at the beginning, middle and end of a word except for the position of its dots:

beginning a word: تـ

in the middle: ـتـ

at the end: ـت

19 Read the following words: بَاتَا بِلَال

(Answers p.45)

You will learn

- how to book a room in an hotel
- how to ask to see people
- how to ask and understand where something is situated
- the numbers 30 - 100

Study guide

Dialogue 1 + Practise what you have learned
Dialogue 2 + Practise what you have learned
Dialogue 3 + Practise what you have learned
Dialogue 4 + Practise what you have learned
Dialogue 5 + Practise what you have learned
Key words and phrases
Grammar
Your turn to speak
Did you know?
Writing

Dialogues

1 *Munir makes a hotel reservation*

Munir	law samaHti, biddna niHjiz ghurfa la shaxS waaHad... mumkin willa mish mumkin?
Nadya	ah Tab9an ... fii Hajiz min 'abil?
Munir	laa lissa, ya9ni halla' biddi aHjiz.
Nadya	OK bas law samaHt biddak ti9abbi lii l-kart.
Munir	Tayyib.
Nadya	ma9luumaat kaamla u t-tawqii9 u laazim ykuun ma9ak jawaaz safar.

Hajaz/yiHjiz to reserve, to book	**bas** but
ghurfa room	**ti9abbi** you fill in
shaxS person	**kart** card
ah yes	**ma9luumaat** (pl) information
Tab9an of course	**kaamil** complete, full
Hajiz reservation	**tawqii9** signature
min 'abil before	**laazim** necessary
lissa not yet	**laazim ykuun** there must be
halla' now	**jawaaz safar** passport

♦ **ghurfa la shaxS waaHad** a single room (lit. room for one person). A double room, on the same principle is **ghurfa la shaxSeen**.

♦ **mumkin willa mish mumkin** [Is that] possible or not?

♦ **fii Hajiz min 'abil?** do you already have a reservation? (lit. is there reservation from before?)

♦ **biddak ti9abbi lii l-kart** you need to fill out this card for me (lit. you want you fill out for me the card). **bidd-** is often the equivalent of English 'need to', 'ought to' as well as 'want'.

♦ **ma9luumaat kaamla** full information. **kaamla** is the feminine of **kaamil** (compare **saakin**, fem. **saakna** in Unit 1). Plural nouns (like **ma9luumaat** [lit. informations] which are *non-human*) usually take feminine singular adjectives, as in this case.

♦ **laazim ykuun ma9ak** you have to have with you.. (lit. necessary is with you...)

Practise what you have learned

1 Listen to the recording. What sort of room does the man book? Mark off the correct answer. (Answers p.59)

   (a) la shaxS waaHad
   (b) la shaxSeen

2 Samir is booking a room in a hotel. Listen and mark off the correct picture that illustrates his response to the receptionist. Remember **kam** how much, how many. (Answers p.59)

1

la kam shaxS?

la shaxSeen.   (a)

la shaxS waaHad.   (b)

2

fii Hajiz min 'abil?

aywa.   (a)

laa.   (b)

3

biddi jawaaz is-safar, min faDlak.

mit'assif, mish ma9ai.   (a)

tfaDDali.   (b)

3 Your turn to speak. You are going to practise booking a room in a hotel. Nadira will prompt you. Then listen to the whole model dialogue.

Dialogues

2 *For how long?*

Munir	Tayyib OK mawjuud, kull shay mawjuud... Tab9an il-mudda biddha tkuun sitt tiyyaam.
Nadya	aywa.
Munir	sitt tiyyaam min sab9a arba9a la itna9sh arba9a ... mumkin willa mish mumkin?
Nadya	ah Tab9an.
Munir	ah.

mawjuud here (lit. found)
kull shay everything (alternative to **kul shii**, with the same meaning)
mudda period (of time)
itna9sh twelve

> ◆ **mawjuud, kull shay mawjuud** it's here, everything's here. **mawjuud** is the normal way of saying 'here' in the sense of 'present' e.g. (on the phone) **muniir mawjuud?** is Munir there? **laa, mish mawjuud** no, he isn't.
>
> ◆ **il-mudda biddha tkuun ...** the period of stay will be ... (lit. ...it wants to be...)
>
> ◆ **min sab9a arba9a la itna9sh arba9a** from 7.4 to 12.4 (i.e. from 7-12 April). This use of numbers for months is common.

3 *And room rates?*

Munir	ah, bafaDDil il-ghurfa t-taanya haadi illi fiiha maktab.
Nadya	aywa, haay xamsa u arba9iin diinaar gheer...
Munir	il-as9aar? il-as9aar, il-as9aar ... i9mali ma9ruuf, keef il-as9aar?
Nadya	il-as9aar min sitta u talaatiin diinaar is-'single' il-9aadi bas haadi l- ... 'semi suite' bitkuun xamsa u arba9iin diinaar.
Munir	haadi biduun Daraa'ib willa...?
Nadya	ah, biduun Daraa'ib ... fii 9ashra bi l-miyya Dariiba.

bafaDDil I prefer	**diinaar** (Jordanian) dinar
taani second, other	**gheer** apart from
illi which, that	**as9aar** (pl) prices, [room] rents
maktab desk	**sitta u talaatiin** thirty-six
haay this (short for **haada**)	**Dariiba**, (pl) **Daraa'ib** taxes
xamsa u arba9iin forty-five	**9ashra bi l-miyya** ten per cent

> ◆ **bafaDDil il-ghurfa t-taanya, haadi illi fiiha ...** I prefer the other room, the one in which there's ... (lit. I prefer the room other, that which in it ...). **taani** 'other' is feminine because **ghurfa** is feminine.
>
> ◆ **i9mali ma9ruuf** do me a favour (and tell me). **i9mali** is a feminine command form, which we will meet in Unit 13. The masculine is **i9mal**.
>
> **is-'single' il-9aadi** the ordinary single [room] **haadi biduun Daraa'ib willa...?** is that without taxes or...?
>
> ◆ **sitta u talaatiin** thirty-six, **xamsa u arba9iin** forty-five. The numbers between the units of ten are formed on the 'one-and-twenty, two-and-twenty, seven-and-sixty' principle, using the unit numbers you encountered in Unit 1, combined with the tens listed in the *Key words and phrases* section of this Unit.

Practise what you have learned

4 A man is booking a room in a hotel. How long does he want it for? From when until when? Mark off the correct answers. (Answers p.59)
Remember: **'addeesh?** how long? how much/many?

sitt tiyyaam   min sab9a xamsa la sitta9sh xamsa
9ashar tiyyaam   min arba9a waaHad la 9ashra waaHad
saba9 tiyyaam   min 9ashra arba9a la xamasta9sh arba9a

5 Suzanne is booking a room. Her part of the conversation has been omitted. Choose the correct replies from the box to complete her part. Then check with the recording for the whole conversation:

> yoomeen; Tayyib; biddi ghurfa la shaxS waaHad; tfaDDali; marHaba

Suzanne _____
Recep.   ahlan.

Suzanne _____
Recep.   aywa. la kam yoom?

Suzanne _____
Recep.   biddi ma9luumaat kaamla. mumkin ti9abbi lii l-kart?

Suzanne _____
Recep.   jawaazik is-safar, iza mumkin?

Suzanne _____

6 Your turn to speak. You are going to book a room for one person for five days. Nadira will prompt you. Note **muftaaH** key, **raqam** number.

7 Listen to the recording. How much does an ordinary room cost? Mark off the correct picture. (Answers p.59)

(a) 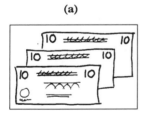   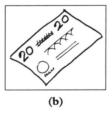   **(c)**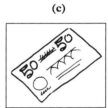

(b)

8 Listen to the recording. The receptionist is on the phone giving the prices of the different kinds of rooms they have at the Jordan Hotel.

(a) What kind of rooms do they have?   **(b)** What are the prices?
(Answers p.59)

Note: **mufrada** single, **ghurfa ma9a 'a9da Sghiira** small suite (lit. a room with a small sitting area)

9 Your turn to speak. Your friend has asked you to find out about the prices of single rooms in some hotels in Jordan, and to book him a room for three days in the cheapest hotel. He is checking with you now. Nadira will prompt you. Then you can listen to the model dialogue.

Dialogues

4 *Samir at the British Council*

Samir	marHaba.
Ma'n	ahleen.
Samir	ballahi mumkin ashuuf il-mudiir is-sayyid Miles Roddis?
Ma'n	Miles Roddis, ah ... 9indak maw9id ma9ah?
Samir	laa wallaahi maa 9indi maw9id bas li'annuh ana misaafir bukra Habbeet ashuufuh bi sha'n bi9tha 'abilla asaafir.

ahleen	hi, hello, welcome	**misaafir**	travelling, leaving
ashuuf	I see	**bukra**	tomorrow
mudiir	boss, manager	**bi sha'n**	about
is-sayyid	Mr	**bi9tha**	scholarship, grant
maw9id	appointment		
li'annuh	because		

> **9indak maw9id ma9ah** do you have an appointment with him?
>
> **bas li'annuh ana misaafir bukra Habbeet ashuufuh...** but because I'm leaving tomorrow I wanted to see him... (lit. I wanted I see him)
>
> **'abilla** is used to mean 'before' with non-past verbs.

5 *The receptionist directs him*

Ma'n	wallah huwwa issa mashghuul bas ida biddak tshuufuh ... ah, mumkin tfaDDal foog 9ala had-daraj btiTla9 foog 9ala iidak ish-shmaal... nihaayit il-mamarr tshuuf sikirtiirtuh muqaabilak bi DH-DHabT.
Samir	eesh isim is-sikritiira?
Ma'n	is-sikritiira isimha hind is-sammaan.
Samir	hind is-sammaan ... shukran jaziilan ... bye bye.
Ma'n	ahlan wa sahlan, yaa hala, tfaDDal.

issa	at the moment	**shmaal**	left
mashghuul	busy	**nihaaya**	end
ida	if (alternative to **iza**)	**mamarr**	corridor
foog (or **foo'**)	upstairs, above	**sikirtiira**	secretary (fem.)
9ala	on	**muqaabil**	opposite
daraj	stairs, steps	**shukran jaziilan**	thanks a lot
btiTla9	you go up	**yaa hala**	welcome

> **tfaDDal foog 9ala had-daraj** please go upstairs by those stairs (lit. be so kind upstairs on these stairs). **tfaDDal** can be used to invite another person to do virtually anything.
>
> **btiTla9 foog** you go up, **9ala iidak ish-shmaal** on the left hand side (lit. on your left hand). **nihaayit il-mamarr** at the end of the corridor, **tshuuf sikirtiirtuh muqaabilak bi DH-DHabT** you'll see his secretary exactly opposite you (lit. opposite you exactly).
>
> **is-sikirtiira isimha hind is-sammaan** the secretary's name is Hind Samman. Grammatically, the structure is as we saw in Dialogue 3 of Unit 1.

Practise what you have learned

10 True or False. Listen and determine which sentence is true and which is false. Note: **ba9d** after, **usbuu9** week. (Answers p.59)

T/F

___ **(a)** The man has an appointment with the boss today.

___ **(b)** The secretary tells the man he can see the boss tomorrow.

___ **(c)** The man is leaving today.

___ **(d)** The man is going to see the boss tomorrow.

11 Complete the dialogue with the words and expressions from the box. Then check with the recording. Note: **mumaththil sharika** company salesman or representative. (Answers p.59)

> il-ism il-kariim; SabaaH il-xeer; mumkin ashuuf il mudiir; aywa; ana

Samir	_____ .
Sec.	SabaaH in-nuur..
Samir	_____ ?
Sec.	9indak maw9id ma9ah?
Samir	_____ .
Sec.	_____ ?
Samir	_____ samiir Hasan, mumaththil sharika.

12 Your turn to speak. You are a company representative, visiting a client. You are going to ask his secretary if you can see the manager. You have no appointment but you would like to see him today. If that's not possible, tomorrow will do. Nadira will prompt you. Note: **miin?** who? New word: **iS-SubuH** in the morning.

13 Listen to the recording. Nahida is asking for some information. Mark off the correct answers. Note: **door** floor, **baab** door. (Answers p.59)

1 Nahida wants to see
(a) the boss ☐
(b) the boss' secretary ☐

2 The secretary's room is
(a) the second door on the first floor ☐
(b) the second door on the second floor ☐

3 The secretary's room is
(a) on the right ☐
(b) on the left ☐

14 Bilaal wants to see Mr Nabiil Bader. Put the following conversation in the right order. Then listen to check your answer.

il-ism il-kariim?	bilaal mahdi.
marHaba.	ahlan.
il-9afu. ahlan wa sahlan.	aywa, mawjuud.
ballah is-sayyid nabiil bader mawjuud?	shukran.
mumkin ashfuuh?	
aywa, sayyid bilaal. tfaDDal foog, id-door	
it-taani, awwal baab 9ala iidak il-yamiin.	

15 Your turn to speak. You have arrived at the reception desk of the Salah Company. Ask to see the assistant manager (**musaa9id il-mudiir**). Nadira will prompt you.

Key words and phrases

To learn

Hajaz/yiHjiz	to reserve or book
Hajiz	reservation
'abil	before
ghurfa, (pl) **ghuraf**	room
shaxS, (pl) **ashxaaS**	person
mawjuud	present, here, in
mumkin ashuuf...?	can I see...?
il-mudiir	the boss, manager, director
si9ir, (pl) **as9aar**	price
il yoom	today
bukra	tomorrow
min... la...	from... to...
talaatiin	thirty
arba9iin	forty
xamsiin	fifty
sittiin	sixty
sab9iin	seventy
tamaaniin	eighty
tis9iin	ninety
miyya (miit before a noun)	hundred

To understand

9aadi	normal, ordinary
9indak maw9id ma9a	do you have an appointment with...?
jawaaz safar	passport
ma9luumaat	information
shmaal	left
yamiin	right
mashghuul	busy
laazim	necessary, obligatory

Note: from this Unit on, verbs listed in the *Key words and phrases* sections are given with the past tense form first, followed by an oblique, followed by the non-past (see above **Hajaz/yiHjiz** to reserve). In both cases the form of the verb given is the third person masculine singular (the 'he' form) as there is no infinitive form in Arabic such as the English 'to go', 'to make', etc.

Grammar

Verbs

You were introduced to the non-past tense of the verb in Unit 3. As we saw, the subject of the non-past verb is indicated by prefixes and suffixes – **a-** for 'I' (**aHibb** I like), **t-** or **ti-** for 'you' (**tHibb** you (m.) like, **tHibbi** you (f.) like, **tHibbu** you (pl) like) and so on. But in the dialogue you hear Munir say **bafaDDil** rather than **afaDDil** for 'I prefer'. In most areas of Jordan, Syria, Palestine (and Egypt) a **b-** or **bi-** prefix is added at the beginning of non-past forms to indicate present and future time. We will call this the 'B-prefix'. Here is the verb 'to like, love' with the B-prefix.

baHibb	I like	**binHibb**	we like
bitHibb	you (m.) like	**bitHibbu**	you (pl) like
bitHibbi	you (f.) like	**biyHibbu** or	they like
biyHibb or **biHibb**	he (or it) likes	**biHibbu**	
bitHibb	she (or it) likes		

Let's look at the verb 'to reserve'

baHjiz	I reserve	**bniHjiz**	we reserve
btiHjiz	you (m.) reserve	**btiHjizu**	you (pl) reserve
btiHjizi	you (f.) reserve	**byiHjizu** or	they reserve
byiHjiz or **biHjiz**	he (or it) reserves	**biHjizu**	
btiHjiz	she (or it) reserves		

To make any verb negative, simply put **maa** before it e.g. **maa baHibb shaay** I don't like tea.

The B-prefix is not used on any verb which follows another non-past verb, or when following certain words like **bidd** want, **mumkin** possible/can, **laazim** must/have to. For example,

after another verb:

bitHibb tishrab shaay?	would you like to drink tea?
baHibb aaxud il-fTuur il-amriiki.	I would like to have the American breakfast.
bafaDDil aHjiz ghurfa la shaxS waaHad.	I prefer to reserve a single room.

after certain words of wanting, possibility, obligation:

biddna naaxud ...	we would like to have ...
mumkin aHjiz ...	can I reserve ...
laazim asaafir bukra.	I have to leave tomorrow.

16 Fill in the correct form of the verbs in the parentheses to complete the conversation. Then check your answers on page 59.

John is booking a room in a hotel in Amman.

John marHaba.

Recep. ahlan.

John biddi _____ (yiHjiz) ghurfa la shaxS, law samaHti.

Recep. _____ (yHibb) ghurfa ma9a 'a9da Sghiira?

John laa, _____ (yfaDDil) ghurfa mufrada, law samaHti.

Recep. maashi. mumkin _____ (y9abbi) il-kart, law samaHt?

John Tab9an. _____ (yHibb) _____ (yshuuf) il-ghurfa, iza mumkin?

Recep. tfaDDal. ghurfa raqam miyya u talaatiin. _____ (yiHki) 9arabi mniiH.

John shukran!

Grammar

The word bidd- bidd- (want), as you will have noticed, combines with the pronoun endings you have met in Unit 3 e.g. **biddi** I want, **biddak** you want, etc. This word, in spite of its verbal meaning, is not grammatically a verb in Arabic. It can be followed by a noun, e.g.

biddi ismak	(to a man) I want your name
biddi ismik	(to a woman) I want your name
biddha sayyaara	she wants a car
biddi l-muftaaH	I want the key

It is also followed by the non-past tense without the B-prefix as we saw earlier, e.g.

biddi ashrab	I want to drink
biddna niHjiz	we want to reserve

The negative is formed with **maa**. For example, **maa biddi** I don't want, **maa biddha** she doesn't want.

17 The following sentences are said about a man. How would you say them about a woman? How would you say them about a group? (Answers p.59)

(a) bidduh yishrab shaay.
(b) bidduh yiTla9 foo'.
(c) maa bidduh yiHjiz ghurfa.
(d) bidduh yshuuf il-mudiir.
(e) bidduh yaaxud Haliib ma9a il-'ahwa.

Your turn to speak

18 You are in Amman and you want to book into a hotel. Decide how long you want to stay, give all the details you want and obtain all the information you need. Then listen to how Nadira books her room and to the questions she asks. Your questions could be different.

19 Imagine that you're in Jordan and that you would like to see the director of the Zaayid Company before you go back home. Try to arrange with his secretary to see him. Then listen to Nadira for comparison. You might want to mention that you have no appointment, but are travelling back tomorrow.

Answers

<table>
<tr><td>**Practise what you have learned**</td><td>Exercise 1 (a) (a single room)</td></tr>
<tr><td></td><td>Exercise 2 1: (a) 2: (a) 3: (b)</td></tr>
<tr><td></td><td>Exercise 4 saba9 tiyyaam (7 days); min arba9a waaHad la 9ashra waaHad (4 Jan. - 10 Jan)</td></tr>
<tr><td></td><td>Exercise 7 (a)</td></tr>
<tr><td></td><td>Exercise 8 (a) single, double, small suite (b) £35, £45, £55</td></tr>
<tr><td></td><td>Exercise 10 (a) F (b) T (c) F (d) F</td></tr>
<tr><td></td><td>Exercise 13 1: (a) 2: (a) 3: (b)</td></tr>
</table>

Grammar

Exercise 16 aHjiz; bitHibb; bafaDDil; ti9abbi; baHibb ashuuf; bitiHki

Exercise 17

about a woman:	about a group:
(a) biddha tishrab shaay	biddhum yishrabu shaay
(b) biddha tiTla9 foo'	biddhum yiTla9u foo'
(c) maa biddha tiHjiz ghurfa	maa biddhum yiHjizu ghurfa
(d) biddha tshuuf il-mudiir	biddhum yshuufu l-mudiir
(e) biddha taaxud Haliib ma9a il-'ahwa	biddhum yaaxdu Haliib ma9a il-'ahwa

Writing

Exercise 20 (a) House 49 (b) House 73 (c) House 106 (d) House 972 (e) House 55 (f) House 823

Did you know?

The Arab world and the Arabic language

There are some twenty-one independent Arab nations, occupying a vast expanse of land from Morocco in the west to Oman in the east, and from the borders of Turkey in the north to Sudan and the Sahara in the south. The total population of these Arabic-speaking countries is about 183 million. The vast majority of Arabs are Muslims (meaning literally 'one who surrenders himself') and profess Islam ('self surrender'). The Muslim holy book is the Qur'an (sometimes spelt Koran in the west), written in Arabic, which was revealed to Muhammad, Islam's prophet, in the early 7th century AD. In some Arab countries of the Near East – Lebanon, Syria, Jordan and Egypt in particular – there are sizeable Christian minorities.

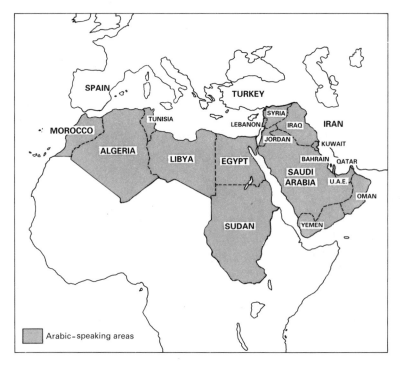

Arabic-speaking areas

Arabic is a member of the Semitic group of languages, closely related to Hebrew and Aramaic, the language Christ spoke. There is a considerable difference between written Arabic – variously known as Literary Arabic, Modern Standard Arabic, or (in its historical form) Classical Arabic – and all varieties of spoken Arabic. Spoken Arabic differs from country to country, and even from town to town, although it is possible to group the dialects into a few major areas within each of which there is virtually total mutual comprehension. Thus the spoken Arabic dialects of north-west Africa (Morocco, Algeria, Tunisia) form a single group, as do those of the Levant (Lebanon, Syria, Jordan). Egyptian, Sudanese and western Saudi Arabian Arabic form another group, as do the dialects of Iraq and the eastern part of the Arabian peninsular. However, even the differences between these groups of dialects are not that great: they all share a great many structural features and there is a high proportion of shared vocabulary. None of the spoken dialects, however, is used more than very marginally in writing: for all formal written communication (and obviously therefore all literature), Modern Standard Arabic is universally used. It is also usually used in formal oral contexts, such as radio and TV news

Did you know?

reading, political speeches, lectures, etc. This form of Arabic (which is learned at school and not as a native language by any Arab) is virtually uniform in its grammar and vocabulary throughout the Arab world. It is a potent symbol of Arab cultural and (in the sense that it is the language of the Qur'an) religious unity.

To many Arabs, Modern Standard Arabic, known as **al-fuSHa** 'the pure' is the only form of the language which has any worth. The dialects, although they are the universal means of everyday conversation, are regarded by many as degraded forms of the language. This feeling is often reflected in attitudes to foreigners' attempts to learn Arabic: many Arabs (especially if they are educated) feel that only the Standard form of the language should be taught, regardless of the fact that Arabs would never themselves use this kind of Arabic for some of the purposes (e.g. chatting, shopping) for which they insist foreigners should use it. It can sometimes seem an uphill battle for foreigners to get Arabs to talk to them in colloquial Arabic. But don't be put off; the less well educated seem to suffer less from this prejudice, and you may well find that they will be more than willing to help you practise.

Writing

In Units 2 and 3 we met the letters ‪ب‬ (**baa**) and ‪ت‬ (**taa**) which consist of the same shape ‪ب‬ but with different numbers and positions of dot placed above or beneath. The shape ‪ى‬ with two dots <u>below</u> it, ‪ي‬ , forms the letter **yaa**, and is pronounced similarly to an English 'y'. At the beginning, or in the middle of a word, it is written eaxctly like **baa** and **taa**, except for the position and number of the dots:

beginning a word ‪ي‬

in the midde ‪ـيـ‬

at the end ‪ـي‬

and on its own ‪ي‬

If we now combine **baa**, **yaa** and **taa**, we get the Arabic word **bayt** house:

‪بَيْت‬

Note that this word just consists of the letters **baa-yaa-taa** joined up; the vowel **a** of **bayt**, being short, is not written as part of the word, but placed above the letter **baa**. The small circle written above the **yaa** (called **sukuun** in Arabic) signifies that there is no short vowel following it. In normal written Arabic, such as you are likely to encounter on shop signs, road signs, advertisements, etc., the short vowels are not written, so you have to recognize a word simply by the shape of the consonants (and long vowels, if any) which make it up.

The letter ‪ي‬ is also used to lengthen a short **i**, in just the same way as ‪ا‬ is used to lengthen a short **a**, as we saw in Unit 1. So if we wanted to write **baytii** (my house) with full vowelling, it would look like this:

‪بَيْتِي‬

Or, more usually, without vowelling, like this:

‪بيتي‬

Arabic numerals   1 ١   2 ٢   3 ٣   4 ٤   5 ٥

6 ٦   7 ٧   8 ٨   9 ٩   0 ٠

Higher numbers are written as they would be in English; strangely although Arabic writing goes from right to left, numbers go from left to right! So 24 is ٢٤ ; 798 is ٧٩٨ ; 65301 is ٦٥٣٠١ .

20 Read the following house numbers (Answers p.59)

(a) بيت ٤٩   (d) بيت ٩٧٢

(b) بيت ٧٣   (e) بيت ٥٥

(c) بيت ١٠٦   (f) بيت ٨٢٣

You will learn

- to ask for directions, on foot and by bus and taxi
- to ask where things are situated
- to understand fairly simple directions
- to check that you've understood correctly

Study guide

Dialogue 1 + Practise what you have learned
Dialogue 2 + Practise what you have learned
Dialogue 3 + Practise what you have learned
Dialogue 4 + Practise what you have learned
Key words and phrases
Grammar
Your turn to speak
Did you know?
Writing

Dialogues

1 *Hind wants some help*

Hind	marHaba yaa 9amm.
Man	marHabteen.
Hind	mumkin tdillni kiif ba'dar awSal la 9ind il-mudarraj ir-ruumaani?
Man	btinzili sirviis jabal 9amman..
Hind	mineen biddi aaxud is-sirviis?
Man	min haada ... shaari9 il-muTraan.
Hind	aywa.
Man	btinzili 9ind jaami9 il-Huseen.
Hind	aha.
Man	btinzili amaant il-9aaSima il-qadiima ... ish-shaari9 duuz 9a sh-shmaal.

tdillni (9ala) you guide me [to]
ba'dar I can
awSal (la 9ind) I arrive [at]
mudarraj amphitheatre
ruumaani Roman
btinzili you (f.) go down
mineen (or **min ween**) from where
shaari9 il-muTraan Mutran Street
jaami9 [main] mosque
amaant il-9aaSima municipality building, town hall
qadiim old, former
9a sh-shmaal on the left

> ♦ **yaa 9amm** oh uncle. Hind uses this polite form of address to the man, who, from his appearance, is old enough to be her uncle.
>
> ♦ **mumkin tdillni kiif ba'dar awsal la 9ind ...** can you show me how I can get to ... (lit. possible you show me how I can I get to ...). The **-ni** 'me' is the object of the non-past verb **tdill** 'you show'. After **ba'dar** 'I can ...', simply add another non-past verb of the same person without the B-prefix: **ba'dar awSal** I can reach ..., **byi'dar yuuSal ...** he can reach, **bti'dar tuuSal** you can reach ... etc.
>
> ♦ **btinzili sirviis jabal 9amman** you go down [by] the Jabal Amman service taxi. Jabal Amman is one of seven **jibaal** (hills) surrounding central Amman, several hundred feet above it. The **sirviis** is a cheap public taxi plying from one fixed point to another. It is a very popular mode of transportation in Jordan, Syria and Lebanon.
>
> ♦ **mineen biddi ...** from where do I need to ...
>
> **btinzili 9ind jaami9 il-Huseen** you get off at the Hussein Mosque. The **jaami9** is the main mosque in a city. The **jaami9 il-Huseen** is the main mosque in Amman city centre.
>
> ♦ **duuz** straight ahead. An alternative, and commoner word with the same meaning is **dughri**.

Practise what you have learned

1 In this exercise you will hear four questions. Show which answers they fit by putting the letters of the appropriate questions in the boxes. (Answers p.74) Note: **ujra** fare [taxi, bus, etc.].

1 laa mish mumkin, laazim tinzili min hoon dughri u taaxdi sirviis min nihaayit ish-shaari9.

2 xud shmaalak min hoon u bitDall dughri.

3 min shaari9 il-haashimi.

4 xamsiin 'irsh.

2 Here are some questions about directions. Underline the word in the parentheses that will fit the blank in the question. (Answers p.74) Remember: **funduq** hotel

(a) kiif ____ awSal la funduq 9amra? [biti'dar, ba'dar, bi'dar]

(b) ween biddi ____ la bank il-urdun? [anzil, tinzili, yinzil]

(c) ba'dar ____ sirviis min hoon la 9ind jaami9 il-Huseen? [taaxud, yaaxud, aaxud]

3 Your turn to speak. You want to get to the Husein mosque by service taxi, so you have to ask where you can find a taxi and where to get off. The first person you ask can't help because she doesn't know: she says **mish 9aarfa** (lit. not know, **mish 9aarif** if it's a man speaking). Nadira will guide you as usual; first as you go up to this woman, and then as you ask a man.

Dialogues

2 *But where exactly is the Roman amphitheatre?*

Hind	ya9ni s-sirviis lamma ywa' 'if ween biywa' 'if?
Man	biywa' 'if 9ind jaami9 il-Huseen.
Hind	biywa' 'if 9ind il-jaami9 u ba9deen aaxud shmaali...
Man	ooxdi shmaalik u bitDalli duuz, Taal9a la amaanat il-9aaSima.
Hind	aDallni maashya dughri, bawSal 9ind amaanat il-9aaSima u il-mudarraj 9ind il-amaana...
Man	u il-mudarraj 9ind il-amaana.
Hind	shukran.

lamma (conj.)   when
ywa' 'if   [it] stops
ba9deen   then
btDalli duuz   you (f.) keep straight on
Taali9, (f.) **Taal9a (la)**   coming out (at)
maashi, (f.) **maashya**   going, walking
dughri   straight ahead

---

ya9ni s-sirviis lamma ywa' 'if ween biywa' 'if?   when the service taxi stops, where does it stop?

▸ **u ba9deen aaxud shmaali...**   and then I go left...? (lit. and then I take my left...?) The man confirms: **ooxdi shmaalik** turn left (lit. take your left). **ooxdi** (or more commonly **xudi**) is the feminine command form 'take!' To a man you would say **xud**.

▸ **aDallni...**   I continue, carry on. Hind is confirming what the man has told her.

The Roman Amphitheatre, Amman

Practice what you have learned

4 You'll hear three short conversations about service taxi routes. Fill in on the table below what you can tell about the routes. Here's a list of names of some areas, streets and buildings in Amman to help you. (Answers p.74)

jabal il-joofa   **shaari9 zahraan**   **bank il-urdun**
jabal il-Huseen   **shaari9 il-haashimi**   **funduq il-balaas**
jabal it-taaj   **jaami9 il-Huseen**
jabal 9ammaan   **il-mudarraj**
Hayy zahraan
il-9abdali
marka l-januubiyya

Service to:	From?	Stops at?	Changes at?
(a) Marka l-Janubiyya	————		————
(b) Jabal Hussein			————
(c) Amphitheatre		————	

5

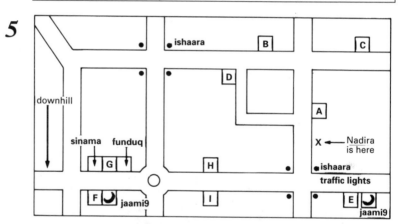

Listen to the two conversations. Nadira is asking directions. Which of the letters on the map is the post office (**maktab il-bariid**)? And which marks the Bank of Jordan (**bank il-urdun**)? Remember you don't need to understand every word, only the gist. (Answers p.74)
New word: **ba9d** after (and remember **jamb** next to).

6 Here's a chance to practise getting someone to clarify the directions he or she gives you. Check that you remember how to ask people to speak more slowly, and to say you don't understand. Notice also how Hind in Dialogue 2 checks that she has understood correctly using **ya9ni** 'that means, so...? So now you're in downtown Amman and you want to find the way to the tourist information office **maktab il-isti9laamaat** (lit. the office of enquiries). You approach an elderly man and ask him if he speaks English. Nadira will tell you what to say, then give you a model version. Remember there's often more than one way to say the same thing, so if you have said something different, it's not necessarily wrong.

Dialogues

3 *Clive wants directions to the University*

Clive   law samaHt il-ax, mumkin tdillni 9ala T-Tariiq la l-jaam9a il-urduniyya?

Man   biddak truuH min... fii Tariiqeen hoon bitwaddiik ... fii Tariiq bitwaddi la l-jaam9a min id-duwwaar il-awwal la th-thaalith u btiTla9 min 9ind jisir ... il-jisir taba9 il-muxaabaraat il-9aamma u bitruuH...

Tariiq (or **Tarii'**)   (m. or f.) road
jaam9a   university
truuH (min)   you go (via)
bitwaddi   [it] takes [you] to, leads [you] to
awwal   first
thaalith (more usually **taalit**)   third
btiTla9 (min 9ind)   [it] comes out (at)
jisir   bridge, flyover
taba9   belonging to
il-muxaabaraat il-9aamma   the General Intelligence [building]
9aamm   general, public

> ♦ **fii Tariiqeen hoon bitwaddiik** there are two roads here, which will take you [there].
>
> ♦ **il-jisir taba9 il-muxaabaraat il-9aamma** the General Intelligence [building] flyover (i.e. the one right next to it). **taba9** is basically used to indicate ownership or close association with someone or something, e.g. **il-maT9am taba9 il-funduq** the hotel restaurant [the restaurant belonging to the hotel].

Practise what you have learned

7 A Jordanian friend is showing you round a town. Listen to his description of what the buildings around you are, then mark the following statements true or false. (Answers p.74) Note: **'uddaam** in front of.

T/F

____ **(a)** You are in the centre of town.

____ **(b)** The Husein mosque is on your friend's left.

____ **(c)** The cinema is on his left.

____ **(d)** The Pasha Hotel is straight ahead.

8 Here are some words to do with finding your way inside a building. You may remember some from the last Unit: **Hammaam** bathroom, toilet; **door** floor.

Now listen to the three short conversations with the receptionist in a hotel. What is being asked about in each case, and where is it? Select your answers from the three lists below and fill in the blanks in the sentences with them. (Answers p.74)

toilet	first floor (i.e. ground floor in Jordan)	on the right
secretary's office	second floor	on the left
manager's office	third floor	straight ahead

(a) The _____ is on the _____ floor _____ .

(b) The _____ is on the _____ floor _____ .

(c) The _____ is on the _____ floor _____ .

9 Your turn to speak. You've just arrived at a hotel, where you've booked a room. Now you're talking to the receptionist. Greet her, tell her you want a room, then answer her questions. When she tells you the room number, ask her where it is and, finally, thank her. This time Nadira will not give you a prompt in English, but after you've paused the recording to make your contribution, you will be given a model version.

Dialogues

4 *There's an alternative*

Man   min il-balad btiTla9 9ala l-9abdali u min hunaak ... btintiqil ... mumkin truuH fi l-baaS aw bi t-taksi la l-jaam9a aw –

Clive   is-sirviis ya9ni.

Man   ah, is-sirviis mumkin ... aw min wasT il-balad mumkin truuH fi l-baaS taba9 il- ... mu'assasit in-naql il-9aamm.

> **il-balad**   city centre, downtown [here]
> **hunaak** (or **hnaak**)   there
> **btintiqil**   you (m.) change [buses, trains, etc.]
> **baaS**   bus
> **taksi**   taxi [private]
> **wasT**   middle, centre
> **mu'assasit in-naql il-9aamm**   Public Transportation Company

---

♦   **min il-balad btiTla9 9ala l-9abdali...**   from the city centre you go up to Abdali... **9abdali** is a suburb situated above central Amman, about two miles from it. There is a large bus and service taxi station there.

♦   **btintiqil** you change. The B-prefix is followed by the **ti**-prefix, signifying the masculine 'you' form. So 'I change' is **bantiqil**, 'he changes' is **byintiqil**, 'they change' is **byintiqlu**, etc.

♦   **il-baaS taba9 mu'assasit in-naql il-9aamm** the Public Transportation Company bus (lit. the bus belonging company the transportation the public). Note again the construction with **taba9** the bus *belonging* to... The word **mu'assasa** 'establishment, institute or (here) company' has the feminine ending **-a**. When it forms the first element in phrases like 'the company of the transportation', as here, this **-a** changes to **-it**. See *Grammar*, this Unit.

Practise what you have learned

10 Here are some questions you might want to ask if you want to go somewhere by bus. Can you work out how to ask them in Arabic? 'The bus-stop' is **maHaTTit il-baaS** and 'the number of the bus' is **raqam il-baaS**. To ask a question beginning with a word like **shu** 'what', **ween** 'where', **eemta** 'when', **leesh** 'why', you put the verb after the question word. For example, **shu byishrab maHmuud?** what will Mahmoud drink? Check your answers on page 74.

(a) Can I get there by bus?

(b) Where's the bus stop for the Husein Mosque?

(c) Where do I get off for the Bank of Jordan?

(d) What's the number of the bus to al-Abdali? (Note: **baaS x** the bus to x)

(e) How much is the fare from here to Irbid?

(f) Does the bus go from here?

(g) Where does the bus go to?

(h) When is the first bus downtown?

11 You ask a woman at a bus-stop how to get downtown. Nadira will prompt you as usual.

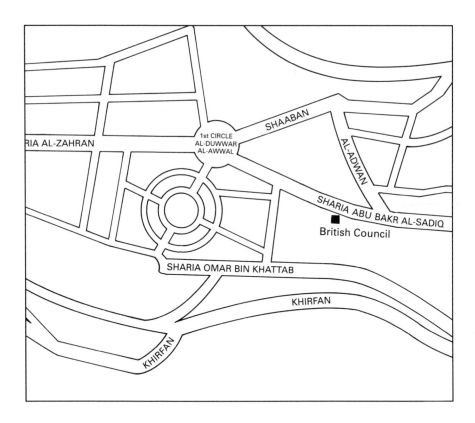

Key words and phrases

To learn

mineen baaxud sirviis...?	Where can I get the service taxi to..?
kiif ba'dar awSal la 9ind...?	How can I get to...?
mumkin tdillni 9ala...?	Can you direct me to...?
(wasT) il-balad	the city centre, downtown
maHaTTit il-baaS	the bus station/stop
il-Hammaam	the bathroom/toilet
wa' 'af/ywa' 'if	to stop
nizil/yinzil	to get off [a bus, etc.]; go down
Tili9/yiTla9 (9ala)	to go up, go out, set out [for]
raaH/yruuH (9ala)	to go [to]
aja/yiiji (9ala)	to come [to]
ba9deen	afterwards
'uddaam	in front of
eemta	when?
hunaak	there
ba9d	after
9a sh-shmaal	on the left
9a l-yamiin	on the right
dughri	straight ahead
taalit	third
bi l-baaS	by bus
ujra	fare
funduq (pl) fanaadiq	hotel

To understand

xud(i) shmaalak/yamiinak	take your left/right
bitDall dughri	go straight ahead
nafs ish-shaari9	the same street
raaH/yruuH mashi	to go on foot, walk
maktab il-bariid	post office
mish 9aarif(a)	I don't know

Grammar

The 'construct'

In Arabic **maktab il-mudiir** is 'the manager's office', literally 'office the manager', and **mat9am il-funduq** is 'the hotel restaurant'. This kind of phrase is called a 'construct' and it has several peculiarities you need to be aware of.

(a) When the first word is feminine and ends in **-a**, this **-a** is replaced by **-(i)t**, e.g. **nihaayit il mamarr** 'the end of the corridor'.

(b) Nothing may be put between the two parts of a construct, except **haada** 'this' and other words meaning 'that', 'these', 'those', e.g **nihaayit haada l-mamarr** the end of this corridor. If you want to say something more about the first word in the construct, the adjective is placed after the whole construct and agrees in gender with the first word. For example, **sayyaart il-mudiir il-kbiira**, is 'the manager's big car', literally 'car [of] the manager the big' where **kbiira** 'big' is feminine to agree with the feminine noun **sayyaara** 'car'.

(c) The first word in a construct phrase can never take **-il**, but is always translatable with 'the' in English. **maktab il-mudiir** is 'the office of the manager', while **maktab mudiir** is 'the office of a manager', or 'a manager's office'.

12 You may like to go back over this Unit and the previous ones and find examples of constructs in them. To check them see p.74

13 Translate into Arabic. (Answers p.74)
(a) the hotel's name
(b) the address of a hotel
(c) the manager's secretary
(d) on the left of the bank
(e) Ahmed's room
(f) Hind's daughter

Ordinal numbers

Except for **awwal** 'first' which we have already met, ordinal numbers 2 - 10 are formed with the vowel pattern **-aa-i-**, like **taalit** third, **saadis** sixth:

taani	second	**saabi9**	seventh
taalit	third	**taamin**	eighth
raabi9	fourth	**taasi9**	ninth
xaamis	fifth	**9aashir**	tenth
saadis	sixth		

These ordinal numbers are used exactly like other adjectives: **ish-shaari9 it-taalit** the third street, **is-sayyaara r-raab9a** the fourth car. The ordinals over 10 are the same as cardinal (i.e. ordinary) numbers: **id-door il-iHda9sh** the eleventh floor, **il-yoom il-arba9iin** the fortieth day.

Note that, if you wish, the ordinal numbers from 1 to 10 may be placed <u>before</u> the noun they qualify, e.g. **taalit sayyaara** the third car, **awwal marra** the first time. This is especially common in giving directions e.g. **xud taani shaari9 9a sh-shmaal** take the second street on the left.

Your turn to speak

Open-ended speaking exercise

14 You want to go to the cinema and have just been told you must go by bus. Think up five questions you might want to ask for clarification, e.g. where to get the bus from, what number it is, etc. Compare your questions with Nadira's.

Answers

Practise what you have learned

Exercise 1   1: (d)   2: (a)   3: (c)   4: (b)

Exercise 2   (a) ba'dar   (b) anzil   (c) aaxud

Exercise 4   (a) stops at the Palace Hotel   (b) from Zahran St., stops at il-Abdali   (c) from Jabal Taj, change at Jabal Amman

Exercise 5   The Post Office is 'F', the bank of Jordan is 'B'

Exercise 7   (a) T   (b) F   (c) T   (d) F

Exercise 8   (a) The manager's office is on the 2nd floor on the right.
(b) The secretary's office is on the 1st floor straight ahead.
(c) The toilet is on the ground floor on the left.

Exercise 10   (a) mumkin awSal la hunaak bil-baaS?
(b) ween maHaTTit il-baaS la jaami9 il-Huseen?
(c) ween banzil la bank il-urdan?
(d) shu raqm baaS il-9abdalii?
(e) 'addeesh il-ujra min hoon la irbid?
(f) il-baaS biyiTla9 min hoon?
(g) ween biyruuH il-baaS?
(h) eemta awwal baaS lil-balad?

Grammar

Exercise 12   Some examples from Unit 5 dialogues:

sirviis jabal 9ammaan	(Jabal Amman Service Taxi)
shaari9 il-muTraan	(Mutran St.)
jaami9 il-Huseen	(The Hussein Mosque)
amaant il-9aaSima l-qadiima	(The old City Hall)
wasT il-balad	(city centre)
mu'assasit in-naql il-9aamm	(Public Transport Establishment)

Exercise 13   (a) ism il-funduq   (b) 9unwaan il-funduq   (c) sikriteerit il-mudiir   (d) 9a shmaal il-bank   (e) ghurfit aHmad   (f) bint hind

Writing

Exercise 15   (a) yaa   (b) abu   (c) binti   (d) tiin   (e) banaat   (f) ana wa anta   (g) lubnaan

Did you know?

Finding your way about

The layout of many Arab cities follows a pattern significantly different from that which is normal in the west. In the oldest Arab cities like Cairo, Damascus and Jerusalem, and to some extent more modern cities like Amman, the central market areas tend to be divided according to the trades carried on there. There are separate, clearly defined streets and areas of markets for the selling of meat, vegetables, spices, clothes, etc. Although western-style supermarket shopping is becoming more common, especially in the newly developed outer suburbs, the medieval pattern still persists in the heart of the oldest cities.

Finding your way around an Arab city can be problematic at first. In Amman, for example, although all the streets bear names which appear on plaques, and are used on official correspondence, in the telephone book, on maps, etc., these names themselves are recent innovations. Many residents still refer to streets by their old names, which often derive from some well-known landmark found there. Thus, what on the map appears as **shaari9 abu bakr as-siddiiq** 'Abu Bakr al-Siddiq Street' is universally known by its old name of **shaari9 reenbo** 'Rainbow Street', after the Rainbow Theatre, now closed, which is found there. So, if you want to go to the British Council, ask the taxi driver to take you to **shaari9 reenbo. shaari9 il-muTraan**, a street in Jabal Amman referred to by one of the speakers in Dialogue 1 of this Unit, appears on the map as **shaari9 9umar ibn al-xaTTaab**. (See the map on page 71.)

Many local people, as can be heard in the dialogues in this Unit, typically describe locations by reference to well-known landmarks rather than street names, official or otherwise. Mosques, palaces and public utilities are typical points of orientation. Here are some common ones:

jaami9 X the mosque of X. **jaami9** ia a large mosque (as opposed to **masjid**, a small one). An example is **jaami9 il-Huseen** in central Amman.

kaniisa church. For example, **il-kaniisa il-urthuduksiyya** the [Greek] Orthodox church, **il-kaniisa il-qubTiyya** the Coptic church.

duwwaar circle/roundabout, e.g. **duwwaar id-daaxiliyya** Ministry of the Interior roundabout. In Amman, traffic roundabouts are among the commonest points of orientation. You might, for example, hear **ween saakin?** where do you live? and the answer **'ariib min id-duwwaar is-saabi9** near the Seventh Circle.

jisir bridge, flyover. For example, **jisir il-muxaabaraat il-9aamma** the flyover next to the General Intelligence building.

bariid post office, e.g. **bariid jabal il-luweebda** Jabal Lweibdah Post Office.

suuq or **suu'** market, e.g. **suu' il-xuDra** the vegetable market. A supermarket is **suubarmarkit**, e.g. **suubarmarkit reenbo** Rainbow Supermarket.

mustashfa hospital. For example, **mustashfa malHas** the Malhas Hospital.

amaana or **baladiyya** municipality, e.g. **amaant il-9aaSima** Municipality of the Capital.

qaSr or **'aSr** palace, e.g. **qaSr zahraan** Zahran Palace.

Writing

The letter و , called **waaw**, sounds like an English 'w'. It never joins up to
any letter which follows it, but if it is preceded by a letter which joins to a
following letter, like ت , it joins onto that letter. Thus:

أُوتيِل

uutiil hotel

Here **waaw** is preceded by an **alif** which, of course, never joins onto a
following letter, so **waaw** stands on its own. But here:

توَاليِت

tawaaliit toilet

waaw is preceded by ت which joins onto the following **waaw**.

As well as serving as the consonant equivalent to the English 'w', **waaw** is
also written to lengthen a short 'u'. Thus **bu**, with the short vowel, looks
like this:

and with the vowel lengthened to **buu**, like this:

Our second letter in this unit is ن , called in Arabic **nuun**. It is identical
in sound with English 'n'. It joins on to both preceding and following letters,
where these allow. At the beginning and in the middle of a word, it has the
same shape as ب , ت , and ي , except that **nuun** has a single dot
written above it.:

نبَات **nabaat** plant

بِنْت **bint** girl

At the end of a word it is more rounded than **baa** and **taa**:

بَيْن **bayn** between

It has a similar shape when written on its own:

بَيَان **bayaan** announcement

15 Read aloud the following words, which have been vowelled. Check your
answers (p.74). Then practise writing the same words, but this time leave
out the vowels.

(a) يَا   (b) أبُو   (c) بِنْتِي

(d) تِين   (e) بَنَات   (f) انَا وَأنْتَ

(g) لُبْنَان

You will learn

- how to ask about the time
- how to tell the time
- how to ask about and understand working hours
- how to ask and understand when shops, stores and banks open and close
- how to ask about the weekend
- some time expressions
- the days of the week

Study guide

Dialogue 1 + Practise what you have learned
Dialogue 2 + Practise what you have learned
Dialogue 3 + Practise what you have learned
Dialogue 4 + Practise what you have learned
Key words and phrases
Grammar
Your turn to speak
Did you know?
Writing

Dialogues

1 *What time is it?*

Clive	law samaHt, 'addeesh is saa9a?
Man	is-saa9a tis9a u xamsa.
Woman	is-saa9a xamsa u nuSS.
Clive	shukran
Woman	ahleen.
Man	tinteen illa rubu9.
Clive	tinteen illa rubu9?
Man	na9am.
Clive	shukran.
Man	9afwan.

saa9a hour, the time, clock, watch
tis9a u xamsa five past nine (lit. nine and five)
xamsa u nuSS half past five (lit. five and a half)
tinteen illa rubu9 quarter to two (lit. two except a quarter)

> When telling the time in Arabic, you use **u** (lit. and) for 'past' and **illa** (lit. except) for 'to'. **tult** 'one third' is used for 20 minutes. Thus **tis9a illa tult** is 8.40 (lit. nine except twenty). 9.25 is **tis9a u nuSS illa xamsa** (lit. nine and half except five), while 9.35 is **tis9a u nuSS u xamsa** (lit. nine and half and five).

'addeesh is-saa9a, min faDlak?

Practise what you have learned

1 Here are four people asking about the times of different things. Listen to the tape and mark the times they mention. (Answers p.87)

(a) **'addeesh is-saa9a?** what time is it?

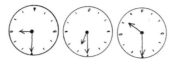

(b) **eemta maw9id il-baaS?** when is the bus due?

(c) **eemta l-fTuur?** when is breakfast?

(d) **eemta maw9id iT-Tayyaara?** when is the plane due?

2 Nadira wants to know Lana's timetable for the day. Listen and mark off the times that Lana mentions. (Answers p.87)

3 Your turn to speak. Look at the clocks below and give the times. Listen to the recording to check your answers.

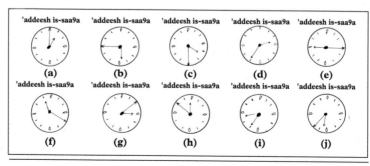

Dialogues

2 Clive wants to know the working hours of a company he's visiting

Man	wallah waqt id-dawaam fi sh-sharika 9indna min is-saa9a tamaanya iS-SubuH la s-saa9a tinteen.
Clive	ah.
Man	u fii iyyaam biykuun fiiha d-dawaam min is-saa9a tamaanya la s-saa9a arba9a ... haadha waqt id-dawaam.
Clive	fi ayy yoom ya9ni?
Man	yoom il-arba9a

wallah by God (mild oath, same meaning as **wallaahi**)
waqt id-dawaam working day, working hours
iS-SubuH [in] the morning
ayy which
yoom il-arba9a Wednesday

> ◆ **is-saa9a tinteen** two o'clock (lit. the hour two). **tinteen** is the feminine form of **itneen**. It is feminine because **saa9a** is feminine.
>
> **fii iyyaam biykuun fiiha d-dawaam min ...** there are days when the working day is from... (lit. there [are] days [which there] is in them working hours from...). **biykuun** is the non-past tense of the verb **kaan/ykuun** 'to be' with the B-prefix.
>
> ◆ **fi ayy yoom ya9ni?** on which day do you mean? **ayy** is used when asking about a particular one of a group or class. For example, **ayy sayyaara?** which car? **fi ayy ghurfa?** in which room?

3 And what about the weekend?

Man	yoom il-jum9a biykuun 9indna 9uTul.
Clive	9uTul.
Man	maa fii dawaam ... dawaamna biykuun min is-sabt la l-xamiis ... il-xamiis biykuun 9indna nuSS in-nhaar.
Clive	nuSS in-nhaar.
Man	nuSS in-nhaar ya9ni la s-saa9a waHda ... binDHall fi sh-shughul, na9am.
Clive	zeen, mashkuur.
Man	il-9afu, ahlan wa sahlan.

yoom il jum9a Friday
9uTul day off, time off, holiday
is-sabt (or **yoom is-sabt**) Saturday
il-xamiis (or **yoom il-xamiis**) Thursday
nuSS in-nhaar half-day
binDHall we stay, remain
shughul work, occupation, business
zeen good, OK (=**kwayyis**)
mashkuur thank you (= **shukran**)
il-9afu don't mention it (= **9afwan**)

Practise what you have learned

4   Widaad is asking a storekeeper about opening and closing hours. Listen and mark off the correct answers. (Answers p.87)
New words: **fataH/yiftaH** to open, **sakkar/ysakkir** to close, **Duhur** noon, **ba9d iD-Duhur** afternoon, **masa** evening.

1   What time does the store open in the morning?
    (a) **sab9a**
    (b) **tis9a**
    (c) **tamaanya**

2   What time does the store close for lunch?
    (a) **is-saa9a itna9sh u nuSS**
    (b) **is-saa9a tinteen**
    (c) **is-saa9a waHda**

3   What time does the store re-open in the afternoon?
    (a) **is-saa9a talaata**
    (b) **is-saa9a arba9a**
    (c) **is-saa9a talaata u nuSS**

4   What time does the store close in the evening?
    (a) **is-saa9a sitta**
    (b) **is-saa9a xamsa**
    (c) **is-saa9a sab9a**

5   Listen to Jane trying to learn the days of the week. Repeat them after her. For help, refer to *Key words and phrases* in this Unit.

6   Your turn to speak. Someone is asking about your working hours at the bank. Nadira will prompt you.

7   Nahid has applied for a job as a secretary. Her boss is telling her about the company's working hours. Listen and decide which sentences are true and which are false. (Answers p.87)

T/F

—— **(a)**   Nahid has to work from Monday to Saturday from 8.00 a.m to 2.00 p.m. only.

—— **(b)**   Nahid has to work on Thursday from 8.00 a.m. to 1.00 p.m.

—— **(c)**   Nahid has to work from Monday to Saturday from 8.00 a.m and from 2.00 p.m. and from 3.30 p.m. to 6.00 p.m.

—— **(d)**   Nahid has to work from Saturday to Wednesday from 8.00 a.m to 2.00 p.m. and from 3.30 p.m. to 6.00 p.m.

—— **(e)**   Nahid has the whole day off on Friday.

8   Your turn to speak. In this exercise you are going to practise the days of the week. Nadira will ask you the question in English and you will give the answer in Arabic. Then listen to the correct answer.

Dialogues

4 Clive asks Abdullah how long he has been doing his present job

Clive	mumkin il-ax as'alak Saar lak kam ya9ni hoon fi l-British Council?
Abdallah	Saar lii ana xams sanawaat illa xams iyyaam.
Clive	illa xams iyyaam.
Abdallah	na9am ... ana min sab9a arb9a l-arba9a u thamaaniin la ithneen arba9a tis9a u thamaaniin - xams sanawaat illa xams iyyaam.

as'al   I ask (a question)
sana, (pl. **sanawaat**)   year

> **mumkin il-ax as'alak ...**   may I ask you, my friend ... (lit. possible the brother I ask you ...)
>
> **Saar lak kam ...**   how long have you been ...? (lit. became to you how much ...?)
>
> **xams sanawaat illa xams iyyaam**   five years all but five days (lit. five years except five days). **xams iyyaam** is quite formal. It is more colloquial to say **xams tiyyaam.**
>
> **min sab9a arba9a l-arba9a u thamaaniin la ithneen arba9a tis9a u thamaaniin**   from 7.4. in '84 to 2.4.89. Note that this speaker says **thamaaniin** and **ithneen** rather than **tamaaniin** and **itneen**, because he is being more 'correct' (i.e. more like written Arabic).

Practise what you have learned

9 Basima and Najwa haven't seen each other for quite a while, and they are catching up on each other's news. Listen and, in English, arrange the information into two columns – in column one the information about Basima, and in column two the information about Najwa.
(Answers p.87)
New words: **il-bank il-9arabi** the Arab Bank, **bashtaghil** I work.

	Basima	Najwa
lives in:	_____	_____
works in:	_____	_____
name of employer:	_____	_____
period of employment:	_____	_____

10 Listen to three people talking about their jobs. Try to note down, in English, the answers to the following questions. (Answers p.87)

  (a) 'addeesh iluh samiir fi shughluh?
  (b) shu awqaat dawaam hind?
  (c) eemta 9uTlit samiir?
  (d) eemta 9uTlit hind?

11 Your turn to speak. You meet an old acquaintance. He wants to know where you are these days and what you're doing. Respond to his questions. Nadira will prompt you.

Key words and phrases

To learn

'addeesh is-saa9a?	what time is it?
is-saa9a ...	it's ... o'clock
is-saa9a ... u ...	it's ... past ...
is-saa9a ... illa ...	it's ... to ...
nuSS	half
rubu9	quarter
tult	third (20 minutes)
il-aHad	Sunday
it-tneen	Monday
it-talaata	Tuesday
il-arba9a	Wednesday
il-xamiis	Thursday
il-jum9a	Friday
is-sabt	Saturday
9uTlit il-usbuu9	weekend
usbuu9 (pl) asaabii9	week
shahar (pl) ashhur	month
iS-SubuH	(in) the morning
il-masa	(in) the evening
ba9d iD-Duhur	in the afternoon
shughul	job, work
sana (pl) sanawaat	year
ayy	which ...?
waqt (or wa't)	time (as in **maa 9indi wa't** I don't have time)

To understand

(awqaat) id-dawaam	working hours
nuSS in-nhaar	half-day

Grammar

The plural

In Unit 2 we met the 'dual', which involved adding **-een** to the end of a word to make two of it e.g. **walad** (one) boy, **waladeen** two boys. Arabic plurals – that is, three or more of something – are of two kinds, called 'sound' and 'broken'. Nouns which take the sound plural simply add an ending to the singular, either **-iin** or **-aat**.

Plurals in **-iin** (or **-yyiin** after nouns ending in **-i**)

These are typically used for male human beings, professions and mixed male/female groups.

singular		plural	
mudarris	⟶	**mudarrisiin**	teachers
muhandis	⟶	**muhandisiin**	engineers ·
urduni	⟶	**urduniyyiin**	Jordanians (people)
lubnaani	⟶	**lubnaaniyyiin**	Lebanese (people)

Plurals in **-aat**

These are used for female human beings, for feminine nouns (those ending in **-a**) and for foreign words imported into Arabic. In the case of feminine nouns, the **-aat** is added after removing the feminine ending **-a** from the singular.

singular		plural	
mudarrisa	⟶	**mudarrisaat**	female teachers
saa9a	⟶	**saa9aat**	hours
ziyaara	⟶	**ziyaaraat**	visits
utiil	⟶	**utiilaat**	hotels
baaS	⟶	**baaSaat**	buses

Grammar

'Broken' plurals

The 'broken' plural is by far the most frequently used method of forming the plural in Arabic. It is formed by taking the <u>consonants</u> of the singular noun and changing the vowel pattern, sometimes doubling one of the consonants or adding another consonant. There are a number of common broken plural patterns in spoken Arabic. It is a good idea to learn the plural of a word along with its singular. Here are some examples of common patterns. 'C' stands for consonant.

(a) singular pattern CaCaC, CiCC or CaCC; plural pattern iCCaaC or aCCaaC

singular		plural	
walad	⟶	iwlaad	boys
'alam	⟶	i'laam	pens
si9r	⟶	as9aar	prices
shaxS	⟶	ashxaaS	persons

(b) singular pattern CaCiiC or CuCiiC; plural pattern CuCaCa

singular		plural	
ra'iis	⟶	ru'asa	president
mudiir	⟶	mudara	boss
waziir	⟶	wuzara	[government] minister

(c) singular pattern CaaCiC; plural pattern CuCCaaC

singular		plural	
saakin	⟶	sukkaan	inhabitant
9aamil	⟶	9ummaal	worker, labourer
zaayir	⟶	zuwwaar	visitor

Note the change from **y** to **w** in the last example here.

Some more common broken plural patterns are dealt with in Unit 7.

Your turn to speak

12 You are visiting a company in Jordan. Introduce yourself to the receptionist and ask to arrange a day and a time to see the director of the company. Then listen to a possible version of what you might say.
Remember: **sharika** company.

13 You have a visitor who would like to know about your working hours. Ask him some questions – his name, where he comes from, if he would like to drink anything. Listen to his responses and answer his questions. Then listen to a possible version on the recording.

Answers

Practise what you have learned

Exercise 1 (a) 7.30 (b) 11.45 (c) 7.00 (d) 10.35

Exercise 2 7.10; 8.00; 9.00; 2.00; 6.20

Exercise 4 1: (c) 2: (c) 3: (a) 4: (c)

Exercise 7 (a) F (b) T (c) F (d) T (e) T

Exercise 9

	Basima	Najwa
lives in:	Amman	Zar'a
works in:	Amman	Amman
employer:	The Arab Bank	Phillips
period of employment:	3 years	2 years

Exercise 10 (a) 6 years (b) 7.30-3.00 (c) Friday (d) Friday and

Did you know?

It's May 1989 in the Christian calendar
It's Ramadan and Shawwal, 1409 in the Muslim one.

Writing

Exercise 14 (a) bayruut (Beirut)   (b) al-yaabaan (Japan)
(c) liibyaa (Libya)   (d) almaanya (Germany)
(e) waziir (minister)   (f) al-yaman (Yemen)
(g) taimz ([The] Times) (h) yuulyuu (July)
(i) zaytuun (olives, as in jabal az-zaytuun, Mount of Olives)
(j) abriil (April)   (k) zamaan (time)
(l) yuunyuu (June)

Did you know?

The calendar

Although the western <u>solar</u> calendar is now used throughout the Arab world in business and most areas of daily life, the Muslim <u>lunar</u> calendar is still used in some countries alongside the western one (most widely in Saudi Arabia and the Gulf States). In all Arab (indeed all Islamic) countries, however, the Muslim calendar is used for religious purposes.

Nowadays, the most commonly used Arabic names for the months in western calendar are simply transliterations of their English equivalents:

yanaayir	January	**yuulyuu**	July
fabraayir	February	**aghustus**	August
maars	March	**sabtambar**	September
abriil	April	**uktuubar**	October
maayuu	May	**nuufambar**	November
yuunyuu	June	**diisambar**	December

However, there is an older set of names which is still much used in the former territories of the Ottoman Empire:

kaanuun ith-thaani	January	**tammuuz**	July
shubaaT	February	**aab**	August
aadhaar	March	**ayluul**	September
niisaan	April	**tishriin il-awwal**	October
ayaar	May	**tishriin ith-thaani**	November
Haziiraan	June	**kaanuun il-awwal**	December

The months of the Muslim calendar are 29 or 30 days long (depending on the sighting of the moon) and are named as follows:

muHarram	**rajab**	
Safar	**sha9baan**	
rabii9 il-awwal	**ramaDaan**	(the fasting month)
rabii9 ith-thaani	**shawwaal**	
jumaada l-awwal	**dhu l-qa9da**	
jumaada th-thaani	**dhu l-Hijja**	(the month of the pilgrimage to Mecca)

Since the lunar year is about ten days shorter than the solar year, fixed Muslim religious festivals occur about ten days earlier each year, as measured by the solar calendar. So, for example, if in a particular year the 'Eid al-Fitr' (fast-breaking at the end of Ramadan) coincides with Christmas Day (as it more or less did in 1968) it will occur 10 days earlier the following year and so on until it once more coincides with Christmas about 35 years later.

The Muslim era began with the flight of the Prophet Muhammad from Mecca to Medina in 622 A.D. This 'flight' is known in Arabic as the **hijra**, and Muslim dates normally appear followed by ﻫ i.e. **hijri** (after the flight). Christian dates are followed by ﻡ standing for **miilaadi** (after the birth). Study the Muslim/Christian calendar on p.89 and see whether you can discover which month of which solar year it is for. Which Muslim year is it? (Answer p.87)

Ramadan

Major Muslim religious festivals

During Ramadan Muslims may not eat, drink or have sexual relations between first light and sundown. Ramadan is a particularly 'holy' period when much time is devoted to prayer and the reading of the Qur'an. Ministries and most businesses work short hours and restaurants close during daylight hours.

Did you know?

At the end of Ramadan comes the feast of 'Eid al-Fitr' (Arabic **9iid al-fiTr**) when the all-day fast is broken. The spotting of the new moon signals the beginning of the month of Shawwal and the start of a three- or four-day holiday when no expense is spared on lavish food and presents for the children. The standard greeting between Muslims and non-Muslims alike is **9iid mubaarak** 'blessed Eid' often with the additional phrase **kul 9aam wa antum bi xeer** 'may you continue to be well with every passing year'.

The Hajj

The Hajj (Arabic **il-Hajj**), or pilgrimage to Mecca, is a duty which every Muslim who can afford it is obliged to perform at least once in his or her lifetime. The Hajj involves a number of rituals over a period of about ten days, the most notable of which is the circumambulation of the **ka9ba** (a cube-shaped building) in the Grand Mosque at Mecca. At the end of the rituals, the pilgrims (and indeed all Muslims whether they have made the pilgrimage or not) slaughter a sheep or goat for their family's consumption. This is called the 'Eid al-Adha' (**9iid il-'aDHa**) or 'Feast of the Sacrifice'. As at the end of Ramadan, there is a three- or four-day holiday of feasting and family visiting.

ه١٤٠٩					رمضان/شوّال					١٩٨٩م				مايو
٢٢	١٥	٨	*(١)		السبت	٢٧	٢٠	١٣	*(٦)	
٢٣	١٦	٩	٢		الأحـد	٢٨	٢١	١٤	٧	
٢٤	١٧	١٠	٣	٢٥	الاثـنـين	٢٩	٢٢	١٥	٨	١
٢٥	١٨	١١	٤	٢٦	الثـلاثـاء	٣٠	٢٣	١٦	٩	٢
٢٦	١٩	١٢	٥	٢٧	الأربعـاء	٣١	٢٤	١٧	١٠	٣
	٢٠	١٣	٦	٢٨	الخميـس		٢٥	١٨	١١	٤
	٢١	١٤	٧	٢٩	الجمعـة		٢٦	١٩	١٢	٥

Writing

In this unit we will learn three more letters. The first is called **miim** and sounds like an English 'm'. Written on its own, it looks like this:

م

as in the word يوم (in spoken Arabic **yoom**)

meaning 'day' At the beginning or in the middle of the word, **miim** loses its tail and always joins on to the letter which follows:

مَايُو

maayuu [the month of] May

مِيمِي

miimii Mimi

We can deal with the next two letters together, as they differ only in the presence or absence of a dot. They are **raa** which is like a rolled 'r' and looks like this:

ر

and **zaa** which sounds like a 'z' and has the same shape as **raa** except that it has a dot above it:

ز

These two letters never join onto a following letter but are joined to a preceding one if it allows. Thus, at the beginning of a word:

رُومَا

ruumaa Rome

زَيْت

zayt oil

and joined to a preceding letter:

تَمْر

tamr [edible] date

رَمْزِي

ramzi Ramzy

14 Read the following. (Answers p.87)

(a) بَيْرُوت

(b) الْيَابَان

(c) لِيبْيا

(d) الْمَانْيا

(e) وَزِير

(f) الْيَمن

(g) «تَايْمز»

(h) يُولْيُو

(i) زَيْتُون

(j) أَبْرِيل

(k) زَمَان

(l) يُونْيُو

SHOPPING (part 1)

You will learn

● to ask for what you want at various shops and stores
● to talk about quantities of things you want
● to understand a storekeeper's questions
● to ask about the price of articles

Study guide

Dialogue 1 + Practise what you have learned
Dialogue 2 + Practise what you have learned
Dialogue 3 + Practise what you have learned
Dialogue 4 + Practise what you have learned
Key words and phrases
Grammar
Your turn to speak
Did you know?
Writing

Dialogues

1 *At the hotel giftshop, Clive is looking for a guide to Jordan and one or two other things*

Clive	SabaaH il-xeer.
Assistant	ahleen, SabaaH il-xeer.
Clive	law samaHt, 9indkum daliil il-urdun?
Assistant	ah, na9am, mawjuud.
Clive	ah ... 'addeesh si9ruh?
Assistant	sab9a danaaniir.
Clive	zeen ... u xarTit 9ammaan kamaan?
Assistant	mawjuud.
Clive	ha ... kam haada?
Assistant	dinaareen.
Clive	u bitbii9u Tawaabi9?
Assistant	na9am.
Clive	9aTni itneen bi xamsiin fils min faDlak.
Assistant	Haadir, tfaDDal.

SabaaH il-xeer good morning
daliil guide, directory
dinaar, (pl) **danaaniir** Dinar (unit of currency)
xarTa map
zeen OK, fine (alternative to **kwayyis** or **mniiH**)
kamaan as well, also, more
bitbii9u you (pl.) sell
Taabi9, (pl) **Tawaabi9** postage stamp
9aTni (or **a9Tiini**) give (m.) me
fils Fils (unit of currency)
min faDlak please (to a man)
min faDlik please (to a woman)
HaaDir certainly (reply to a request or command)

Practise what you have learned

1 John wants to try reading an Arabic newspaper – **jariida** (pl **jaraayid**) **9arabiyya** – and asks for one in a store. Later the storekeeper asks him if he wants anything else – **shii taani?** (lit. another thing?). Here's the conversation between John and the storekeeper. Select phrases from the box below the conversation to fill the blanks. Check your answers by listening to the recording. Note: **ir-ra'y** is the name of a newspaper.

John	SabaaH il-xeer.
Storekeeper	_____ .
John	_____ jariida 9arabiyya kwaysa _____ .
Storekeeper	biddak urduniyya _____ suuriyya?
John	urduniyya, _____ .
Storekeeper	_____ ir-ra'y, kwaysa jiddan.
John	_____ ?
Storekeeper	_____ talaatiin _____ .
John	kwayyis, _____ .
Storekeeper	shii taani?
John	shukran ilak.

> iza mumkin, baaxudha, shu fii 9indak?, SabaaH il-xeer, 'irsh, fii, willa, 'addeesh si9rha?, biddi, xamsa u

2 In this exercise you will hear Fadya doing some shopping. Here is a list of some things she buys and some things she doesn't. Mark (✓) the items she buys and put a cross (✗) against those unavailable or which she doesn't ask for. Write the quantities in. (Answers p.102)

	✓ or ✗	quantity
cigarettes		
Coca Cola		
newspapers		
packets of tea		
packets of biscuits		
chocolate		

Fadya begins with the greeting **masa l-xeer** 'good afternoon, evening', used after about 3 o'clock in the afternoon. Note also how she uses **'addeesh il-Hisaab** 'what's the bill' to ask how much the items she's buying come to altogether.

3 Your turn to speak. You go into a shop in the late afternoon and ask the assistant if they have English newspapers. You want *The Times* and a packet of biscuits (**biskoot**). Nadira won't prompt you this time, but all you need to do is reply appropriately to the store assistant and ask at the end how much the items come to. After you've spoken each time, you'll hear a version of the same thing – if it's a bit different from yours, that doesn't necessarily mean that yours is wrong.

Dialogues

2 *Munir needs some colour film*

Munir	wallaahi law samaHt biddi as'al - fii 9indkum aflaam? filim sitta u talaatiin Suura?
Assistant	na9am.
Munir	u mulawwan?
Assistant	mulawwan, na9am.
Munir	iza mumkin biddi filim.
Assistant	HaaDir.

filim, (pl) **aflaam**   film
Suura, (pl) **Suwar**   picture, photograph
mulawwan   colour (film)

---

filim sitta u talaatiin Suura   a film with thirty-six exposures

---

Practise what you have learned

4 Here are some things you might find yourself wanting to say in connection with shopping. Fill in the missing non-past verbs, with or without **bi-**, to give the meaning of the English translation. (Answers p.102)

(a) **ween _____ Tawaabi9?** where do they sell stamps?

(b) **ayy jaraayid _____ ?** which newspapers do you sell?

(c) **mit 'asfiin, maa _____ 9arabi kwayyis.** sorry, we don't speak Arabic very well.

(d) **biddna _____ il-jaraayid.** we'd like to see the papers.

(e) **_____ jariidit it-taimz, iza mumkin.** we'll have *The Times*, please.

5 On the tape you will hear Mohamed talking to a man in the street. Mark off the version of the sentences below that correctly describes their conversation. (Answers p.102)

1 Mohamed wants to know where he can ask about
 (a) cinema hours.
 (b) bus times.
 (c) taxis to Irbid.

2 The man directs him to
 (a) the bus station.
 (b) the hotel reception.
 (c) the tourist office.

3 Malik Abdallah Street is
 (a) the second street on the right.
 (b) at the end of the third street on the right.
 (c) at the end of the second street on the right.

4 Mohamed asks if
 (a) they sell guides and maps to Jordan.
 (b) he can look at a map of Jordan there.
 (c) they sell bus tickets there.

6 Your turn to speak. Here's some practice at saying amounts of Jordanian money. You need to read the *Did you know?* section first. You will also need to look at the numbers from 100 to 1000 in the *Key words and phrases* section. Here's an example: **talaat talaaf u arba9miyya u xamsa u sittiin dulaar** $3,465. Now look again how Clive asks for two 50 fils stamps. (In fact it is more common to hear **xamas 'uruush** for this amount.) Here are some amounts for you to practise, as if you're asking for stamps. First work out how to say them, then say them, and check with the recording, line by line.

(1) 1 x 0.10JD + 2 x 0.20JD
(2) 1 x 0.500JD + 3 x 0.250JD
(3) 1 x 1JD + 1 x 0.15JD
(4) 4 x 0.38JD

Dialogues

3 *Munir needs some black and white film*

Munir	ba9deen ... u ba9deen biddi kamaan filim arba9a u 9ishriin Suura abyaD u aswad.
Assistant	HaaDir.
Munir	mawjuud kamaan, law ...? iza mumkin shu as9aarhum matalan?
Assistant	as9aarhum dinaareen u xamsa u talaatiin il-9aadi –
Munir	il-abyaD u il-aswad?
Assistant	il-abyaD u il-aswad dinaareen u nuSS u il-9aadi dinaareen u xamsa u tamaaniin.
Munir	Tayyib shukran.

ba9deen and then
kamaan as well
abyaD white
aswad black
matalan for example

> ◆ **mawjuud kamaan law ...** do you have that as well, or ...? (lit. existing as well, or ...)
>
> ◆ **dinaareen u xamsa u talaatiin** 2 Dinars 35. The official units of currency in Jordan are the Dinar and the Fils (1,000 to the Dinar). The '35' is 35 **'irsh,** a denomination of the old Ottoman currency still very much in colloquial use in Jordan, Syria, Palestine and Egypt. An **'irsh** (pl **'uruush**) in Jordan is equal to 10 Fils, so the price in the official units of currency would be JD 2.350. In fact the assistant gets confused and quotes 2 Dinars 85 (= JD 2.850) in his next sentence for the same item. See *Did you know?* this Unit.
>
> **il-9aadi** the ordinary one. A reference to colour film, as this is what most people use nowadays.

Practise what you have learned

7 Listen to Sahar buying bus tickets **tazkara,** (pl) **tazaakir,** then fill in what she wants on the table. (Answers p.102)
New word: **sarii9** express (lit. fast).

	Price	Number of tickets
ordinary		
express		

8 Fill in the blanks in this telephone conversation to give the same meaning as the English. Then check your answers on page 102.

Samir	**aloo?**	Hello?
Ashraf	**samiir? ana ashraf.**	Samir? This is Ashraf,
Samir	**ahlan yaa ashraf, kiifak?**	Hi, how are you?
Ashraf	**allah yisalmak. shu ra'yak tiiji ma9ai 9ala s-siinama _____ ? _____ filim Annie Hall.**	OK. What do you think of coming with me to the cinema this afternoon? We can see the film 'Annie Hall'.
Samir	**ma9leesh, mish mumkin 9ashaan SaaliH laazim _____ hoon _____ .**	Sorry, I can't, because Salih's supposed to be coming (lit. must come) here at two o'clock.
Ashraf	**_____ kamaan. _____ btaaxdu taksi u btuuSalu _____ ana min il-maktab.**	He can come too. As soon as he comes, you take a taxi and you'll arrive before I get there from the office.

9 Your turn to speak. You want to buy some postcards **kart,** (pl) **kuruut.**

Dialogues

4 *Hind buys a few things from the corner grocery store*

Hind	marHaba nabiil
Nabil	ahleen marHaba.
Hind	ijakum il-laHma l-yoom?
Nabil	laHma lissa ... lissa la s-saa9a waHda ta'riiban.
Hind	ah, allah yxalliik, fii imkaaniyya txalliihum lamma tiiji l-laHma yi9malu lii tneen laHma kabaab u iza byib9atu lii ma9aha itneen kiilo banduura ... ruzz u sukkar kamaan itneen kiilo.
Nabil	da'ii'a waHda bas asajjilhum ma9leesh? ... itneen kiilo laHma u itneen kiilo banduura, itneen kiilo ruzz u itneen kiilo sukkar ...

ijat (it) came
laHma meat
il-yoom today
lissa not yet
ta'riiban about, approximately
imkaaniyya possibility
txalli you allow, make
   (someone do something)
lamma when, at the time when
tiiji (it) comes
yi9malu they make
laHma kabaab kebab meat
bib9atu they send
banduura tomato(es)
ruzz rice
sukkar sugar
da'ii'a (pl) **da'aayi'** minute
bas just
asajjil I note down
kiilo kilogramme

> • **allah yxalliik ...** God preserve you .. This phrase is used here as a way of 'softening' a request to someone to do something, and functions in a similar way to **law samaHt** 'if you wouldn't mind' or **iza mumkin** 'if possible'. We met the same phrase in Unit 1, but used in a different context.
>
> • **fii imkaaniyya txalliihum lamma tiiji l-laHma yi9malu lii ...** when the meat arrives, is there any possibility you could have them make for me ... (lit. is there possibility you let them, when comes the meat, they make for me ...) The 'them' and 'they' here refers to the storekeeper's assistants. **fii imkaaniyya ...** is another way of making a request sound polite.
>
> • **itneen kiilo** two kilos. With kilos, litres and kilometres the noun stays in the singular, and the numbers are used in their counting forms with **-a** on the end. The same applies to ordering food and drinks, e.g. **talaata litir** 3 litres, **xamsa 'ahwa** 5 coffees, etc.
>
> • **u iza byib9atu lii ...** and could they send me ... (lit. and if they send to me ...)
>
> • **da'ii'a waHda bas asajjilhum ma9leesh?** just one minute while I note that down, all right? The **-hum** refers to the things Hind has ordered.

Practise what you have learned

10 On the recording you will hear Nadira checking over what she has bought. Check it against her shopping list below and see what she still needs to get. (Answers p.102)

small packet of cocoa

1½ Kg sugar

litre Pepsi

3 tins beans

3 packets biscuits

4 Packets tea

2 big bottles of orange Juice

11 Your turn to speak. Buying tickets for a film. Note that 'the film x' is a 'construct' phrase: you say **filim x**, as in **filim Annie Hall**, the film Annie Hall. Nadira will guide you, as usual.

Key words and phrases

To learn

SabaH il-xeer	Good morning
masa l-xeer	Good afternoon, good evening
ma9a s-salaama	Goodbye
itneen kiilo ruzz	two kilos of rice
litir Haliib	a litre of milk
9ilbit shukalaaTa	a box of chocolates
sagaayir	a packet of cigarettes
banduura	a can of tomatoes
bakeet biskoot	a packet of biscuits
'azaazit 9aSiir	a bottle of fruit juice
tazkara, (pl) tazaakir	ticket
Suura, (pl) Suwar	picture, photograph
jariida, (pl) jaraayid	newspaper
kamaan	also, as well
9imil/yi9mal	to make, do
ba9at/yib9at	to send
a9Ta/ya9Ti	to give
lamma yiiji	when he comes, gets here
'abil maa aaji	before I come
awwal maa yuuSal	as soon as he/it arrives
miiteen	200
talaatmiyya	300
arba9miyya	400
xamasmiyya	500
sittmiyya	600
saba9miyya	700
tamaanmiyya	800
tisa9miyya	900
alf, (pl) alaaf	a thousand (the plural becomes **talaaf** after a number)
shii taani?	anything else?
min faDlak/faDlik	please

Grammar

More on verbs

In Unit 3 we gave the non-past tense of verbs like **yHibb** 'he likes' and **yiHjiz** 'he reserves'. Now we'll look at two other kinds. First there are some verbs which have a long vowel (**uu, ii** or **aa**) in the middle of their non-past form. In all other respects, they go like **yHibb**:

aruuH	I go	**nruuH**	we go
truuH	you (m.) go	**truuHu**	you (pl) go
truuHi	you (f.) go	**yruuHu**	they go
yruuH	he (or it) goes		
truuH	she (or it) goes		

Other examples of **uu** non-pasts we've met are **yshuuf** he sees and **ykuun** he is. An example of an **ii** non-past in this Unit is **ybii9** 'he sells' which occurs in Dialogue 1 with the B-prefix in the you (pl) form: **bitbii9u** you (pl) sell.

Another common type of non-past verb ends in a vowel, **-i** or **-a**, e.g. **yiHki** he speaks, **yibda** he begins. The **-i** or **-a** is kept throughout the non-past, except where another vowel is added as part of the ending:

aHki	I speak	**niHki**	we speak
tiHki	you (m.) speak	**tiHku**	you (pl) speak
tiHki	you (f.) speak	**yiHku**	they speak
yiHki	he (or it) speaks		
tiHki	she (or it) speaks		

abda	I begin	**nibda**	we begin
tibda	you (m.) begin	**tibdu**	you (pl) begin
tibdi	you (f.) begin	**yibdu**	they begin
yibda	he (or it) begins		
tibda	she (or it) begins		

12 Fill in the blanks with the right form of **yiHki** or **yibda**. (Answers p.102)

A law samaHtu b _____ ingliizi?

B laa ma9leesh, b _____ 9arabi bas.

A mumkin as'alkum eemta b _____ il-filim?

B b _____ ba9d xamas da'aayi'. b _____ 9arabi kwayyis ktiir.

A shukran

Negatives

As we have already seen, negatives of all kinds of words except verbs are made with **mish**. For example, **huwwa mish mawjuud** he isn't there, **ana mish amriiki** I'm not American. There are three ways you can say 'not' with a verb. Use whichever you like, but you will have to understand all three. So, to negate **baHibb** I like, you can put **maa** before and **-sh** after: **maa baHibbish**; or just **maa** before: **maa baHibb**; or just **-sh** after: **baHabbish**. They all mean exactly the same thing: 'I don't like'. **9ind** and **fii** are negated by **maa**. For example, **maa 9indi waqt** I haven't time, **maa fii maay** there's no water.

Broken plurals

We saw in Unit 6 that nouns of the pattern CaaCiC often have the broken plural CuCCaaC. This is usually with words where a profession or regular activity is designated, like 'inhabitant' or 'worker'. Other nouns with the CaaCiC singular pattern, but with a non-human meaning, have a different plural pattern:

singular		*plural*	
Taabi9	────►	**Tawaabi9**	postage stamps
shaari9	────►	**shawaari9**	streets
jaami9	────►	**jawaami9**	mosques

The plural pattern here is CawaaCiC.

Your turn to speak

13

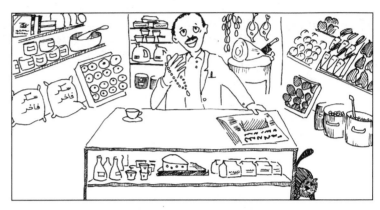

You have just walked into this store. Ask for at least five things you want, remembering to give quantities. Then compare with Nadira doing the same on the recording.

Answers

Practise what you have learned

Exercise 2 She buys 1 packet of tea (large).
She buys 1 packet of biscuits.
She does not buy cigarettes (only American are available), and does not ask for CoCa-Cola, newspapers or chocolate.

Exercise 4 (a) biybii9u
(b) bitbii9u
(c) bniHki
(d) nshuuf
(e) biddna

Exercise 5 1. (b) 2. (c) 3. (c) 4. (a)

Exercise 7 2 'ordinary' at 500 fils each
1 'express' at 750 fils each

Exercise 8 ba9d iD-Duhr; binshuuf; yiiji; is-saa9a tinteen; mumkin yiiji; awwal maa yiiji; abil maa awSal

Exercise 10 She still needs to get 3 tins of beans and 2 big bottles of orange juice.

Grammar

Exercise 12 A: btiHku
B: baHki
C: byibda
B: byibda ... btiHki

Writing

Exercise 14 (a) saalim (b) saliim (c) maryam (d) samiira
(e) sabtambar (f) shaay (g) liira (h) liira suuri
(i) salaam (j) shiiratuun (k) maaryuut (l) wizaara

Did you know?

Money

In the modern Arab world, the currencies of all countries are decimal. The designations of the units, however, differ from one country to another. Below are some you are likely to encounter.

Jordan	1,000 fils	= 1 dinar (JD)	dinaar urduni
Iraq	1,000 fils	= 1 dinar (ID)	dinaar 9iraaqi
Kuwait	1,000 fils	= 1 dinar (KD)	dinaar kweeti
Bahrain	1,000 fils	= 1 dinar (BD)	dinaar baHreeni
Egypt	100 piastres	= 1 pound (£E)	gineeh maSri
Syria	100 piastres	= 1 pound (£S)	liira suuri
Lebanon	100 piastres	= 1 pound (£L)	liira lubnaani
Saudi Arabia	100 halala	= 1 riyal (SR)	riyaal sa9uudi
Qatar	100 dirhams	= 1 riyal (QR)	riyaal qaTari
Oman	1,000 baisa	= 1 riyal (OR)	riyaal 9umaani
UAE	100 fils	= 1 dirham	dirham

The pound is called **gineeh,** (pl) **gineehaat** (from English 'guinea') in Egypt, and **liira,** (pl) **liiraat** (from Italian 'lira' via Turkey) in Lebanon and Syria. The smaller denomination **'irsh** (or **qirsh**), (pl) **'uruush** (or **quruush**) 'piastre' is used in all these countries, and also colloquially in Jordan. Prices in colloquial Arabic in Egypt are generally expressed in terms of the **gineeh** and **'irsh**. In Lebanon and Syria, the **'irsh** is in normal use as one hundredth of the **liira,** though galloping inflation in Lebanon has so devalued the currency that the **'irsh** is no longer in use.

In Jordan the **'irsh**, while no longer part of the official currency, is commonly used as equivalent of 10 fils, so **xamsa u 9ishriin 'irsh** '25 qirsh' is equal in Jordan to **miiteen u xamsiin fils** '250 fils' or alternatively **rubu9 dinaar,** 'a quarter of a dinar'. All of these variants are encountered in normal conversation. Obviously, the other currency names noted above – the **riyaal,** (pl) **riyaalaat,** the **dinaar,** (pl) **danaaniir,** the **dirham,** (pl) **daraahim** – have different values in different countries. For example, a Qatari riyal is worth about ten times a Saudi riyal, and a UAE dirham is worth about a hundred times a Qatari one.

When speaking about dinars, riyals, etc., it is not usually necessary to use the adjective 'Jordanian', 'Saudi', etc. However, if you have cause to in order to make your meaning clear, the adjective always stays the same and doesn't agree with its noun in either gender or number. For example, **dinaareen urduni** two Jordanian dinars, **tamaanya liiraat suuri** eight Syrian pounds.

A number of other words are used in conversation to refer to money in a general sense. In Lebanon. Syria and Jordan the word **maSaari** is commonly used, e.g. **ma9ak maSaari?** got any money on you? An even commoner alternative, used in all the above countries and the rest of the Arab world as well, is **fluus,** e.g. **il-fluus mish ma9aha?** doesn't she have the money?

Writing

The letter **siin** is pronounced like the English 's' in 'see'. On its own it is written like this: س

It joins on to a following letter and also to a preceding one where this is possible. At the beginning or in the middle of a word it loses its tail, but retains it when it is at the end:

سَامِي   السَبْت   نَاس

saami Sami (man's name)   **as-sabt** Saturday   **naas** people
(Note that **as-sabt** in written Arabic is pronounced **as-Sabt** in spoken.)

The same basic shape is used for our next letter, **shiin**, which sounds like the English 'sh' in 'sheep'. The difference is that **shiin** is written with three dots above the first part of it: ش

For example:

شَمْس   بَشِير   مِشْمِش

shams sun   **bashiir** Bashir (man's name)   **mishmish** apricot

The feminine ending **-a** which we have already met is written like this:

ة

as in

زِيَارَة

ziyaara visit

When it is preceded by a letter which joins onto a following one, like **nuun**, it looks like this:

سَنَة

sana year

14 Practise reading the following. (Answers p.102)

(a)	man's name	سالم	(b)	man's name	سليم
(c)	woman's name	مريم	(d)	woman's name	سميرة
(e)	September	سبتمبر	(f)	tea	شاي
(g)	pound	ليرة	(h)	Syrian pound	ليرة سوري
(i)	peace	سلام	(j)	Sheraton	شيراتون
(k)	Marriott	ماريوت	(l)	ministry	وزارة

SHOPPING (part 2)

You will learn

- how to buy presents
- how to understand a storekeeper's questions
- how to make a comparative statement
- how to buy clothes
- more about shopping
- the colours

Study guide

Dialogue 1 + Practise what you have learned
Dialogue 2 + Practise what you have learned
Dialogue 3 + Practise what you have learned
Dialogue 4 + Practise what you have learned
Key words and phrases
Grammar
Your turn to speak
Did you know?
Writing

Dialogues

1 *Clive is looking for presents for his family at a gift shop. What about an ornament?*

Clive	SabaaH il-xeer.
Assistant	SabaaH in-nuur, ahleen.
Clive	ahleen ... ah, mumkin tfarjiini eesh illi 9indkum ya9ni ... ana biddi ashtiri hadaaya la zoojti u la iwlaadi.
Assistant	fii 9indna ashya ktiira ... hoon fii mathalan jmaal, il-jmaal haadool min xashab.
Clive	min xashab.
Assistant	aywa.
Clive	ya9ni shu bni9mal fiih?
Assistant	haadool la z-ziina.
Clive	la z-ziina.
Assistant	Hilwiin.

SabaaH il-nuur good morning
(reply to **SabaaH il-xeer**)
tfarjiini you (f.) show me
illi (that) which
ashtiri I buy
hadaaya presents
zooja wife
shii or **ishii**, (pl) **ashya** thing
jmaal (here) toy, camels
haadool (or **haadoola**) these
xashab wood
ziina decoration
Hilw nice, pretty

▸ **hadaaya la zootji** presents for my wife. **la** means 'for' in the sense of 'for the benefit of'.

▸ **mathalan** for example (alternative pronunciation of **matalan**).

il-jmaal haadool these camels (lit. the camels these).

▸ **shu bni9mal fiih?** what is it for? (lit. what do we do with it?)

la z-ziina for decoration.

Hilwiin (they're) nice. The plural **-iin** on the adjective **Hilw** is because the noun it refers to, **jmaal** camels, is plural. See *Grammar*, this Unit.

Practise what you have learned

1 Samir is at a grocer's. He is planning to visit his friend and wants to take something with him. Listen and mark off the right answer. (Answers p.116) New word: **sharaab** drink

1 What does he buy?
   (a) biskoot
   (b) sharaab
   (c) shukalaaTa

2 How much does he pay?
   (a) talaat danaaniir
   (b) dinaareen u nuSS
   (c) xamas danaaniir
   (d) talaat danaaniir u nuSS

2 Jamila is a storekeeper. Her supplier is delivering her order. Listen to the tape and then match the items with their prices. (Answers p.116)

(a) 9ilbit xashab kbiira   1 dinaar u nuSS
(b) 9ilbit xashab Sghiira   2 dinaareen
(c) jamal kbiir   3 dinaar
(d) jamal Sghiir   4 talaat danaaniir

3 Your turn to speak. You want to buy a present. Find out what the store has – they may not have what you want. Nadira will prompt you.

Dialogues

2 *Or perhaps a cushion or two?*

Clive	u haadi eesh?
Assistant	haadool fii kamaan maxaddaat.
Clive	maxaddaat.
Assistant	maxaddaat filasTiiniyya.
Clive	filasTiiniyya, ah ... haada shughul iid?
Assistant	shughul iid haadoola, Hilwiin ktiir.
Clive	'addeesh', ya9ni, si9ruh?
Assistant	xamsa u 9ishriin dinaar.
Clive	laa, haada ktiir.
Assistant	mahuwwa shughul iid u bti9raf shughul iid byaaxud wa't ktiir!
Clive	bas ya9ni mish miHtaajiin ila maxaddaat.

maxadda (pl) **aat** cushion
filasTiini Palestinian
shughul work
iid hand
bti9raf you know
byaaxud [it] (m.) takes
miHtaaj (ila) in need of

➤ **haadool fii kamaan maxaddaat** these – there are cushions as well.

➤ **maxaddaat filasTiiniyya** Palestinian cushions. See *Grammar*, this Unit, for notes on noun – adjective agreement.

shughul iid hand-made. This is a 'construct' phrase (see again *Grammar*, Unit 5) literally 'work (of) hand'.

➤ **laa haada ktiir** no that's too much (lit. ... a lot). This is a common first response in trying to beat down the price.

mahuwwa shughul iid ... but it's hand-made ... When **ma-** is put in front of a pronoun like **huwwa** (or **hu**), it's a way of emphasizing a statement of contradiction. Here, Clive says the cushions cost too much; the assistant protests on the contrary that they are hand-made and therefore don't come cheap.

bas ya9ni mish miHtaajiin ila maxaddaat but we don't need any cushions. The 'we' is understood, hence the **-iin** plural ending on the adjective **miHtaaj** (needful).

Practise what you have learned

4 Samiira is buying a present. Listen and mark off the correct answers.
(Answers p.116) New word: **taTriiz** embroidery

1 What does she want to buy?
  (a) maxaddaat
  (b) ashya la z-ziina
  (c) taTriiz
  (d) jmaal

2 What is the price of one camel?
  (a) dinaar
  (b) arba9 danaaniir
  (c) nuSS dinaar
  (d) dinaareen

5 Samya is buying clothes. Listen and mark off the correct answer. Refer to
the *Key words and phrases* section for colours and clothes.
New word: **ma'aas** size. (Answers p.116)

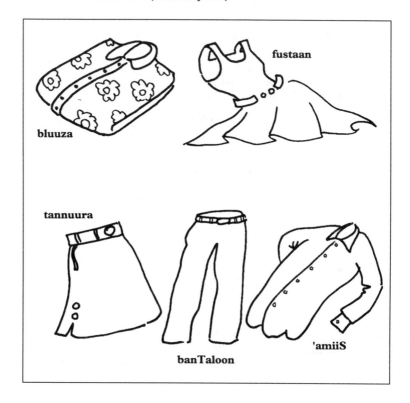

1 What did Samya buy?
  (a) a blouse
  (b) a dress
  (c) a pair of trousers

2 What size did she ask for?
  (a) thirty-five
  (b) forty
  (c) thirty-eight

3 What colour(s) doesn't she like?
  (a) yellow
  (b) blue
  (c) black

4 How much does she pay?
  (a) forty
  (b) thirty
  (c) thirty-five

6 Your turn to speak. You are at a souvenir shop and you want to buy a
present. Nadira will prompt you.

Dialogues

3 *The silver necklaces look nice, but...*

Assistant	fii kamaan shii taani ... shuuf matalan haadool il-9u'uuda ... il-9u'uuda ktiir Hilwiin haadool.
Clive	Hilwa ... mniiHa, bas aftakir, ghaali?
Assistant	shwayya ghaalya ... haada matalan haada l-9u'ud haada min fiDDa.
Clive	min fiDDa xaaliS?
Assistant	fiDDa, fiDDa xaaliS ... ah, bi xamsa u talaatiin dinaar.
Clive	laa ghaalya, ghaalya.
Assistant	mahu barDuh kamaan shughul iid.
Clive	mm.
Assistant	bitHibb ishii arxaS?
Clive	arxaS shwayy.

shuuf look!
9u'ud, (pl) **9u'uuda** necklace
aftakir I think
ghaali expensive
shwayya a little
fiDDa silver
xaaliS pure (of metals)
barDuh also, as well
arxaS cheaper

---

haadool il-9u'uuda these necklaces (lit. these the necklaces).

il-9u'uuda ktiir Hilwiin haadool these necklaces are really pretty (lit. the necklaces very pretty, these). **haadool** 'these', like **haada**, can either precede or follow the definite noun it goes with. So both **haadool il-9u'uuda** and **il-9u'uuda haadool** mean 'these necklaces'.

Hilwa ... mniiHa, bas aftakir, ghaali Here Clive makes a mistake. He should have said **ghaalya** with the feminine ending (as the assistant does in the next line) because he is referring to **9u'uuda** (necklaces)

9u'ud min fiDDa a silver necklace (lit. necklace from silver). **min** 'from' is used to describe the material something is made of. In Dialogue 1 we saw **jmaal min xashab** wooden camels.

mahu barDuh kamaan shughul iid but that's hand-made as well! Again, as in Dialogue 2, the assistant protests, using **mahu** but it's ...!

Practise what you have learned

7 Put the following in the right order to form a dialogue. Then listen to the recording to check your version.

fii 9indkum fasatiin filasTiiniyya?
ahlan.
Hilw. shu si9ruh?
marHaba.
ma9a s-salaama
laa. ghaali ktiir
fii taTriiz ktiir u kulluh shughul iid.
aywa fii. fii fasatiin Hilwa ktiir. tfaDDali.
arba9iin dinaar.
ghaali ktiir. ma9leesh, shukran.

8 Samira is buying her friend a birthday present. Fill in Samira's part from the box below. You need to know these words: **9uTur** perfume, **dahab** gold. (Answers p.116)

> law samaHti; biddi hidiyya; saba9 danaaniir; shu si9ir;
> shu fii 9indkum; fii ishii arxaS; a9Tiini; marHaba

Samira   _____

Hoda   ahlan.

Samira   _____ . _____ hadaaya?

Hoda   fii 9uTur, u fii 9u'uuda min fiDDa u min dahab.

Samira   _____ il-9u'ud il-fiDDa?

Hoda   il-9u'ud bi xamasta9shar dinaar.

Samira   shu, ghaali _____ ?

Hoda   fii il-9uTur. saba9 danaaniir.

Samira   _____ . kwayyis. _____ il-9uTur_____ .

Hoda   tfaDDali.

9 Your turn to speak. You want to an embroidered blouse (**bluuza mTarraza**). Nadira will prompt you.

Dialogues

4 *Finally Clive finds something nice but not too expensive*

Assistant	shuuf, fii haadi 9ilba, haadi arxaS min il-9u'ud.
Clive	haadi eesh ya9ni.
Assistant	9ilba min Sadaf haadi.
Clive	min Sadaf? ... u eesh bni9mal fiiha ya9ni?
Assistant	haadi matalan binHuTT fiiha l-mujawharaat ... iza matalan zootjak biddha tHuTT fiiha l-mujawharaat ... Hilwa ktiir, kamaan shughul iid.
Clive	biykuun arxaS.
Assistant	Tab9an arxaS min il-9u'ud.
Clive	'addeesh ya9ni?
Assistant	haadi 9ashar danaaniir.
Clive	9ashar danaaniir?
Assistant	aywa.
Clive	ya9ni ma9quul.
Assistant	bitHibb aliffha?
Clive	liffii lii yyaaha.
Assistant	HaaDir ... tfaDDal!
Clive	shukran.
Assistant	mabruuk!

Sadaf sea-shell
nHuTT we put
mujawharaat jewels
Tab9an of course
ma9quul (or **ma9'uul**) reasonable
aliffha I wrap it up
liffii lii yyaaha wrap (f.) it up for me!
mabruuk congratulations!

◆ **shuuf, fii haadi 9ilba ...** look, there's this, a box ...

◆ **haadi arxaS min ...** this is cheaper than ... See *Grammar*, this Unit.

iza matalan zoojtak biddha tHuTT fiiha l-mujawharaat ... your wife might want to put her jewels in it (lit. if, for example, your wife, she wants she put in it the jewels). **yHuTT** 'he puts' goes like **yHibb**, which we saw in Unit 3.

bykuun arxaS it'll be cheaper

◆ **bitHibb aliffha?** do you want me to wrap it up? (lit. you want I wrap it?). The verb **yliff** 'he wraps up' goes like **yHibb**. The **-ha** 'it' (f.) on the end of **aliff** is feminine because it refers to the feminine noun **9ilba**.

◆ **liffii lii yyaaha** wrap it up for me! **liffii lii** is the feminine command for 'wrap for me!' The masculine form is **liff lii** is 'for me'. The use of **yyaa-** in **yyaaha** 'it' is explained in *Grammar* this Unit.

◆ **mabruuk** congratulations. This is said to anyone who has just bought some new item like a car, a computer, or, as here, even a small jewel box. It is also used in the way we use 'congratulations' – on passing exams, getting a new job, the birth of a baby, etc.

Practise what you have learned

10 Samar has bought some presents on holiday. She's going over the list with her husband. Mark off the five items that she bought. (Answers p.116)

(a) 9u'ud min fiDDa
(b) tannuura
(c) bluuza
(d) 9u'ud min dahab
(e) banTaloon

(f) taTriiz
(g) 'amiiS
(h) 9uTur
(i) fustaan
(j) 9ilba min Sadaf

11 True or false. Listen to the conversation between two women about prices in the market and decide which sentences are true and which are false. (Answers p.116)

T/F

_____ (a)   kiilo l-bandoora bi sab9iin 'irsh

_____ (b)   9ilbit il-Haliib bi dinaareen

_____ (c)   kiilo s-sukkar bi talaatiin 'irsh

_____ (d)   9ilbit ish-shukalaaTa bi talaat danaaniir

_____ (e)   bakeet ish-shaay bi dinaar

12 Your turn to speak. Once more you are in a gift shop. You aren't sure what to buy, but you would like something hand-made. Nadira will prompt you.

Key words and phrases

To learn

SabaaH in-nuur	good morning (reply to **SabaaH il-xeer**)
hidiyya, (pl) hadaaya	present
ghaali	expensive
raxiiS	cheap
fii ishii arxaS?	is there anything cheaper?
si9ir, (pl) as9aar	price
'addeesh si9ir ...?	what's the price ...?
laff/yliff	(here) to wrap up
mabruuk	congratulations

Clothes

bluuza, (pl) -aat	blouse
'amiiS, (pl) 'umSaan	shirt
banTaloon, (pl) -aat	trousers
tannuura, (pl) -aat	skirt
fustaan, (pl) fasatiin	dress
jakeet, (pl) -aat	jacket
kundara, (pl) -aat	a pair of shoes

Colours

masculine	*feminine*	*plural*	
abyaD	**beeDa**	**biiD**	white
aswad	**sooda**	**suud**	black
aHmar	**Hamra**	**Humur**	red
azra'	**zar'a**	**zuru'**	blue
aSfar	**Safra**	**Sufur**	yellow
axDar	**xaDra**	**xuDur**	green
binni	**binniyya**	**binni**	brown

To understand

maxadda, (pl) maxaddaat	cushion/pillow
shughul iid	hand-made
9u'ud, (pl) 9u'uuda	necklace
xashab	wood
fiDDa	silver
jamal, (pl) jmaal	camel
Sadaf	sea-shell

Grammar

Noun-adjective agreement

You learned in Unit 4 that adjectives have three forms – masculine, feminine and plural – and that adjectives agree with nouns in gender. You also learned that with plural nouns denoting human beings the adjective is plural. With plural nouns that do not denote human beings the adjective is usually feminine singular, but may also be plural. For example:

jmaal Hilwa or **jmaal Hilwiin**   nice toy camels
maxaddaat Hilwa or **maxaddaat Hilwiin**   nice cushions

With dual nouns, the adjective is plural. For example:

waladeen kwaysiin   nice boys (2)
iwlaad kwaysiin   nice boys (more than 2)

Dual nouns generally also require plural verbs: **il-binteen byiHku 9arabi** the two girls speak Arabic.

The comparative

The comparative in Arabic usually has the same root as its underlying adjective and has a predictable pattern. With regular roots the comparative form is: aCCaC. For example:

raxiiS   **arxaS**   cheaper
kbiir   **akbar**   bigger, older

With 'weak' roots (having a vowel, y or w at the end) the comparative form is: aCCa. For example:

ghaali   **aghla**   more expensive
Hilw   **aHla**   sweeter, nicer

The Arab equivalent to 'than' is **min**. For example: **9amman aSghar min landan** Amman is smaller than London.

The particle yyaa-

The function of **yyaa-** is to carry a pronoun ending. It is otherwise empty of meaning. It is needed because Arabic does not permit two pronoun endings to be attached to one word. If two are needed, one is added to the verb or verb-like word, and the other is attached to **yyaa-**. For example:

liffii lii yyaaha   wrap it for me

This is literally 'wrap for me (particle) it'.

13 Give the correct form of the adjectives in parentheses in the following sentences. (Answers p.116)

(a) biddi arba9 9ilab _____ (*kbiir*).

(b) fii 9indna hadaaya shughul iid u _____ (*raxiiS*).

(c) il-fasatiin _____ (*ghaali*).

14 Give the comparative form of the adjectives in parentheses in the following sentences. (Answers p.116)

(a) haada l-banTaloon Sghiir, biddi ma'aas_____ (*kbiir*) iza mumkin.

(b) haadi l-9ilba kbiira, fii 9ilba _____ (*Sghiir*) ?

(c) haada il-9u'ud Hilw, bas biddi ishii _____ (*Hilw*).

Your turn to speak

15   You have done your grocery shopping. Go over the list with a member of your family. You could start by saying: **ishtareet ...** I have bought ... Tell her/him what you've bought, the quantities and how much you have paid for each item. Then listen to a model version. (You might need to revise Unit 3.)

16   You have bought some presents, and you are showing them to a friend. Again, you could start by saying: **ishtareet ...** Tell her/him what they are, what they cost and whether you found something expensive but had to settle for something cheaper. Then listen to the recording.

Answers

<table>
<tr><td rowspan="7">Practise what you
have learned</td><td>Exercise 1</td><td>1. (b); 2. (c)</td></tr>
<tr><td>Exercise 2</td><td>(a) 4 (b) 1 (c) 2 (d) 3</td></tr>
<tr><td>Exercise 4</td><td>1. (d); 2. (a)</td></tr>
<tr><td>Exercise 5</td><td>1. (b); 2. (c); 3. (a); 4. (c)</td></tr>
<tr><td>Exercise 8</td><td>marHaba; biddi hidiyya; shu fii 9indkum; shu si9ir; fii ishii arxaS; saba9 danaaniir; a9Tiini; law samaHti</td></tr>
<tr><td>Exercise 10</td><td>(c) (e) (a) (i) (h)</td></tr>
<tr><td>Exercise 11</td><td>(a) T (b) F (c) T (d) T (e) F</td></tr>
</table>

<table>
<tr><td rowspan="2">Grammar</td><td>Exercise 13</td><td>(a) kbiira (b) raxiiSa (c) ghaalya</td></tr>
<tr><td>Exercise 14</td><td>(a) akbar (b) aSghar (c) aHla</td></tr>
</table>

<table>
<tr><td>Writing</td><td>Exercise 17</td><td>(a) Kodak (b) Pepsi (c) Canada Dry (d) Coca-Cola
(e) Mitsubishi</td></tr>
</table>

Did you know?

In the older, less westernized parts of Arab markets, it is still normal to negotiate the price of whatever you want to buy by bargaining. Foodstuffs are normally sold at fixed prices, but articles like carpets and rugs, cushions, ornaments, pots and crafted items are often bargained for. The price of articles sold at the roadside is almost always negotiable. Bargaining is a game, and it is one which is fun and good for your Arabic. The 'moves' in this game usually go something like this:

1 Buyer asks the price: **'addeesh haada?**
2 Seller names his initial price: **haada yaa axi bi talaatiin dinaar** it's thirty dinars, my friend. He may add some kind of follow-up comment to justify the price: **shuuf, haay shughul iid, Hilw ktiir** look it's hand-made, very nice.
3 Buyer offers no more than a half of the asking price, but if it seems much too high, a third: **laa, haada ktiir, ba9Tiik xamasta9sh bas, maa byiswa talaatiin** no that's too much, I'll only give you fifteen, it's not worth thirty.
4 Seller feigns lack of interest: **laa, yiftaH allah** no, God will open (another source of income); or perhaps **allaah yirzi'ni** God sustain me! (implying what has been offered is insufficient).
5 Buyer makes his first move: **ba9Tiik 9ishriin u haadi aaxir kilma** I'll give you twenty, and that's my last word.
6 Seller responds: **laa, maa biykaffiini** no it's not enough for me.
7 Buyer feigns lack of interest and makes for the door or walks away saying: **mniiH, bashtiri min gheerak** OK I'll buy from someone else.
8 Seller calls him back and makes his first move: **istanna shwayy máa bitlaa'i arxaS fi s-suu', laakin babii9 bi si9r xaaSS min shaan xaaTrak** wait a bit, you won't find cheaper in the market, but I'll sell at a special price just for you.
9 Buyer responds: **Tayyib, 'addeesh?**
10 Seller names new price: **xamsa u 9ishriin, maa bykaffi aqall min heek** twenty-five, less than that is not enough!
11 Buyer counters: **laa, yaa axi, xamsa u 9ishriin mish ma9'uul** no my friend, twenty-five isn't reasonable.
12 Seller protests: **mahu shughul iid, 9amaluh byaaxud wa't ktiir** but it's hand-made, making it takes a long time.
13 Buyer names his real last price: **itneen u 9ishriin u waafa't, haay aaxir kilma. shu bit'uul?** twenty-two and I agree. That's my last word. What do you say?
14 Seller accepts: **Tayyib, xalaaS, tfaDDal** OK, that's it, take it.
15 Buyer pays: **tfaDDal, xud!** here, take (the money)!

Obviously, this is no more than the bare bones of an example. In practice, bargaining can be a very long, drawn-out process with feigned protestations, lengthy descriptions of where and how the article was manufactured, compliments on the buyer's Arabic and his beautiful children (if present), often accompanied by a glass of tea or coffee. The seller knows exactly how far he is prepared to go down from the word go, so it as well to get an idea of a reasonable price range beforehand and to decide exactly what your real 'last word' price is. Provided this is within reason, you will probably, with persistence, get what you want at the price you're prepared to pay!

Writing

In this unit we meet two more letters for which we have close equivalents in English. The first is **kaaf**, which sounds like the English 'c' in 'cup', or the 'c' and 'k' in cake. On its own it looks like this:

ك

At the beginning and in the middle of a word it has a diagonal 'hat':

كباب **kabaab** kebab

سكر **sukkar** sugar

At the end of a word, it looks like it does when written alone:

شيك **shiik** cheque

The next letter, **daal**, sounds similar to an English 'd' in words like 'do' and 'did'. It is written alone like this: د

It joins onto preceding letters which allow joining, but never joins onto a following letter (just like **raa** and **zaa**). It looks like this joined:

بلد   بريد

balad town, village   **bariid** post office

and like this not joined:

مراد   دليل

muraad Murad (man's name)   **daliil** guide, guidebook

When a letter is doubled in Arabic and no vowel comes between each occurrence of the doubled letter, it is not written twice. Instead, a small sign resembling a 'w' is written above it:

سكّان   زوّار

sukkaan inhabitants   **zuwwaar** visitors

17 The following are all Arabic versions of western product names which can be seen on advertisement boards in any Arab city. See if you can puzzle out what they are? (Answers p.116)

(a) <div dir="rtl">كوداك</div>   (b) <div dir="rtl">بيبسي</div>

(c) <div dir="rtl">كندا دراي</div>   (d) <div dir="rtl">كوكا كولا</div>

(e) ميتسوبيشي

MAKING TRAVEL ARRANGEMENTS

You will learn

- to arrange journeys with taxi drivers
- to rent a car
- to ask for information about buses
- to accept an offer of a lift
- to ask about distances

Study guide

Dialogue 1 + Practise what you have learned
Dialogue 2 + Practise what you have learned
Dialogue 3 + Practise what you have learned
Dialogue 4 + Practise what you have learned
Dialogue 5 + Practise what you have learned
Key words and phrases
Grammar
Your turn to speak
Did you know?
Writing

Dialogues

1 *Clive wants to get a taxi*

Clive	SabaaH il-xeer.
Man	SabaaH in-nuur.
Clive	biddi aruuH 9ala d-duwwaar il-awwal.
Man	na9am.
Clive	kam il-ujra ya9ni?
Man	iHna 9indna 9addaad ... murtabTiin fi 9addaad.
Clive	murtabTiin fi 9addaad.
Man	na9am ... binshaghghil il-9addaad ... fatHa xamst ... miyya u xamsiin fils u biy9idd il-9addaad ... 9ala l-masaafa, kam il-masaafa min hoon la hunaak.
Clive	u kam il-masaafa min hoon la d-duwwaar il-awwal?
Man	il-masaafa min hoon la d-duwwaar il-awwal xamsa kilomitir.
Clive	xamsa kilomitir.
Man	na9am.

ujra	fare	**fatHa**	opening (here,
iHna (alternative to **niHna**)	we		a 'click' on a meter)
murtabTiin (pl), **fi** connected to		**biy9idd**	(the meter) counts
binshaghghil we turn on, operate		**masaafa**	distance

> ♦ **binshaghghil il-9addaad ... fatHa xamst ... miyya u xamsiin fils**
> we operate the meter ... a click is fif-[teen] ... is 150 fils. The hesitation is
> between 15 piastres and 150 fils. (See *Did you know?* in Unit 7).
>
> **9ala l-masaafa** according to distance.
>
> ♦ **kam il-masaafa?** how far is it? **kam** is an alternative to **'addeesh**.

2 *Where exactly is the British Council?*

Clive	u ti9raf ween shismah, il-majlis ith-thaqaafi l-briiTaani?
Man	na9am..
Clive	aftikir haada fi shaari9 –
Man	shaari9 ir-reenbo.
Clive	shaari9 ir-reenbo.
Man	shaari9 ir-reenbo.
Clive	haada 'ariib min id-duwwaar il-awwal?
Man	min id-duwwaar il-awwal ... ba9d id-duwwaar il-awwal bi Hawaali thalaath miit mitir.
Clive	ah shukran.
Man	ahleen il-9afu

ti9raf	(do) you know?	**aftikir**	I think
il-majlis ith-thaqaafi		**Hawaali**	approximately
	l-briiTaani the British Council	**mitir**	metre

> ♦ **ti9raf ween shismah ...** do you know where the ... what-do-you-call-it
> ... British Council is? **shismah** or **shismuh** (lit. what its name) is an
> extremely useful phrase when you can't remember the name of something.
>
> ♦ **ba9d id-duwwaar il-awwal bi Hawaali ...** about 300 metres past the
> 1st Circle ... (lit. after the 1st circle by about ...).

Practise what you have learned

1 In this exercise you will hear four questions. Write the number of the question next to whichever of the answers below makes sense. (Answers p.130)

(a) 9ishriin dinaar bi l-9addaad.

(b) xamsa illa rubu9.

(c) talaata kiilo.

(d) saa9teen u nuSS.

2 Listen to the conversation and mark the following statements true or false, as appropriate. (Answers p.130)
New word: **raayiH**, (f.) **raayHa** going

(a) The taxi is going to Abdali.

(b) The taxi does not have a meter.

(c) The driver explains that each kilometre costs 9 qirsh.

(d) The man takes the taxi.

3 Your turn to speak. You want to go to the centre of town, so you stop a taxi by shouting '**taksi**'. Negotiate with the driver. Nadira will guide you.

4 Mahmoud's car is getting very low on petrol. Listen to him talking to a passer-by. What is the Arabic for 'petrol station'? Where is the nearest one? How far is it? (Answers p.130)
New words: **a'rab** the nearest, **ba9iid (9an)** far (from).

5 A conversation at a petrol station. Fill in the blanks in the conversation below with words and phrases from the box, then check your answers on page 130.

iza mumkin	mumkin tdillni	'abilmaa	'addeesh	biddi
	il-litir	SabaaH in-nuur	a'rab	

A SabaaH il-xeer.

B _____ .

A _____ 9ashra litir banziin _____ .

B HaaDir, shii taani?

A shukran, _____ haada?

B dinaareen u nuSS.

A ya9ni _____ bi miiteen u xamsiin fils?

B aywa.

A Tayyib, u _____ 9ala _____ bank?

B ba9iid shwayy, laazim truuH bi s-sayyaara, xud taani shaari9 9a sh-shmaal u btimshi Hawaali kiilo _____ tiiji la l-bank 9ala iidak il-yamiin.

A u shu ism il-bank?

B bank 9ammaan.

A shukran.

B il-9afu yaa siidi.

6 Your turn to speak. You want to go to Hayy Zahran in Amman, so you stop a bus at a bus stop and talk to the driver. Nadira will guide you as usual.

Dialogues

3 *Yousif, a student, wants a taxi to take him to the Jordanian University from outside Amman*

Yousif	marHaba yaa ax.
Driver	yaa hala, Hayyaak allah.
Yousif	keef Haalak?
Driver	yaa marHaba biik.
Yousif	ballah biddi aruuH 9a l-jaam9a l-urduniyya, mumkin?
Driver	mumkin ... il-jaam9a l-urduniyya?
Yousif	na9am.
Driver	ah, bas sayyaarti haadhi bitwaSlak min haan la awwal 9ammaan, ya9ni manTigit ish-sharg il-awsaT, duwwaar ish-sharg il-awsaT ... ba9deen inta btooxidh sayyaara thaanya ... btinzil la l-balad taHat?

sayyaara car
bitwaSlak will take you
haan here (alternative to **hoon**)
manTiga area
ish-sharg il-awsaT the Middle East (here, name of a roundabout
designating an area of Amman)

Hayyaak allah God give you life. This is a common formula which can be used to thank, to greet, to take one's leave, and in many other circumstances.

keef Haalak? (or **keef il-Haal?**) how are you? (lit. how is your state?)

awwal 9ammaan the outskirts of Amman (lit. [the] first of Amman)

ba9deen btooxidh sayyaara thaanya then you take another car. This speaker, from the east of Jordan, says **btooxidh** 'you take' instead of **btaaxud**. He also uses **th** instead of **t** in certain words like **thaani** 'second, other' instead of the usual city-dweller's pronunciation, **taani**.

btinzil la l-balad taHat? are you going right down into the city centre? (lit. are you going down to the city below?)

Practise what you have learned

7

Najwa wants to get from a small village in northern Jordan to Jabal Amman, a suburb of Amman. Listen to her making enquiries at the bus station, then answer the following questions. (Answers p.130)

New words: **il-baaS il-jaay** the next bus (lit. the coming bus); **aaxir baaS** the last bus; **ghayyar/yghayyir** to change (e.g. buses); **makaan** place

(a) Give as much information as you can about how she should get to Jabal Amman – what transportation she can take, whether she needs to change and, if so, where.

(b) What time does the next bus leave?

(c) Where can she buy a ticket?

8

John, who's on holiday in Jordan, and Fuad come out of a café late in the evening, and Fuad offers John a lift. For each line of the conversation select the appropriate sentence or combination of sentences. Then check your version by listening to the recording.

New phrases: **balaash at9ibak** I don't want to trouble you; **naazil (fi)** staying (at).

1 *Fuad* (a) mumkin twaSSilni bi-sayyaara? (b) ma9i sayyaara
     (c) mumkin awaSlak?

2 *John* (a) shukran   (b) bafaDDil aaxud il-baaS
     (c) mumkin aruuH bi l-baaS   (d) balaash at9ibak

3 *Fuad* (a) ween bitruuH?   (b) ween naazil?

4 *John* (a) saakin fi funduq 9amra   (b) naazil fi funduq 9amra
     (c) inshaallaah.

5 *Fuad* (a) ba9iid shwayy
     (b) laazim truuH maashi
     (c) bas maa fii baaS halla' 9ala hunaak.

6 *John* (a) eemta awwal baaS?
     (b) fii baaS biyruuH kul rubu9 saa9a, mish heek?
     (c) iza biddi baaS, baruuh bi l-baaS?
     (d) leesh?

7 *Fuad* (a) bas aaxir baaS raaH is-saa9a 9ashra
     (b) laazim tghayyir il-funduq
     (c) xalliini awaSlak u xalaaS

8 *John* (a) Tayyib   (b) alf shukr
     (c) ta9aala ma9i iza biddak

9

Your turn to speak. You want to get from Amman to Yarmuk (University) and are making enquiries at the bus station. Here is a list of the information you need:

(a) whether there's a direct bus
(b) if not, how you can get there
(c) the times of the next bus and the last bus
(d) the cost of a ticket
(e) whether you can book a place

You start by greeting the man in the information office and then work your way through the list. Stop the recording after each answer to work out your next line. You will hear Nadira give a version of it after the pause. At the end check you have the right information, by looking on p.130.

Dialogues

4 *How much will it cost?*

Yousif	ah, kam widdak?
Driver	min haan la l-jaam9a l-urduniyya bnaaxud minnak thalaath danaaniir.
Yousif	thalaath danaaniir.
Driver	na9am
Yousif	Tayyib ... mu ghaali?
Driver	wallah haadha 9aadi, haadha ajaar is-sayyaara li'annuh s-sayyaara btimshi 9ala 9addaad.
Yousif	ya9ni raxiiS.
Driver	ee na9am haadha l-9aada.
Yousif	Tayyib, twakkalna 9ala llah, inshaallaah.
Driver	inshaallaah.
Yousif	yallah.
Driver	Hayyaak allah, tfaDDal.
Yousif	shukran.
Driver	iTla9, yaa marHaba.

9aadi normal
ajaar is-sayyaara the rental of the car
li'annuh because
btimshi goes, runs
9aada custom, norm
iTla9 get in!

---

kam widdak how much do you want? **widd** is used in the same way as **bidd**. This is a more 'Bedouin'-sounding way of asking the question than would be normal in Amman, where one typically hears **'addeesh biddak** how much do you want?

mu ghaali? isn't that a bit expensive? **mu** is the rural Arabic equivalent of Amman **mish**. City-dwellers would say **mish ghaali?**

is-sayyaara btimshi 9ala 9addaad the car is metered (lit. the car goes on a meter)

twakkalna 9ala llah we put our trust in God. This is a phrase uttered at the beginning of a journey (often seen on dashboard stickers in taxis). Here, it is a signal from Yousif that he is starting the journey with the driver, and has therefore accepted the demanded fare of 3 dinars.

yallah let's go! This is a very common phrase of general encouragement.

iTla9, yaa marHaba jump in! hi! **iTla9,** (f.) **iTla9i** is the command form of this verb which is used for getting on buses, cars, taxis, trains and planes. **marHaba** is used here to welcome the passenger into the driver's company now that he has agreed to go with him.

Practise what you have learned

10 Renting a car. Listen to the conversation, and then indicate what information the woman wants by marking off the appropriate phrases below. (Answers p.130) New words: **ruxSit swaa'a** driving licence; **ista'jar/yista'jir** to hire, rent.

(a) how to get to the centre of town
(b) how to drive a Fiat
(c) how old the hire cars are
(d) how much it costs to hire a car
(e) where the nearest petrol station is
(f) where she can get the car key from
(g) whether she has to pay in advance
(h) whether the car rental company needs proof of her identity

11 Your turn to speak. You want to rent a car for two days. Nadira will guide you through the negotiations in the usual way.

Dialogues

5 *Yousif is trying to get from Al-Azraq in eastern Jordan, to Irbid in the north*

Yousif as-salaam 9aleekum

Driver wa 9aleekum as-salaam wa raHmat allah, ahlan wa marHaba biik.

Yousif keef Haalak?

Driver hala.

Yousif ballah biddi 'irbid ... idha samaHt ... mineen arkab, aw idha twaSSilni int, ya9ni ...

Driver iHna l-aan fi l-azrag ... widdak 'irbid tiTla9 ma9i min haan la 9ammaan.

Yousif la 9ammaan ... kwayyis.

Driver ee, awaSlak safariyyaat 'irbid.

Yousif kwayyis.

Driver safariyyaat 'irbid fi l-9abdali ... bawaSlak iyyaaha u min hunaak btiTla9 ... idha tabgha baaS, tiTla9 bi baaS.

Yousif na9am.

Driver u idha tabgha tiTla9 bi t-taksi, taksi.

Yousif na9am.

mineen	from where	**safariyyaat**	travel agency,
arkab	I catch (a bus, taxi, etc.)		ticket office
il-aan	now (alternative to **halla'**)	**tabgha**	you want (= biddak)

♦ **as-salaam 9aleekum** peace be upon you (and its invariable response **wa 9aleekum as-salaam** and on you be peace) is the traditional greeting of the desert Arab, nowadays considered a rather 'correct', somewhat formal, opening (see *Did you know?*, Unit 2). Here the driver gives an even more elaborate response, involving the additional phrase **wa raHmat allah** 'and the mercy of God (also be upon you)'.

♦ **biddi 'irbid** I want to go to Irbid. (lit. I want Irbid). Irbid is a town in northern Jordan, about an hour's drive from Amman.

idha samaHt would you mind (telling me). This is an alternative to the phrase we have already met, **law samaHt. idha** 'if' is an alternative pronunciation to **iza**, which we have already met.

aw idha twaSSilni int or if *you* will take me (lit. or if you will take me, you). The use of **int** (short for **inta**) at the end of the sentence is a way of emphasizing *you* (as opposed to some other taxi-driver).

il-azrag a town in eastern Jordan containing a large medieval fort whose stones are a blackish-blue, hence the name ('The Blue').

♦ **widdak 'irbid tiTla9 ma9i min haan la 9ammaan** if you are heading for Irbid, I'll take you as far as Amman (lit. you want Irbid, you get in with me from here to Amman).

safariyyaat 'irbid fi l-9abdali the Irbid ticket agency in al-Abdali. Abdali is the main bus and taxi-station to Amman.

bawaSlak iyaaha I'll take you to it

u idha tabgha tiTla9 bi t-taksi, taksi and if you want to go by taxi, (you can go by) taxi. A **taksi** is a private (often metred) taxi plying for individual hire, rather than the **serviis** a 'service' taxi which is a form of public transportation plying over a fixed route for modest fixed fares.

Practise what you have learned

12 You want to get from your hotel to the Mosque of Al Husein as cheaply as possible. Listen to the information Nadira gives you on the tape, then note the details of how much each method costs. You may need to listen more than once. (Answers p.130)

method	how?	cost?
1		
2		
3		

13 A short practice exercise in replying to greetings. You will hear Nadira giving a number of common greetings. After each one, pause and give the appropriate response. You will then hear the response too, so you can check.

Key words and phrases

To learn

keef (or **kiif**) **Haalak?**	how are you?
kiilomitir (or **kiilo**)	kilometre
'ariib min	near (to)
a'rab maHaTTa	the nearest station/bus stop
ba9iid 9an	a long way from
kam il-masaafa min ... la?	how far is it from ... to?
Hawaali	about
sayyaara, (pl) **sayyaaraat**	car
sayyaara taanya	another car
yallah	let's go! come on!
iza	if
aaxir baaS	the last bus
il-baaS il-jaay	the next bus
ween raayiH (raayHa)	where are you going?
makaan	place, room (for something)
9irif/yi9raf	to know
ghayyar/yghayyir	to change (buses, money)
waSSal/ywaSSil	to give someone a lift, take someone somewhere by car
naazil fi	staying at/in
iftakar/yiftikir	to think
balaash at9ibak	I don't want to put you to any trouble
inshaallaah	God willing
taHat	down, downstairs, below, under

Grammar

The structure of Arabic words

Most Arabic words are built from two elements: a 'root', usually three consonants, and a 'pattern' of vowels with or without further consonants. For example **ktb** is a root with the meaning of 'writing'. When **ktb** is combined with the verb pattern **yiCCiC** (C stands for the place of a root consonant) it forms the non-past verb **yiktib** 'he writes'. With the noun pattern **CiCaaC** it forms the noun **kitaab** 'book'. With the pattern for places **maCCaC** it forms the noun **maktab** 'office' – a place of writing, and so on. It is worth trying to note the roots of words as you come across them, because it can be a great help both in learning vocabulary and in understanding words you have never met before.

For non-past verbs the commonest patterns are **yiCCiC**, **yiCCaC** and **yiCCuC** (yiktib, yi9mal, etc.), which is the 'simple form', but there are also 'derived' forms, of which **yishtiri**, **ysaafir** and **yista'jir** are examples you have already met. The most useful one to know about is the one where the middle consonant of the root is doubled, as in **yTalli9** (root **Tl9**), and which usually has the meaning of causing something to happen. So **yTalli9** means to make someone or something go out (or up) and is derived from **yiTla9**, the 'simple' form, meaning to go out or up.

Active participles

Words like **raayiH** (f. **raayHa**, pl **raayHiin**) – going or gone – and **faahim** (f. **faahma**, pl **faahmiin**) – understanding – are examples of the active participle pattern of the simple verb, often equivalent to English forms ending in -ing like: going, living, coming. Note that 'hollow verbs' – with a long vowel in the non-past, like **yshuuf** – have a **y** in the place of the second root letter, (**shaayif** 'seeing'). Verbs ending in vowels have participles ending in **-i** like **maashi** walking, going. **jaay** (coming) is the participle from **yiiji** he comes. The active participle may refer to a state – knowing, living, staying, needing, seeing – or an act of motion that is in process or about to happen – going, coming, going out, etc. Participles are a kind of adjective and are negated with **mish**.

14 Fill in the blanks with the appropriate non-past form or participle of the verb in parentheses. Translate the sentences. (Answers p.130)

(a) il-bint _____ (*yruuH*) is-suu' kul yoom.

(b) ana _____ (*yiiji*) min wasT il-balad.

(c) A: ween _____ (*yruuH*) yaa salwa?

B: ana _____ (*yinzil*) ashuuf il-mudir.

(d) A: shu _____ (*yi9mal*) yaa aHmad?

B: ana _____ (*yiktib*) (= 'write') la zoojti.

(e) A: ana _____ (*maa yshuuf*) sayyaarti, ween hiyya?

relative adjectives and nouns

If you take a place name (or many other kinds of noun) and add **-i** to the end (after removing the **-a** ending of feminine nouns) you turn the word into a 'relative' adjective or noun. For example:

briiTaanya	Britain	⟶	briiTaani	British (as an adj. or noun)
9arab	Arabs	⟶	9arabi	Arab, Arabic (as an adj. or noun)
9aada	custom	⟶	9aadi	customary, normal
thaqaafa	culture	⟶	thaqaafi	cultural

The feminine of these adjectives ends in **iyya**, and plurals normally in **-iyyiin**: **briiTaaniyyiin** British (people), **amriikiyyiin** Americans, **il-majlis ith-thaqaafi l-briiTaani** The British Council.

Your turn to speak

15 You want to get from Amman Airport to a hotel in town. Think of a few questions you might ask at the information desk about transportation to the hotel. Then compare them with Nadira's. (Hints: fare? by taxi? by bus? bus number?)

Answers

Practise what you have learned	Exercise 1 (a) 4 (b) 3 (c) 2 (d) 1
	Exercise 2 (a) F (b) F (c) T (d) T
	Exercise 4 maHaTTit banziin; just past the large mosque; half a kilometer away
	Exercise 5 SabaaH in-nuur; biddi; iza mumkin; 'addeesh; il-litir; mumkin tdillni; a'rab; 'abilmaa
	Exercise 7 (a) Bus to Irbid, second bus to Abdali bus station, then change there to another bus or take a taxi (b) 2.45 (c) on the bus or at the information office
	Exercise 9 (a) No direct bus (b) bus to Jerash, and then change (c) next bus 2.20, last bus 8.30 (d) quarter Dinar to Jerash (e) it is possible to book in advance
	Exercise 10 (d), (g), (h)
	Exercise 12 Method 1 private taxi – 1.500 J. Dinars Method 2 bus (No 110) & 2nd bus – 40 fils (= 4 qirsh) Method 3 service taxi – 70 or 80 fils (= 7 or 8 qirsh)

Grammar

Exercise 14 (a) bitruuH (b) jaay (c) raayHa; naazila
(d) bti9mal; baktib (e) mish shaayif

Writing

Exercise 16 (a) Amman and Irbid (b) 1. bank (bank) 2. shaari9 (street)
3. duwwaar (circle, roundabout) 4. taksii (taxi)
5. suubarmarkit (supermarket) 6. mamnuu9 (prohibited,
'No...') 7. banziin suubar (super grade[4-star] petrol)
8. banziin 9aadi (ordinary grade [2-star] petrol)

Did you know?

Travel in the Arab world

In most parts of the Arab world there is a well-developed public transportation system, whose practicalities differ from one country to another. Public transportation is generally very cheap and good value in comparison with what is available in western countries. In Syria, Egypt, Jordan, Iraq and the West Bank, there are good national and international bus services between major towns with express air-conditioned services now becoming more common. Even these luxury buses are still remarkably cheap. Within major towns, and between some of them, the standard method of public transportation is the service taxis (**sarviis**) which follow fixed itineraries and have fixed fares between picking up and dropping off points. Service taxis are faster and more comfortable to use in large towns than buses, and they are not much more expensive. The disadvantage is that you usually have to wait, if you get on the starting point, until the driver has filled up his taxi. In the case of long distance buses, and some of the larger service taxi companies, you buy your ticket from a ticket office near the taxi stop rather than give the driver your fare.

The private taxi (**taksi xuSuuSi**) is relatively expensive and although some cities, like Amman, have metered taxis, the norm is to negotiate with the driver how much the journey will cost before you start, so you need to get some idea roughly what is reasonable before you set out. Obviously taxi pick-up points near international hotels tend to try to charge more, but you can always take a walk to the nearest major intersection and wave one down. The first thing to do is to greet the driver and tell him where you want to go, for example: **marHaba ... biddi aruuH 9ala wasT il-balad** hi, I want to go downtown. He may ask you **9ala ween?** to where? After you tell him, ask him how much it will cost: **'addeesh biddak?** By this stage it will be apparent that you speak Arabic, which usually has two consequences: the driver will not attempt to overcharge you by a vast amount since you will already have shown yourself not to be just another gullible foreigner; and in many cases he will be interested to chat more, find out where you're from, find out what you think of his country, complain about the traffic, solicit your views on the world scene, England's chances in the World Cup (if you're English), and so on. For this reason also you will look less like a walking pound or dollar sign to him and more like an interesting fellow human being. Arabic-speaking foreigners using public transportation have great curiosity value, and you will get excellent opportunities for chatting and general small talk which will improve your Arabic. Squashed in buses and service taxis you also get the opportunity to listen at close quarters to everybody else's conversations!

Writing

In this unit, we shall learn one new letter only, generally reckoned to be the most difficult for English speakers to pronounce correctly (to remind yourself of the pronunciation, see Hints on Pronunciation, p.5). This letter is called **9ayn**, and is symbolized in this book by the letter **9**, as in the name of the letter itself, and in words we have encountered so far like **si9ir** price, **9ammaan** Amman, **saa9a** hour, (wrist) watch, clock. By itself – that is, when not joined to the letter before – it looks like this:

ع

In initial position it joins onto a following letter and loses its 'tail':

عالم   **9aalam** world

When joined to a previous and a following consonant, it looks different again:

سعر   **si9ir** price

When in final position and joined to the letter before, it looks like this:

ربع   **rubu9** quarter

16 (a) Look at the bus ticket on p.131. Can you find the names of two Jordanian cities on it?

(b) Here are a few names you might see on signs and billboards in the street. Try to read and translate them. (Answers p.130)

(1)	بنك	(2)	شارع
(3)	دوار	(4)	تكسي
(5)	سوبر مركت	(6)	ممنوع
(7)	بنزين سوبر	(8)	بنزين عادي

10 ORDERING A MEAL

You will learn

- to order hors d'oeuvres (starters) in a restaurant
- to order a meal in a restaurant
- to order drinks
- the names of various dishes

Study guide

Dialogue 1 + Practise what you have learned
Dialogue 2 + Practise what you have learned
Dialogue 3 + Practise what you have learned
Dialogue 4 + Practise what you have learned
Key words and phrases
Grammar
Your turn to speak
Did you know?
Writing

Dialogues

1 *Shahir and Muhammad go out for lunch at the Al-Andalus restaurant in Irbid. What about the recommendations of the patron?...*

Shahir shu biddak tghaddiina l-yoom?
Patron shu illi btu'muru iHna HaaDriin fiih!!
Shahir shu, ya9ni, 'uul ilna.
Patron fii il-muqabbilaat u il-mashaawi, il-'mixed grill' Tab9an...

tghaddiina you give us for lunch (lit. you lunch us)
illi which, that which
btu'muru you (pl) order
HaaDriin fiih ready (pl) for it
'uul ilna tell us (lit. say to us)
muqabbilaat hors d'oeuvres, starters, appetizers
mashaawi roast/grilled meats

▶ **shu biddak tghaddiina l-yoom** what are you going to give us for lunch today? (lit. what do you want to lunch us today?). **bidd** is often used in the sense of 'intending' or 'going to' as well as 'wanting'. If it had been in the evening, Shahir might well have said **shu biddak t9ashshiina?** what are you going to give us for dinner? (lit. what do you want to dinner us?)

▶ **shu illi btu'muru iHna HaaDriin fiih** whatever you order, we're ready to prepare it (lit. what that you order, we are ready for it). By itself, **tu'mur** (lit. you order) is often used, like **HaaDir** as an acknowledgement of an instruction from a boss, customer or other 'superior'.

Practise what you have learned

1 What does the customer in the dialogue order? Listen and mark off the correct answer. (Answers p.143)
New word: **ghada** lunch

(a) mashaawi
(b) muqabbilaat
(c) fTuur

2 Listen to the next dialogue in which a man is asking for directions to a restaurant. Mark off the correct answers. (Answers p.143)
New word: **maT9am** restaurant, and remember: **Taawla** table

(a) What is the man asking about?
● a foreign restaurant
● an English restaurant
● an Arabic restaurant

(b) Which road was the man told to take?

● the first street on the left
● the first street on the right
● the second street on the right

(c) How far was he directed to walk?
● thirty metres
● fifty metres
● a hundred metres

3 Your turn to speak. Imagine you are in a restaurant. You want to ask about hors d'oeuvres. Nadira will prompt you in English.

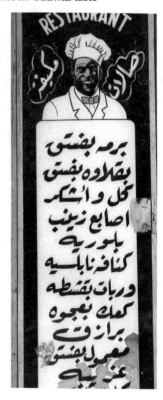

Dialogues

2 *Muhammad asks for more details of the hors d'oeuvres.*

Muhammad haadha jayyid bas ya9ni eesh il-muqabbilaat, law ta9Tiina asmaa'ha.

Patron muqabbilaat ... fii 9indak il-HummuS, il-mtabbal, it-tabbuula, is-salaTa l-gharbiyya u ish-sharqiyya, fii 9indak salaTa ruusi, fii 9indak salaTa iiTaali, fii 9indak salaTa turki ... salaTit il-xass bi l-malfuuf bi l-mayuneez, 9indak l-kubba il-HamiiS, il-kubba n-nayya.

Muhammad il-kubba l-eesh?

Patron kubba nayya.

jayyid   good, OK
law ta9Tiina asmaa'ha   if you would give us their names
mtabbal   spiced purée of roasted eggplant pulp
tabbuula   salad made of cracked wheat, mint, parsley, oil and lemon juice
salaTa salad   **gharbi** western   **sharqi** eastern
ruusi Russian   **iiTaali** Italian   **turki** Turkish
xass lettuce   **malfuuf** cabbage   **mayuneez** mayonnaise
kubba HamiiS   deep-fried meatballs containing pine kernels
kubba nayya   raw meatballs (like steak tartare)

> **bi** with (as in **malfuuf bi l-mayuneez** but not in the sense of 'in the company of')
>
> **il-kubba l-eesh?** kubba what? Muhammad is asking for clarification.

3 *The Patron explains what one of the hors d'oeuvres is, and then says what is available for main courses.*

Patron kubba HamiiS ... hiyya 9ibaara 9an kubba maqliyya bi z-zeet.

Muhammad ah na9am, muHammaSa haay.

Patron hiyya maqliyya bas-

Muhammad maqliyya kathiir SaHiiH.

Patron kalima shaamiyya ... isimha kubba HamiiS.

Muhammad wallah il-HamiiS haadha kwayyis akiid.

Patron fa haadi tashkiilit il-muqabbilaat ... 9indak il-mashaawi 9indna illi hiyya binsammiiha 'mixed grill', ya9ni mashaawi mushakkala btiHwi 9ala shugaf laHmit xaruuf wa kabaab wa shiish tawuk illi huwwa laHmit dajaaj bi l-bhaaraat wa sharHaat steek ...

9ibaara 9an in other words   **mHammaS** toasted
maqliyya bi z-zeet   fried (f.) in oil   **kalima** word (same as **kilma**)
SaHiiH   true, correct   **akiid** certainly
shaami Syrian   **wallah** by God   **binsammiiha** we call it
tashkiila variety, selection   **btiHwi 9ala** it contains
mashaawi mushakkala   mixed grill
shughaf chunks   **laHmit xaruuf** lamb (lit meat [of] sheep)
shiish tawuk   chicken cooked on a spit
laHmit dajaaj   chicken meat (lit meat [of] chicken)
bhaaraat spices   **sharHa** slice   **steek** (western style) steak

Practise what you have learned

4 Here is the menu for the hors d'oeuvres. Listen and mark off what the waiter names. Then circle what the man orders. (Answers p.143)

HummuS	☐	mtabbal	☐
kubba nayya	☐	kubba HamiiS	☐
salaTa sharqiyya	☐	salaTa gharbiyya	☐
tabbuula	☐	salaTa ruusi	☐

5 Next, complete the part of the customer in the dialogue below by choosing from the jumbled sentences in the box. Then check your answer on page 143.

P ahlan.

C _____ .

P tfaDDal. shu btu'mur?

C _____ ?

P tfaDDal. haay il-minyu.

C _____ .

P HaaDir. bitHibb tishrab shii?

C _____ .

P tikram.

C _____ .

P tfaDDal.

> 1 9aSiir burt'aan;
>
> 2 il-Hisaab law samaHt;
>
> 3 shu fii muqabbilaat 9indkum;
>
> 4 Taawla la shaxS waaHad min FaDlak;
>
> 5 waaHad HummuS, waaHad mtabbal, waaHad salaTa sharqiyya.

6 Your turn to speak. You have invited a friend to a restaurant. You know this restaurant. You have been here before. Ask your friend what he would like to start with and tell your friend what hors d'oeuvres they have got. When you have had a try, listen to a model version of it.

7 A couple are ordering a meal. Listen and then answer the questions. (Answers p.143) You need to know these words: **dajaaja mHammara** roast chicken; **xuDra** vegetables.

(a) What does the woman order?
- xuDra
- shugaf laHmit xaruuf
- nuSS dajaaja mHammara
- kabaab

(b) What does the man order?
- nuSS dajaaja mHammara
- shugaf laHmit xaruuf
- kabaab
- xuDra

(c) What do they order for drinks?
- 9aSiir manga
- 9aSiir tuffaaH
- bibsi
- 9aSiir burtu'aan

(d) How do they like their coffee?
- Hilwa
- sukkar 'aliil
- saada (no sugar)

8 Put the following jumbled parts of a dialogue in a restaurant in the right order. Then listen to check your answer. New words: **il-qaa'ima** menu.

bitHibb tishrab shii?
aywa, 9aSiir tuffaaH, law samaHt.
il-Hisaab, law samaHt.
Taawla la shaxS waaHad, min faDlak.
mumkin il-qaa'ima?
waaHad mashaawi mshakkala
u waaHad HummuS.

ahlan.
laa, bas.
tfaDDal. shu btu'mur?
tfaDDal. haadi T-Taawla.
shii taani?
HaaDir, tikram.
tfaDDal.

Dialogues

4 *And after more details, they finally give their order...*

Muhammad   u il-xubiz haadha l-xubiz ya9ni min intaaj 'irbid willa ...
Patron   intaaj 'irbid na9am ... maxaabiz 'irbid il-aaliyya ... iHna binqadmuh,
             binqadmuh noo9een - xubiz mHammaS u xubiz 9aadi.
Muhammad   wallah il-mHammaS kwayyis haada.
Shahir   il-mHammaS aHsan shii ... bas il-muqabbilaat biddna l-
             muqabbilaat il-9arabiyya min faDlak illi hiyya illi 9addeethum ...
             kamaan marra.
Patron   mtabbal, tabbuula, salaTa xishna u salaTa naa9ma illi hiyya baba
             ghannuuj, il-kishka ... it-tashkiila illi xalliina nguul il-muqabbilaat
             ish-sharqiyya ...

> **xubiz** bread
> **min intaaj 'irbid** baked in Irbid (lit. the production of Irbid)
> **maxbaz** bakery
> **maxaabiz 'irbid il-aaliyya** Irbid Automated Bakeries
> **binqadmuh noo9een** we serve it in two (different) ways
> **xubiz mHammaS** toasted bread
> **xubiz 9aadi** ordinary bread
> ♦ **aHsan shii** preferable (lit. best thing)
> **9addeet** you listed
> **kamaan marra** once again
> **xishna** rough (f.) (i.e. containing whole or roughly chopped ingredients,
>   like a European salad)
> **naa9ma** smooth, soft (i.e. finely chopped or processed)
> **baba ghannuuj** purée of roasted eggplant pulp, sesame seed oil and
>   lemon juice
> **il-kishka** dish made from cracked wheat and yoghourt

♦ **illi hiyya illi 9addeethum** ... which are those which you listed.

it-tashkiila illi xalliina nguul il-muqabbilaat ish-sharqiyya the
selection which let's say is the 'eastern hors d'oeuvres' (lit. the selection
which let us say ...) 'Let' in expressions like 'let me say', 'let's say' is
xalli. The **-i** at the end is lengthened when a pronoun is added: so
xalliini 'let me...' **xalliiha** 'let her...' **xalliih** 'let him...'. An appropriate
form of the non-past verb is then added: **xalliiha truuH** 'let her go! (lit.
let her she goes), **xalliini ashuuf** 'let me have a look! (lit. let me I see).

♦   Notice that the restaurant patron says **nguul** for 'we say', rather than
n'uul. the g pronunciation instead of ' in this verb is typical of rural areas
of Jordan, and has a somewhat Bedouin ring; the ' has a more urban ring.
There are many other words in which it occurs such as, **'alam** pen
(**galam**) **'abil** before (**gabil**), **'uddaam** in front of (**guddaam**). In your
own pronunciation you can use either, though be sure that a word which
you hear with ' can also be pronounced with a **g**, since this is not always
the case.

Practise what you have learned

9 A woman is ordering her breakfast. Listen and mark what she orders on the menu below. (Answers p.143)
New words: **masluu'** boiled. You might need to review Unit 3.

```
                          MENU

   beeD masluu'              9aSiir tuffaaH

   beeD maqli                9aSiir burtu'aan

   fuul                      9aSiir manga

   xubiz mHammaS             'ahwa

   xubiz 9aadi               shaay

   fTuur amriiki             Haliib

   HummuS
```

10 Samira has invited some foreign friends to her house to taste Arab food. She is familiarizing them with the dishes. Listen and mark off the correct answers to the questions. (Answers p.143)

(a) Which dish was a type of salad?
● malfuuf
● HummuS
● tabbuula
● mtabbal

(b) Which dish was with rice and meat?
● mtabbal
● HummuS
● malfuuf
● tabbuula

(c) Which word gives you the impression that the guest liked the food?
● min luTfik
● shukran
● zaaki
● tfaDDalu

11 Your turn to speak. You are in an Arab restaurant with a friend. You've decided what you want to eat. You are doing the ordering. Start by saying you want some hors d'oeuvres first. Nadira will prompt you as usual.
maay ma9daniyya is mineral water.

Key words and phrases

To learn

'aal/y'uul	to say, tell (**la** = to)
aHsan	better, best
aHsan shii	the best thing
muqabbilaat	hors d'oeuvres (starters, appetizers)
xubiz	bread
mHammaS	toasted
mashwi	grilled/roasted
maqli	fried
masluu'	boiled
mHammar	roast(ed)
dajaaj	chicken
HummuS	chick peas purée
mtabbal	spiced purée of roasted eggplant pulp
kubba HamiiS	cracked wheat balls stuffed with meat, onions and fried pine nuts
salaTa	salad
mashaawi mshakkala	mixed grill
haat, (f.) haati	bring!
gharbi	western
sharqi	eastern

To understand

shu btu'mur? (-i [f.], -u [pl])	what would you like? (lit. what do you order?)
shu bitHibb taakul	what would you like to eat?
ghada	lunch
9asha	dinner
tashkiila	variety, selection
laHmit xaruuf	lamb
laHmit baqar	beef

Grammar

Passive Participle

The active participle of the simple verb was discussed in Unit 9. Active participles work like verbs and follow a pattern, as you have noticed. Passive participles are usually adjectives, but they sometimes function as nouns (often with a special meaning). You have come across many in previous units. Often, they function like English past participles in, for example, the door was <u>locked</u>; <u>toasted</u> sandwich; or <u>broken</u> glass.

The passive participle of the simple verb has the pattern:

maCCuC

mawjuud (from **wajad** to find): present, in existence
mashghuul (from **shaghal** to occupy): busy
maftuuH (from **fataH** to open): opened
masluu' (from **sala'** to boil): boiled

Verbs that end in vowels have the pattern:

maCCi

mashwi (from **shawa** to grill): grilled
maqli (from **qala** to fry): fried

The passive participles of derived verbs have a stem pattern similar to that of the past tense with a prefix **m-** or **mu-** (occasionally **mi-**) added:

mHammaS (from **HammaS/yHammiS** to toast): toasted
mtabbal (from **tabbal/ytabbil** to season): seasoned (eggplant purée dish)
mlawwan (from **lawwan/ylawwin** to colour): coloured

Active participle of derived verbs

The active participle of derived verbs has the same basic pattern as the non-past tense, except that instead of a **y-** prefix, it has a **mi-** or **mu-** prefix:

mudiir director, boss	(from **ydiir** he directs)
misaafir traveller, travelling	(from **ysaafir** he travels)
mumkin possible	(from **yumkin** it is possible)
mitzawwij married	(from **yitzawwaj** he gets married)

illi

In sentences like:

9indak il-mashaawi illi hiyya binsammiiha 'mixed grill'
There are the grills which we call 'mixed grill'. (lit. you have the grills which it we call it 'mixed grill')
   The word **illi** works in Arabic like the words 'which, who, that' in English phrases such as: the dish <u>which</u> you ordered; the man <u>who</u> came to dinner; the letter <u>that</u> arrived. Here are some further examples from the dialogues.

shiish tawuk illi huwwa ... shiish tawuk, <u>which</u> is ...
salaTa naa9ma illi hiyya ... smooth salad, <u>which</u> is ...
it-tashkiila illi xalliina nguul ... the variety <u>which</u> let us call ...

If the noun is indefinite (that is, it has no **il-** and is not a name) the **illi** is left out, for example: **noo9 binsammiih kufta** a kind which we call 'kufta' (lit. [a] kind we call it 'kufta').

Grammar

The other point to note is that sentences with **illi** usually contain a pronoun which refers back to the noun being described and agrees with it grammatically: **il-bint illi shuftha** the girl I saw (lit. the girl who I saw her)

il-mashaawi illi binsammiiha the grills which we call ...

(lit. the grills which we call it).

Note in this last example that as **mashaawi** is a non-human plural, it requires feminine singular agreement, as we saw earlier.

12 Use the passive participles of the verbs in parentheses to translate these sentences: (Answers p.143)

The restaurant is closed.	(**sakkar/ysakkir** to close)
That's prohibited.	(**mana9/yimna9** to prohibit)
This seat (maq9ad) is reserved.	(**Hajaz/yiHjiz** to reserve)
The hotel isn't open.	(**fataH/yiftaH** to open)
The toilet is engaged.	(**shaghal/yishghil** to occupy)

13 Use the active participle of the verbs in parentheses to translate the following sentences: (Answers p.143)

We are very sorry.	(**ta'assaf/yit'assaf** to be sorry)
I'm very grateful.	(**tashakkar/yitshakkar** to be grateful)
I'm not married.	(**tazawwaj/yitzawwaj** to get married)
Are you (m.) ready to go?	(**ista9add/yista9idd** to be ready)
Where do you (m.) live?	(**sakan/yiskun** to live)

Your turn to speak

14 You have invited an Arab couple for lunch in a restaurant. How will you ask them what they want for hors d'oeuvres and main course, what they would like to drink and what they want for dessert. Practise asking them, and ordering the meal. You can listen for a possible version of how the conversation might go.

Answers

Exercise 1 (b)

Exercise 2 (a) an Arab restaurant (b) the first street on the left
(c) fifty metres

Exercise 4 Mark off: kubba HamiiS, tabbuula, HummuS, salaTa
sharqiyy Circle: HummuS, tabbuula, salaTa sharqiyya

Exercise 5 4; 3; 5; 1; 2

Exercise 7 (a) nuSS dajaaja mHammara u xuDra (half roast chicken
and vegetables) (b) shugaf laHmit xaruuf u kabaab u
xuDra ([grilled] lamb chunks with kabab and vegetables)
(c) 9aSiir tuffaaH u 9aSiir burtu'aan (apple juice and orange
juice) (d) sukkar 'aliil (a little sugar)

Exercise 9 beeD maqli (fried egg), xubiz mHammaS (toasted bread),
9aSiir burtu'aan, 'ahwa

Exercise 10 (a) tabbuula (b) malfuuf (stuffed cabbage)
(c) zaaki (delicious)

Grammar

Exercise 12 il-maT9am msakkar; haada mamnuu9; hal-maq9ad
maHjuuz; il-funduq mish maftuuH; it-tawaaliit mashghuula;

Exercise 13 iHna mit'asfiin ktiir; ana mitshakkir ktiir; ana mish
mitzawwij; inta mista9idd truuH?; ween saakin?

Writing

Exercise 15 (a) maT9am il-andalus   The Andalus Restaurant
(b) il-maT9am il-9arabi   The Arab Restaurant
(c) maT9am is-sulTaan   The Sultan's Restaurant
(d) funduq 9amrah   The Amra Hotel
(e) funduq ambasadoor   The Ambassador Hotel
(f) funduq ish-sharq il-awsaT The Middle East Hotel
(g) funduq il-quds   The Jerusalem Hotel

Did you know?

Restaurants

As in the rest of the world there is an enormous range of eating establishments in Arab cities from the most 'popular' hole-in-the-wall shops selling a single type of dish (usually delicious!) to western-style, 5-star restaurants with European chefs and prices to match. A single word **maT9am** (pl **maTaa9im**) loosely 'restaurant', but covering any kind of 'eating place' (the word's literal meaning) is used to describe all of these.

At the cheapest end of the range, there is the **kushk** (derived from a Turkish word from which we get the English word 'kiosk'), which is a small hut or tiny shop selling take-away dishes. These usually sell a very limited range of simple things like doner kebab, **falaafil** – in Egypt called **Ta9amiyya** – or sandwiches (**sandwiitshaat**). Fresh pressed fruit juices (**9aSiir**) are also often sold, for example, **9aSiir burtu'aan** orange juice, **9aSiir farawla** strawberry juice or **9aSiir manga** mango juice.

Somewhat more varied fare, though invariably local, is served in the large number of cheap restaurants, sometimes open to the street, where you can sit down. Usually there is no menu, and the waiter, in reply to the question **shu fii 9indkum?** what do you have? will reel off a long list of possibilities. Some of the commonest of these featured in Dialogues 4 and 5 of Unit 3, and also in this unit. The normal way of ordering is simply to say **a9Tiini ballah ...** Please give me ... or **a9Tiina ballah ...** Please give us ... Bread (**xubiz**) comes as a matter of course and is not normally charged for. In such restaurants, unlike the more expensive one in this unit, there is no talk of 'hors d'oeuvres' (**muqabbilaat**). All orders (**Talabaat**) are served at the same time (**ma9a ba9D**), or as they emerge from the kitchen. The only drinks available are mineral water (**maay ma9daniyya**), cold soft drinks (generically called **baarid** 'cold', as in **bitHibb tishrab baarid?** Would you like a soft drink?), tea (**shaay**), Arab coffee (**'ahwa**), and perhaps milk (**Haliib**). Usually in such restaurants there are no written bills, and you simply settle the bill (**il-Hisaab** the account) at a cash register as you leave. It is not expected that you leave a tip (**baxshiish**).

Further up the price range, air-conditioned, European-style restaurants serve both Arab and western fare from written menus (**minyu**). Depending on the local law and the intended clientele, it is often possible in this kind of establishment to have your hamburger (**hamburgar**) and chips (**baTaaTis maqli**) with a variety of western-style drinks. Tipping here is more usual, though a service charge (**xidma**) may already have been added in addition to the government taxes (**Daraa'ib Hukuumiyya**) which are automatically added in many countries to bills in more expensive restaurants and hotels.

Did you know?

Contrary to popular misconception, you can eat very well in the Middle East if you are a vegetarian (**nabaati**). Since meat was once expensive and a relative luxury, many of the dishes which make up the traditional **mazza** are based on spiced pulses, cereals or vegetables: **HummuS** (chick peas), **tabbuula** (wheat), **falaafil** (broad beans), **baba ghannuuj** and **mtabbal** (eggplant) and **mjaddara** (lentils and rice), to name but a few.

BEVERAGES

COFFEE 0.500
TEA 0.500
DECAFFEINATED COFFEE 0.500
HOT CHOCOLATE 0.800
MILK SHAKES 1.100
MILK 0.500

المشروبات

قهوة ٥٠٠,٠
شاي ٥٠٠,٠
قهوة بدون كافيين ٥٠٠,٠
شوكولا ساخنة ٨٠٠,٠
مخفوق حليب ١,١٠٠
حليب ٥٠٠,٠

Writing

In this unit we have encountered the word **maT9am** restaurant. This word is written like this:

مطعم

You already know the letters **miim** and **9ayn** which occur in this word – can you spot the shape which must correspond to **T** (called **Taa**)? It's:

ط

which is formed by making the rounded part of the letter first, then adding a downward stroke. It looks the same wherever it is written in a word, and joins both sides if appropriate. Refer back to *Hints on Pronunciation* to remind yourself what this difficult letter sounds like.

The next letter, **faa**, sounds like the English 'f' in 'fish', and looks like this on its own:

ف

At the beginning and in the middle of a word, it loses its 'tail':

فطور   سفريات

fTuur breakfast   **safariyyaat** travel agency

At the end of a word, it is written with its tail:

كيف

kayf (spoken Arabic **kiif**) how?

The next letter, **qaaf**, is a similar shape to **faa**, except that it has two dots written above it, not one. Again, this is a difficult sound for most non-Arabs, so refer back to *Hints on Pronunciation*. In the colloquial Arabic of Amman, Cairo, Beirut and Jerusalem, **qaaf** is replaced in many common words by ' (see *Hints on Pronunciation*) which is like the sound in Cockney or Glaswegian English which replaces the 't' in words like 'bu'er' (butter), 'wa'er' (water). People from country areas, on the other hand often pronounce **qaaf** like the English 'g' in 'go'. On its own it looks like this:

ق

When it begins a word, or is preceded by a letter which does not join with the following one, it looks like this:

قرية   رقم

qarya village   **raqam** number

In the middle of a word, after a letter which joins:

النقل العام

in-naql il-9aamm public transport

In final position it has a somewhat deeper tail, compared with **faa**:

العراق

il-9iraaq Iraq

15 Here are some restaurant and hotel signs. See if you can work out what they say and mean. (Answers p.143)

(a) مطعم الاندلس   (b) المطعم العربي

(c) مطعم السلطان   (d) فندق عمره

(e) فندق امبسادور   (f) فندق الشرق الأوسط

(g) فندق القدس

LIKES AND DISLIKES

You will learn

- to say how much you like something
- to state preferences
- to talk about sports
- to give your opinion of things you have done or seen

Study guide

Dialogue 1 + Practise what you have learned
Dialogue 2 + Practise what you have learned
Dialogue 3 + Practise what you have learned
Dialogue 4 + Practise what you have learned
Dialogue 5 + Practise what you have learned
Key words and phrases
Grammar
Your turn to speak
Did you know?
Writing

Dialogues

1 *Iman and Ahmad are having a chat*

Iman maa baHibbish 9aadaat iS-SubuH illi bas bitkuun la shurb il-'ahwa u il-kalaam ... baHibb innuh astafiid min wa'ti akthar min heek ...

Ahmad maa bitdaxxini?

Iman laa, maa baHibb it-tadxiin.

Ahmad kwayyis, ana barDu heek ... ana maa badaxxin wala baHibb ashrab 'ahwa willa ... bas baHibb ashrab shaay!

Iman btishrab shaay ... kwayyis!

9aadaat habits, customs	**shurb** drinking
kalaam talking, chatting	**astafiid** I benefit, use profitably
wa't time	**heek** like this
bitdaxxini you (f.) smoke	**tadxiin** smoking

> **maa baHibbish 9aadaat iS-SubuH illi bas bitkuun la shurb il-'ahwa u il-kalaam ...** I don't like morning habits which just consist of drinking coffee and chatting. (lit. I don't like habits of the morning which only are for drinking the coffee and the talking.)
>
> **baHibb innuh astafiid ...** I like to profit ... (lit. I like that I profit ...) **innuh** is the equivalent of the English 'that' in phrases involving verbs of thinking, feeling and saying, such as: 'I think <u>that</u> ...', 'I believe <u>that</u> ...', 'he told me <u>that</u> ...'
>
> **akthar min heek** more than that (lit. more than like this)
>
> **ana barDu heek** I'm like that as well
>
> **ana maa badaxxin wala baHibb ashrab 'ahwa** I neither smoke nor like to drink coffee (lit. I don't smoke or like...)

2 *Transportation can be a problem...*

Iman u ba9deen lamma batna' 'al baHibb tkuun ma9ai sayyaarti li'ann it-taksiyyaat ... it-taksi ghalaba.

Ahmad ghalaba.

Iman Sa9b innak tlaa'i taksi fi l-wa't il-Haali.

Ahmad Sa9b haada 9alashaan il-jaw baarid aw shii ...

ba9deen then, after, also	**tlaa'i** you find
lamma when, at the time when	**il-wa't il-Haali** the present time
batna' 'al I move around	
taksi (pl. **taksiyyaat** or **takaasi**) taxi	**9alashaan** (here) because
ghalaba problem, nuisance	**il-jaw** the weather
Sa9b difficult	**baarid** cold

> **lamma batna' 'al, baHibb tkuun ma9ai sayyaarti...** when I move around, I like to have my car (lit. ...I like it be with me my car).
>
> **it-taksi ghalaba** taxis are a pain. Almost anything that causes you problems can be called **ghalaba**.
>
> **Sa9b innak tlaa'i ...** it's difficult to find ... (lit. difficult that you find).

Practise what you have learned

1 Listen to the conversation between Zeinab and Munir, who are trying to decide what to do this evening, and answer the questions below. (Answers p.158) New words: **ra'S shar'i** belly dancing (lit. Eastern dancing); **tafarraj/yitfarraj 9ala** to watch; **gharbi** Western

Which things does Zeinab like doing and which does she dislike - Tick or cross the pastimes below.

(a) watching belly dancing
(b) watching television
(c) watching Westerns

(d) watching old films
(e) listening to Western music
(f) listening to Arab music?

2 Your turn to speak. Here you can practise talking about what food you like. You will need to understand the new word **a9jab/yi9jib** to please (for example: **byi9jibni ktiir** I like it a lot) and the word **akil** food. You need also to remember **shu ra'yak fi ...?** what do you think of ...?, and that when talking about something in general you need to put **il-** in front of the word (for example: **is-sbaaHa** swimming). Nadira will guide you through the conversation in the usual way.

3 Fill in the blanks in the sentences below with words from the box. (Answers p.158) New expression: **bi sur9a** quickly

> **Sa9b**   **sahil** (easy)   **tiftikir**   **biy'uul**   **mit'assif**   **9aarif**

(a) _____ innak tlaa'i s-sinama 9alashaan hiyya janb il-jaami9 il-kbiir.

(b) _____ innuh maa byifham 9arabi, bas ana _____ innuh byifham kwayyis.

(c) _____ inni afham kalaam il-urduniyyiin lamma byiHku bi sur9a.

(d) _____ innuh haada l-jamal ghaali shwaay?

(e) _____ innuh maa fii 9indna HummuS il-yoom.

4 Your turn to speak. Mu'nis is asking you about Jordan, so you can practise giving your views. Nadira will guide you as usual.

Dialogues

3 *Iman likes sport, and so does Ahmad.*

Ahmad Tab shu 9indik hiwaayaat, shu fii hiwaayaat, zayy eesh matalan?

Iman ah ... baHibb al9ab riyaaDa iS-SubuH bakkiir aktar shii u s-sbaaHa.

Ahmad is-sbaaHa, kwayyis.

Iman u inta shu bitHibb?

Ahmad wallaahi ana baHibb is-sbaaHa ktiir ... 9indi Hatta l-madaalya l-broonziyya bi s-sbaaHa!

Iman kwayyis.

> **Tab** short for Tayyib (OK)
> **hiwaayaat** hobbies
> **zayy eesh** like what
> **matalan** for example
> **al9ab** I play
> **riyaaDa** sport
> **iS-SubuH bakkiir** in the early morning
> **aktar shii** mostly
> **sbaaHa** swimming
> **Hatta** (here) even
> **madaalya** medallion, medal
> **broonzi** bronze

> **shu 9indik hiwaayaat?** what hobbies have you got?
>
> **baHibb al9ab riyaaDa** I like to play sport. **riyaaDa** signifies sports and exercise in general.
>
> **9indi Hatta ...** I've even got a ...

Practise what you have learned

5 In this exercise you will hear Salah and Salim talking about sport. Below
there is a list of statements about Salah's likes and dislikes in sport, arranged
in his order of preference, but with the actual sport omitted. Can you fill in
the blanks with the appropriate sports, according to the conversation?
(Answers p.158)
New words: **rikib/yirkab xeel** to ride a horse; **rukuub il-xeel** horse-
riding.

(a) biyHibb _____ aktar shii.

(b) biyHibb _____ ktiir.

(c) biyHibb _____ nuSS u nuSS.

(d) maa biyHibbsh _____ bi l-marra (not ... at all).

6 In this conversation John is talking to Hanan and Ashraf about riding
horses. Fill in the blanks with the appropriate forms of the verbs and
pronouns in parentheses. Don't forget the B-prefix before the verb where
appropriate. (Answers p.158)
New words: **SaHra** desert; **byi9raf yil9ab** he knows how to play

Hanan yaa John, _____ _____ (yi9raf yirkab) xeel?

John laa, maa _____ (yi9raf), bas _____ _____

(yHibb yitfarraj). inti _____ _____ (yi9raf yirkab)?

Hanan aywa, _____ _____ (yHibb yirkab) ktiir, ana u
ashraf.

John ween _____ (yirkab)?

Ashraf _____ _____ (yHibb yirkab) fi S-SaHra aktar

shii, 9ashaan Hilwa u _____ (yi9jibuh) ktiir. u inta, shu

noo9 ir-riyaaDa lli _____ (yHibbuh)?

John wallaahi _____ _____ (yHibb yil9ab) golf.

Ashraf _____ _____ (yi9raf yil9ab) kwayyis?
John ya9ni, nuSS u nuSS.

*Riding horses at
Petra in Jordan*

Dialogues

4 *Ayda went to a reunion yesterday of some old friends...*

Haifa	inbasaTti mbaariH? eesh ra'yik kaan?
Ayda	bti9rafi inbasaTit ktiir maZbuuT, il-jam9a kaanat Hilwa ...
Haifa	Tab, eesh illi kaan Hilw mawjuud?
Ayda	bti9rafi aktar shii inbasaTit – min waHda illi aktar min 9ashar sniin mish shayfatha, u awwalmaa shaafatni 'yiii inti 9ayda mish ma9'uul!!'.

inbasaTti   you had a good time
mbaariH   yesterday (alternative to **ams**, with same meaning)
ra'y   opinion, view
inbasaTit   I had a good time
maZbuuT   true, exact(ly)
jam9a   gathering
sniin   years (pl of **sana**, alternative to **sanawaat** with same meaning)
mish shayfatha   I haven't seen her
awwalmaa   as soon as
shaafatni   she saw me
mish ma9'uul   incredible

♦ **inbasaTti mbaariH?**   did you have a nice time yesterday? The verb **inbasaT/yinbasiT** is very commonly used, and is equivalent to English expressions like 'have a good/nice time', 'enjoy yourself'. Here the verb is in the past tense, and the **-ti** ending indicates that the person addressed is a woman (feminine singular). Ayda's reply is of course 1st person (I): **inbasaTit** I had a good time.

♦ **eesh ra'yik kaan**   what did you think of it? (lit. what your (f.) view was?). **eesh ra'yak?** or **shu ra'yak?** are the normal ways of asking someone's opinion about (**fi**) something.

bti9rafi inbasaTit ktiir maZbuuT ...   you know, I <u>did</u> have a really good time, it's true ... Ayda sounds as if she's going to say 'but ...' when she is interrupted by Haifa.

♦ **aktar shii inbasaTit – min waHda illi aktar min 9ashar sniin mish shayfatha**   the thing I was really happy about was a woman who I hadn't seen for more than ten years (lit. mostly I was happy from one [woman] to me more than ten years not having seen her).

shayfatha   is made up of **shayfa**, meaning 'seeing' or 'having seen' (for a man this would be **shayif** – see *Grammar*, Unit 9), with the pronoun **-ha** her. The **t** (part of the feminine ending) has to be added at the end of **shayfa** and before a pronoun suffix (such as **-ha**) is added.

Practise what you have learned

7 Listen to George and Salwa talking about George's trip to Petra.You're
thinking of going there yourself, so you're interested in the practical details:
(a) how he got there
(b) what time he set off and arrived back
(c) whether he enjoyed himself.
You can check if you have understood correctly by looking at p.158.
New words: **riHla, -aat** journey; **Haarr** hot (weather)
(Note also that **Haarr ktiir** means 'too hot' as well as 'very hot'.)

8 Fuad is telling someone what he did yesterday, and here is his story
jumbled up. Arrange it in the right order, by writing 1 in the box against
what should be the first sentence, and so on. You can check your answers
on page 158.
Remember: **'aabal/y'aabil** to meet someone; **waafa'/ywaafi'** to agree.

(a) nizilt il-balad bi l-baaS. ☐

(b) ba9deen 'aabalt fariida 'uddaam maT9am il-baasha. ☐

(c) mbaariH ittaSalt bi SaaHibti fariida bi t-tilifoon. ☐

(d) waafa'at. ☐

(e) u ishtareet tazkarteen la s-sinama. ☐

(f) sa'altha iza kaan biddha truuH ma9i 9a s-sinama bi l-leel. ☐

9 Your turn to speak. You will hear Habiiba asking you about the trip to Syria
you came back from yesterday. After each question she will pause, to give
you time to stop the recording and answer based on the information below.

You went to Damascus and stayed five days, returning yesterday. It was a
long journey, but not hard, and you enjoyed Damascus a lot. You saw the
Ummayad Mosque (**il-jaami9 il-umawi**) and the famous bazaar or Suq
suu' (f.) **il-Haamidiyya**. You liked the mosque best.
New word: **bi'i/yib'a** to stay.

Dialogues

5 *Samira is feeling a bit irritated about the behaviour of some people she saw in the park...*

Karim	shu, maa lik il-yoom, shaayif mish mi9jbiitni!
Samira	wallaahi inni shway mitDay'a.
Karim	min eesh?
Samira	bti9raf ana mbaariH heek, ah, kunt rayHa 9a l-Hadiiqa u 'a9adit heek – kaan jaay 9a baali a'9ud il-9aSir shway heek bi Haali – shuft manaaZir ktiir maa a9jabatni ... fii 9indna Hadaa'iq 9aama, bas in-naas maa 9am ti'dar-
Karim	shu ya9ni?
Samira	ya9ni ti9raf innu hal-Hadiiqa la l-jamii9 u biyxarbuuha byi'Ta9u z-zrii9a u iS-Sghaar biykasruuh bi l-al9aab ... haada ishii mulk la kull in-naas mish laazim iHna nxarbuh heek.
Karim	haadha ghalaT Tab9an, ana bawaafig ma9ik.
Samira	u haadha l-ishii illi ana za99alni u bas.

mitDay'a (f.) irritated		**kunt rayHa** I (f.) was going	
Hadiiqa pl. **Hadaa'iq (9aamma)** (public) park, gardens		**'a9adit** I sat down	
il-9aSir the afternoon		**a'9ud** I sit down	
manaaZir sights, things seen		**bi Haali** by myself	
il-jamii9 everyone, all		**in-naas** people	
byi'Ta9u they cut, pick		**biyxarbuuha** they ruin it	
biykasruuh they break it, smash it		**zrii9a** plants	
mulk property		**al9aab** games	
ghalaT wrong		**kull in-naas** all the people, everyone	
Tab9an of course		**bawaafig** I agree (with = **ma9a**)	
za99alni it annoyed me, upset me			

---

shu, maa lik il-yoom what's the matter with you today? (lit. what, what to you today?).

shaayif mish mi9jibiitni I see you're not yourself (lit. [I] seeing [you] not pleasing me). **mi9jib** is the active participle of the verb **a9jab/yi9jib** to please. The feminine form with **t** is used here because the participle is describing a woman – it is she who is doing the pleasing (or rather the lack of it!); the **-ni** is the object 'me'.

kaan jaay 9a baali a'9ud il-9aSir shway heek bi Haali I felt like sitting down for a bit in the afternoon by myself (lit. [it] was coming to my mind [that] I sit the afternoon a bit by myself).

manaaZir maa a9jabatni sights which didn't please me. The verb **a9jab/yi9jib** is frequently used in the sense of 'like, please': **bti9jibak il-urdun willa laa?** do you like Jordan or not?

in-naas maa 9am ti'dar.. people are incapable ... **9am** is used with a non-past verb to indicate that the action is happening now.

ti'dar can, are capable. This is feminine singular because **naas** is often classed as a non-human plural, and thus takes feminine singular agreement.

mish laazim iHna nxarbuh heek we shouldn't ruin it like that.

Practise what you have learned

10 Read the following conversation and answer the questions below.
(Answers p.158)

New word: **rijjaal** (pl.**rjaal**) man (it is important to pronoun the **jj** in
the singular properly as this is the main difference from the plural – see
Hints on Pronunciation.)

Anwar shufti filim sindibaad yaa bushra?
Bushra aywa, shuftuh min santeen heek.
Anwar u shu kaan ra'yik?
Bushra bi SaraaHa maa a9jabni ktiir.
Anwar leesh?
Bushra maa Habbeetsh ir-rijjaal illi kaan byil9ab door sindibaad. mish
9aarfa, kaan mish mi9jibni heek. ba9deen il-filim kaan Tawiil ktiir.
Anwar u maa kaan fii ishii yi9jibik fi l-filim?
Bushra ya9ni, manaaZir iS-SaHra a9jabatni aktar shii, kaanat kwaysa, u
inta, shu ra'yak? shuft il-filim?
Anwar laa, kaan biddi ashuufuh, bas iza kaan heek, mithil maa bit'uuli,
xalaaS, biddiish.

(a) Which phrases indicate (i) things that Bushra did not like about the
film, and (ii) things she did like?

(b) What do you think **kaan byil9ab door sindibaad** means?

(c) Underline the phrases that mean a) *there wasn't anything* and b) *I
wanted to see it*.

(d) Underline the phrase that says how long ago Bushra saw the film. How
long ago was it?

11 Your turn to speak. You are talking to Yusif about your hotel, which you
are not very happy with. Nadira will guide you in the usual way.

Key words and phrases

To learn

baHibb (x) aktar shii	I like (x) the most
a9jabni/byi9jibni	I like it
is-sbaaHa	swimming
il-jaw Haarr	It's/the weather's hot
baarid ktiir	very/too cold
riHla (pl. -att)	trip, journey
Sa9b	difficult
muxtalif (9an)	different (from)
9alashaan	because
inbasaT/yinbasiT	to enjoy oneself
inbasaTt min ir-riHla	I enjoyed the trip
laa'a/ylaa'i	to find
tafarraj/yitfaaraj 9ala	to watch
rikib/yirkab	to ride, get on/in
kaan/ykuun	to be
zaar/yzuur	to visit
mbaariH	yesterday
rijjaal (pl. rjaal)	man
sitt (pl. -att)	woman
SaaHib (f. SaaHiba, pl. aSHaab)	friend
Tariiq or Tarii' (pl. Turuq or Turu')	road
kull	all, every

To understand

nuSS u nuSS	so so
maa byi9jibni bi l-marra	I don't like it at all
bti9raf til9ab...?	do you know how to play...?
bitdaxxin?	do you smoke?

Grammar

The past tense

The past tense in Arabic is equivalent to the English 'did' or 'has done', depending on the context. Here is an example of a regular verb in the past: **9imil/yi9mal** to do, make. You are familiar with several of the forms already, for example, **law samaHt/samaHti/samaHtu**. Some verbs have an **i-i** vowel pattern (like **9imil**) and some an **a-a**, like **samaH**.

9imilt	I did	**9imilna**	we did
9imilt	you (m.) did	**9imiltu**	you (pl.) did
9imilti	you (f.) did		
9imil	he did	**9imilu**	they did
9imilat	she did		

You may also hear, in regular verbs, forms like **9imilit** for 'I/you (m.) did', in which the ending is **-it**, rather than **-t**. For example, Ayda says **inbasaTit** rather than **inbasaTt** for 'I enjoyed myself'. This is a variation which you should try to recognise.

As with the non-past tense, the past tense endings are the same for all verbs. In some types of verbs, the bit the endings are added to (the 'stem') may change, depending on whether the ending begins with a consonant or not. Here is the past of **kaan/ykuun** to be.

kunt	I was	**kunna**	we were
kunt	you (m.) were	**kuntu**	you (pl.) were
kunti	you (f.) were		
kaan	he was	**kaanu**	they were
kaanat	she was		

kaan/ykuun is a so-called 'hollow' verb. All this means is that in some parts of the past tense ('he', 'she', 'they'), there is a long **-aa-** vowel in the middle of the stem, e.g. **kaan** 'he was', **kaanat** 'she was', **kaanu** 'they were'. In the rest of the past tense of such verbs, the stem has a short vowel which in some verbs is **-u-** and in some **-i-**: so **kaan** 'he was' but **kunt** 'I was', **raaH** 'he went', but **ruHt** 'I went', **naam** 'he slept' but **nimit** 'I slept'.

In the non-past, 'hollow' verbs always have a stem containing a long vowel, which maybe **-aa-**, **-ii-** or **-uu-**, e.g.

aruuH	I go	**yruuH**	he goes	**yruuHu**	they go
abii9	I sell	**ybii9**	he sells	**ybii9u**	they sell
anaam	I sleep	**ynaam**	he sleeps	**ynaamu**	they sleep

'Hollow' verbs, like ordinary ones, are listed under the 'he' forms of the past tense and non-past tense, e.g. **raaH/yruuH** to go, **baa9/ybii9** to sell. Other kinds of verbs in the past will be dealt with in Unit 12.

The negative of the past tense is formed in the same way as that of the non-past, e.g. **maa 9imilt** or **maa 9imiltsh** I didn't do.

12 Fill in the blanks with the appropriate form of the verbs in parentheses. (Answers p.158) New word: **maHall (m.-aat)** place.

min sana _____ (saafar) ana u zoojti 9ala l-urdun u _____ (nizil) fi

funduq 9amra. zoojti _____ (raaH) ktiir 9ind SaaHbitha illi _____

(kaan) saakna fi 9ammaan, u _____ (zaar) maHallaat ktiira ma9a

ba9D. u ana _____ (raaH) riHla 9ala l-bitra u _____ (zaar)

maHallaat taanya bi T-Tariiq, u _____ (kaan) riHla mumtaaza. u

niHna _____ (shaaf) filim 9arabi 'adiim. _____ (kaan) fi9lan

filim 9aZiim.

Your turn to speak

13   Mention three things you like doing and three things you do not like doing, in Arabic of course. You will hear Nadira tell you her likes and dislikes on the recording.

Answers

Practise what you have learned

Exercise 1	Tick: (a), (b), (d); Cross: (e)
Exercise 3	(a) sahil (b) biy'uul, 9aarif (c) Sa9b (d) tiftikir (e) mit'assif
Exercise 5	(a) is-sbaaHa (b) is-sbaaHa (c) it-tinis (d) rukuub il-xeel
Exercise 6	bti9raf tirkab?; ba9raf or ba9rafsh; baHibb atfarraj; bti9rafi tirkabi?; binHibb nirkab; btirkabu? binHibb nirkab; bti9jibna; bitHibbha? baHibb al9ab; bti9raf til9ab
Exercise 7	(a) by bus (b) 6.00 a.m., 9.15 p.m. (c) yes, a lot
Exercise 8	(a) 4 (b) 5 (c) 1 (d) 3 (e) 6 (f) 2
Exercise 10	(a) (i) ir-rijjal illi kaan byil9ab door sindibad or il-filim kaan Tawiil ktiir (ii) manaaZir iS-SaHra (b) He played/was playing the role of Sinbad (c) (i) maa kaan fii ishii (ii) kaan biddi ashuufuh (d) min santeen = 2 years ago

Grammar

Exercise 12	saafarna; nizilna; raaHat; kaanat; zaaru; ruHt; zurt; kaanat; shufna; kaan

Writing

Exercise 14	(a) Ma'iin (b) Jerash (c) Aqaba (d) al-Azraq (e) al-mudarraj ar-ruumaani = The Roman Amphitheatre

158   UNIT 11

Did you know?

Sports and pastimes

In the modern Arab world, the most popular sports are the same as those in the West. As we saw in the dialogues of this Unit, **riyaaDa** is the general word for sport, but the most popular individual games (**li9b** pl. **al9aab**) or sports are **it-tanis** tennis, **ir-rakaD** jogging, running, **kurat il-qadam** soccer, **kurat is-salla** basketball, **il-kura iT-Taa'ira** volleyball, as well as **is-sbaaHa** swimming, which we saw earlier. Other popular spectator sports are **sibaaq il-xeel** horse-racing, and, in Bedouin areas, **sibaaq il-jmaal** camel-racing. Betting on the result of a race or match (**muqaamara**) is specifically prohibited in Islam.

Musical evenings (**saharaat** or **Haflaat musiiqiyya**) are enormously popular in all parts of the Arab world, and recordings of concerts account for a considerable proportion of the output of all Arab TV and radio stations. Although the music and songs performed at such evenings can be termed 'popular', it is wrong to equate them with western concepts of 'pop' music. In the Arab world until very recently, there was not really any distinction between 'classical' and 'popular' music. Egyptian popular singers such as Umm Kulthum, Farid al-Atrash (both now dead), and Lebanese such as Fayruz and Sabah have an enormous and universal appeal among all ages and social groups. Their songs treat the timeless themes of love, betrayal and loss, and are constructed on a grand scale, with the performance of a single song sometimes lasting up to an hour. The great singers occupy a unique place in the national and pan-Arab psyche. The funeral of Umm Kulthum, the doyenne of Egyptian singers, was the occasion for a mass outpouring of grief, attended by several million Egyptians, and brought Cairo to a complete standstill.

Day trips to sites of natural beauty are as popular in the Arab world as they are in the West. In Jordan, for example, popular destinations for a family day out (**riHla**) are the hot springs at Ma'in south of Amman (**Hammaamaat ma9iin**), and the forts (**quSuur**) on the road east to al Azraq (**qaSr il-xaraanah, qaSr 9amra**). Day return tickets by bus (**tazkira rooHa raj9a**) are cheap. In Amman and its immediate vicinity, there are extensive Roman remains: the Roman amphitheatre (**il-mudarraj il-ruumaani**) in Amman itself and the ruins (**aathaar**) at Jerash, to the north of Amman, where every September an international festival (**mahrajaan dawli**) of the performing arts is held.

The theatre (**il-masraH**) is perhaps less well established in most Arab countries than in the West, being a relatively recent cultural importation. The cinema (**is-siinama**), on the other hand, is as popular as it is in the West, and there is a thriving film industry, particularly in Egypt, which exports its films to the rest of the Arab world. Although their paramount position in the popular arts is now less than it was twenty years ago, Egyptian film stars and singers still have the largest general following throughout the Arab world, rather in the way that American film actors and popular singers dominated the English-speaking countries in the 1930's to 1950's.

Writing

In Unit 9 we met the letter **9ayn**: ع

The same shape with a dot above it is a different letter called **ghayn** and is symbolised in the spoken part of the course by the two letters **gh**. On its own it looks like this: غ

This is a difficult letter to pronounce (see *Hints on Pronunciation*), but sounds something like a Parisian French 'back r' or the sound you make in your throat when gargling. It is written in all positions exactly like **9ayn**, the only difference being the dot. Here are some examples:

Initial position	*Medial position*	*Final position*
غرفة	شغل	تبغ
ghurfa room	**shughl** work, job	**tibigh** tobacco

Our next letter is called **jiim** and sounds like the English 'j' in 'John', though some Lebanese and Syrians pronounce it like the 's' in 'pleasure', and Egyptians pronounce it like the 'g' in 'go'. On its own, when not joined, it looks like this: ج

Initially and medially it loses its 'tail' when joining onto a following letter:

نجّار **najjaar** carpenter (also family name)   جعفر **ja9far** Ja'far (male name)

In the final position, when preceded by a 'joining letter', it retains its tail:

برنامج **barnaamij** programme

In final position, when not joined, it has a similar shape:

كراج **karaaj** garage

15 The following are names of tourist places and sites in Jordan. See if you can make them out.

(a) معين

(b) جرش

(c) عقبة

(d) الازرق

(e) المدرّج الروماني

You will learn

- how to make appointments
- how to arrange to meet someone
- more ways of talking about future plans and events
- some irregular verbs

Study guide

Dialogue 1 + Practise what you have learned
Dialogue 2 + Practise what you have learned
Dialogue 3 + Practise what you have learned
Key words and phrases
Grammar
Your turn to speak
Did you know?
Writing

Dialogues

1 *Hala, a student, would like to arrange an appointment to see Miles Roddis, a British Council Representative, about a scholarship application to a British university. She goes to his Personal Assistant...*

Hala	marHaba.
PA	ahlan.
Hala	HaDirtik sikritiirit il-mudiir?
PA	aywa, tfaDDali.
Hala	biddi a'aabil Mr Roddis, law samaHti.
PA	bi xSuuS eesh biddik t'aabliih?
Hala	Talab 'addamtuh la bi9tha 'abil talaat tashhur...
PA	aywa.
Hala	u-...
PA	maa ijaaki l-jawaab 9aleeh.
Hala	maa ija lii radd la ghaayit halla'.
PA	Haawalti tshuufi Mrs Farah, il-mas'uula 9an il-bi9thaat?
Hala	Haawalt 'abil fatra u dayman mashghuula mashghuula.

a'aabil I see, meet, have a meeting with	
bi xSuuS concerning, about	
t'aabliih you (f.) meet him	**Talab** application
'addamtuh I presented it, put it in	**bi9tha** (pl. -aat) scholarship
jawaab answer, reply	**radd** answer, reply
la ghaayit halla' up till now	**Haawalti** you (f.) tried
mas'uul (f. mas'uula) (9an)	**Haawalt** I tried
person responsible (for)	**fatra** a period of time
dayman always	

> **Talab 'addamtuh la bi9tha** an application I made for a scholarship. **'addamtuh** means literally 'I presented it'. You say in Arabic: an application I presented <u>it</u>, a man I saw <u>him</u> in the street, a book I read about <u>it</u> in the newspaper. **illi** (which), we saw in Unit 10 *Grammar*, is only used in Arabic if the noun is definite: **iT-Talab illi 'addamtuh** <u>the</u> application <u>which</u> I made it, for example.

> **'abil talaat tashhur** three months ago. **'abil** by itself means 'before', but when followed by a period of time it is equivalent to the English 'ago': **'abil yoomeen** two days ago, **'abil fatra** some time ago. You have met **min** (from) with the same meaning: **min yoomeen** two days ago.

> **maa ijaaki l-jawaab 9aleeh** you haven't had a reply (lit. not came (to) you the reply to it). The PA's completion of Hala's sentence overlaps on the recording with Hala's sentence which means the same: **maa ija lii radd la ghaayit halla'** I haven't had a reply up to now.

> **Haawalti tshuufi...** have you tried to see... (lit. you tried to see...). After the verb **Haawal/yHaawil** you simply use a non-past verb as the equivalent of the English 'to try to.../to try and...': **Haawalt ashuufuh** I tried to see him.

Practise what you have learned

1 Listen to a conversation between a personal assistant and someone seeking an appointment with her boss. Answer True/False (T/F). (Answers p.170)

(a) She can see the director. ☐

(b) She can see him tomorrow. ☐

(c) She is asked to come in after a month. ☐

(d) She can see him in a week. ☐

(e) She cannot see him because he is not in. ☐

(f) She is told he is busy. ☐

2 Listen to the conversation in which an enquirer is given directions. Then mark off the correct answers. (Answers p.170)

(a) Who does the lady want to see?
● the manager
● the manager's assistant
● the manager's secretary

(b) The room is on:
● the first floor, second door on the right
● the second floor, first door on the left
● the second floor, first door on the right

3 Your turn to speak. You are on a business trip to Jordan. You would like to see the director of Salah Company. Speak to the receptionist. Nadira will prompt you as usual.

Dialogues

2 *Later, Raghda, a secretary in one of the ministries, comes into the office to set up a meeting for her boss with Mr Roddis...*

PA	tfaDDal.
Raghda	marHaba hind.
PA	ahleen, kiifik?
Raghda	kiif Haalik?
PA	ahlan wa sahlan.
Raghda	biddi aaxud maw9id ma9a Mr Roddis.
PA	aywa.
Raghda	la mudiiri bi l-wizaara.
PA	bi l-wizaara... er... eemta biyHibb yiiji?
Raghda	id-duktuur 9ali Talab minni innuh aaxud luh maw9id ayya yoom – ya9ni yoom it-tneen, ayya yoom ba9d is-sabt, il-aHad aw it-tneen is-saa9a Hda9sh...
PA	il-aHad aw it-tneen is-saa9a iHda9sh... bi n-nisba la yoom il-aHad, raghda, Mr Roddis mashghuul bas bi n-nisba... la yoom it-tneen ahlan wa sahlan, mumkin...

wizaara ministry
Talab he asked
ayya yoom any day
bi n-nisba la... as far as... is concerned

♦ **biddi aaxud maw9id ma9a Mr Roddis** I want to make (lit. take) an appointment with Mr Roddis. In Arabic you usually 'take' an appointment to see someone.

♦ **eemta biyHibb yiiji** when would he like to come?

♦ **Talab minni innuh aaxud luh maw9id** he asked me to make him an appointment... (lit. he required from me that I make for him appointment...). To 'ask someone to do something' (as opposed to 'ask someone a question' = **sa'al**) is always with the verb **Talab** (to require), which is used with **min** (from): **Talab minha truuH ma9uh** he asked her to go with him (lit. he required from her she goes with him). Note that the 'he' form of the verb, **Talab**, is the same as the noun **Talab** (application, requirement), which you met in Dialogue 1 of the Unit.

it-tneen Monday: an alternative to **il-itneen** with the same meaning.

Practise what you have learned

4 The manager is asking his secretary about appointments for the week. Listen to their conversation and fill in his pocket diary for him. Write down in English the days and the times he is engaged, and with whom. (Answers p.170)

SUNDAY 29	WEDNESDAY 2
	THURSDAY 3
MONDAY 30	
	FRIDAY 4
TUESDAY 1	SATURDAY 5

5 Listen to the dialogue between a visitor and a receptionist. Mark off the correct answer to the questions. (Answers p.170)

(a) Why can't he see the director?
● The director is busy.
● He does not have an appointment.
● The director is not in.

(b) What was he asked to do?
● To come tomorrow.
● To wait.
● To make an appointment.

(b) When is the appointment for?
● Thursday at 10.30 am.
● Monday at 9.30 am.
● Thursday at 11.30 am.

6 Your turn to speak. You are phoning to make an appointment to see the manager of **shaa9ir wa shurakaa'** (Sha'ir and Partners). Nadira will prompt you as usual.

Dialogues

3 *What is the meeting to be about...?*

Raghda	mumkin it-neen is-saa9a Hda9sh?
PA	aywa Tayyib... 9aarfa leesh bidduh yshuuf Mr Roddis?
Raghda	aZunni innuh biddhun yibHathu tafaaSiil istiqdaam xabiir min briiTaanya, bidduh yfarjiih il-'proposals' illi ma9uh.
PA	ah, OK... lakaan il-, er-, it-tneen, talaata ish-shahar is-saa9a Hda9sh, ahla u sahla.
Raghda	OK, shukran.
PA	ahlan.

9aarif (f.**9aarfa**) knowing
aZunni I think
yibHathu they discuss
tafaaSiil details
istiqdaam summoning, inviting out
xabiir expert
lakaan so, then

> ♦ **9aarfa leesh bidduh yshuuf Mr Roddis?** do you know why he wants to see Mr Roddis? **9aarfa** is the feminine active participle (m. = **9aarif**) of the verb **9irif** to know.
>
> ♦ **aZunni innuh biddhun yibHathu...** I think that they want to discuss... The **hun** in **biddhun** (they want) is an alternative to **biddhum** with the same meaning.
>
> Notice that in the English-speaking atmosphere of the British Council Office, even two Arabic-speakers may occasionally use English words like 'proposals' in the middle of an Arabic conversation. If you get stuck, it is worth a try! (Incidentally, in Arabic, 'proposals' is **iqtiraaHaat**).
>
> **talaata ish-shahar** the third of the month.
>
> ♦ **ahla u sahla** instead of **ahlan wa sahlan**: a more relaxed, informal way of saying the same thing.

Practise what you have learned

7 Two secretaries are arranging appointments for their bosses. Complete the dialogue using the words from the box below. (Answer p.170)

> eemta   l-usbuu9   maw9id   ahlan   is-saa9a Hda9sh
> kwayyis   keef Haalik

Su'ad   marHaba baasima.

Basima   ————————— su9aad, ————————— ?

Su'ad   il-Hamdu lillaah, biddi aaxud ————————— la mudiiri ma9a mudiirik.

Basima   ————————— biyHibb yiiji?

Su'ad   ayy yoom haada ————————— ba9d is-saa9a 9ashra.

Basima   yoom il-xamiis is-saa9a Hda9sh kwayyis?

Su'ad   aywa, —————————. lakaan il-xamiis ————————— .

8 Samira wants to invite her friend, Hanadi, to lunch. Hanadi is looking at her diary. Fill in the three engagements that she mentions. When can she fit Samira in? Where will they have lunch? (Answers p.170)

FRIDAY

12.00 Noon

1.00 p.m.

5.00 p.m.

___

SATURDAY

12.30 p.m.

3.00 p.m.

5.00 p.m.

___

SUNDAY

10.00 a.m.

1.00 p.m.

9 Your turn to speak. A business acquaintance wants to invite you to dinner. She is trying to arrange a day and a time. Nadira will prompt you as usual. New word: **biynaasbak** it suits you, is convenient to you.

Key words and phrases

To learn

biddi aaxud maw9id	I want to make an appointment (lit. I want to take...)
ba9d bukra	the day after tomorrow
leesh	why?
halla'	now
Talab/yiTlub	to ask something (**min** = from)
Haawal/yHaawil	to try, attempt
'aabal/y'aabil	to meet
'abil fatra	some time ago
dayman	always

To understand

bixuSuuS eesh?	concerning what?
bi n-nisba la	in relation to, concerning
wizaara	ministry
xabiir	expert
tafaaSiil	details
baHath/yibHath	to discuss
eemta biynaasbak?	when would suit you?

Grammar

The past of the weak verb

Remember that some verbs are called 'weak' verbs. These verbs end in a vowel **-a** or **-i** in the past 'he' form. (look back to the Grammar section of Unit 7 for the non-past forms.) For example:

Haka   to speak   **bi'i**   to stay

The **-a** in verbs like **Haka** drops before endings that begin with a vowel. For example:

Hakat   she spoke   (from **Haka** + at)
Haku   they spoke   (from **Haka** + u)

The **-a** is replaced by **-ee-** before endings that begin with a consonant. For example:

Hakeet   I spoke   (from **Haka** + t)
Hakeeti   you (f.) spoke   (from **Haka** + ti)

Here are the full forms for **Haka**:

Hakeet	I spoke	**Hakeena**	we spoke
Hakeet	you (m.) spoke	**Hakeetu**	you (pl) spoke
Hakeeti	you (f.) spoke		
Haka	he spoke	**Haku**	they spoke
Hakat	she spoke		

When the 'he' form of a verb ends in **-i**, this becomes **y** before endings that begin with a vowel. For example:

bi'yat   she stayed   (from **bi'i** + at)
bi'yu   they stayed   (from **bi'i** + u)

And it becomes **-ii-** before endings that begin with a consonant. For example:

bi'iit   I stayed   (from **bi'i** + t)
bi'iiti   you (f.) stayed   (from **bi'i** + ti)

Here are the full forms for **bi'i**:

bi'iit	I stayed	**bi'iina**	we stayed
bi'iit	you (m.) stayed	**bi'iitu**	you (pl) stayed
bi'iiti	you (f.) stayed		
bi'i	he stayed	**bi'yu**	they stayed
bi'yat	she stayed		

The verb **aja** to come

The verb **aja** (to come) is an irregular verb which you have occasionally met. Here are its forms:

Past		Non-past	
ijiit	I came	**aaji**	I come/am coming/will come
ijiit	you (m.) came	**tiiji**	you (m.) come/are coming/will come
ijiiti	you (f.) came	**tiiji**	you (f.) come/are coming/will come
ija (or **aja**)	he came	**yiiji**	he comes/is coming/will come
ijat (or **ajat**)	she came	**tiiji**	she comes/is coming/will come
ijiina	we came	**niiji**	we come/are coming/will come
ijiitu	you (pl.) came	**tiiju**	you (pl.) come/are coming/will come
iju (or **aju**)	they came	**yiiju**	they come/are coming/will come

Remember that if you want to say 'Come (here)!' as a command, you use **ta9aala** (m.), **ta9aali** (f.), **ta9aalu** (pl.).

Your turn to speak

10   You have an acquaintance in Jordan, and you think he might be able to help you with your business. You would like to invite him for lunch. Phone him and, when his wife answers, ask if he is in and if you can speak to him. When he comes to the phone, ask how he and the children are. Invite him, stating the day, the time, and the place. Then check with the recording for a model version.

When you want to invite him to lunch you can say: **shu ra'yak nitghadda sawa?** (lit. what is your view we have lunch together?).

Answers

<table>
<tr><td rowspan="2">**Practise what you
have learned**</td><td>Exercise 1</td><td>(a) F (b) F (c) F (d) T (e) F (g) T</td></tr>
<tr><td>Exercise 2</td><td>(a) the manager's secretary (b) 2nd floor, 1st on the right</td></tr>
<tr><td></td><td>Exercise 4</td><td>Sunday, 10.00 a.m. the Ministry; Tuesday, 3.00 p.m. the manager of the Zayid Company; Wednesday, 11.00 a.m. Dr Hamid</td></tr>
<tr><td></td><td>Exercise 5</td><td>(a) He hasn't got an appopintment (b) to make an appointment (c) Thursday, 10.30 a.m.</td></tr>
<tr><td></td><td>Exercise 7</td><td>Su'ad: marHaba baasima!
Basima: ahlan su9aad, kiif Haalik?
Su'ad: il-Hamdulillaah. biddi aaxud maw9id la mudiiri ma9a mudiirik.
Basima: eemta biyHibb yiiji?
Su'ad: ayy yoom haada l-usbuu9 ba9ad is-saa9a 9ashra.
Basima: yoom il-xamiis is-saa9a Hda9sh kwayyis?
Su'ad: aywa, kwayyis, lakaan il-xamiis, is-saa9a iHda9sh</td></tr>
<tr><td></td><td>Exercise 8</td><td>Friday lunch with Maha.
Saturday 12.30 meeting at the Ministry.
Sunday 10.00 shopping.
Lunch with Samira: Sunday 1.00 at Al-Basha restaurant.</td></tr>
</table>

<table>
<tr><td>**Writing**</td><td>Exercise 11 1. = (f), 2. = (b), 3. = (d), 4. = (a), 5. = (c), 6. = (e)</td></tr>
</table>

Did you know?

Business hours

The working week in the Arab world – at least in all government offices and most businesses – runs from Saturday to Thursday, with Friday being the Muslim day of rest. Thursday is often a shorter working day than the others. In many countries the office day begins early at 7.30 a.m. and ends at one or two in the afternoon. Stores tend to open again at five and stay open until seven or eight in the evening. 'Working hours' are called **id-dawaam, waqt id-dawaam** or **awqaat id-dawaam**. So **shu awqaat id-dawaam 9indkum?** means 'What are your opening/working hours?' As we have seen in this Unit, in Arabic you 'take' (**taaxud**) an appointment (**maw9id**) to meet someone.

Politeness at meetings

When meeting someone for the first time, especially if that person is of high rank or status, it is normal to use a few polite expressions. You normally call the other person **HaDirtak** your presence (**HaDirtik** for a woman) rather than just **inta** you, (which would sound rather rude), or by some other honorific, depending on his/her rank and on the conventions of the country you are in, for example, **sa9aadtak** your excellency (lit. your happiness) (undersecretaries, ambassadors), **jalaaltak** your majesty (royalty in some countries). Expressions like **tasharraft** I am honoured (to meet you), **sharraftuuna bi ziyaartak** you have honoured us with your visit, are freely bandied about. A relatively formal interchange at the beginning of a business might go something like this:

A (entering) **as-salaam 9aleekum.**
(Peace be upon you.)
B **wa 9aleekum as-salaam! tfaDDal, udxul! sharraftna!**
(And on you peace! Please, come in! You have honoured us!)
A **allah ysharrifak.**
(May God honour you.)
B **kiif Haal HaDirtak?**
(How are you?)
A **al-Hamdu lillah, Tayyib. u HaDirtak kiif iS-SiHHa?**
(Praise be to God, well. And how is your health?)
B **al-Hamdu lillah, allah yiHfaZak... tfaDDal, istariiH.**
(Praise be to God, God preserve you... please, sit down.)

Exchanges of this kind may continue for some time longer, and are an important part of the meeting ritual before the participants get down to business. Although things are slowly changing, particularly among the younger generation of Arabs, the western 'businesslike' approach which dispenses with this elaborate politeness is perceived by many as merely rude, although it is appreciated that western ways are different.

Did you know?

Westerners are often disconcerted, particularly at meetings in Ministries with lower-ranking officials, when they are interrupted by other visitors simply popping in and sitting down, or when they are shown in for their meeting only to find that a previous visitor is still there and shows no sign of leaving, and indeed, joins in the elaborate ritual exchanges of courtesies. This is a vestige of the tradition that an important person's **majlis** reception area (lit. place of sitting) is always open to any visitor at any time. This, again, is changing but it is as well to be aware of the conservative way of doing things.

١٤٠٩هـ	جمادى ١ / جمادى ٢					١٩٨٩م					يناير
٢١	١٤	٧	٢٩		السبت	٢٨	٢١	١٤	٧		
٢٢	١٥	٨	(١)	٢٣	الأحد	٢٩	٢٢	١٥	(٨)	*١	
٢٣	١٦	٩	٢	٢٤	الإثنين	٣٠	٢٣	١٦	٩	٢	
٢٤	١٧	١٠	٣	٢٥	الثلاثاء	٣١	٢٤	١٧	١٠	٣	
	١٨	١١	٤	٢٦	الأربعاء		٢٥	١٨	١١	٤	
	١٩	١٢	٥	٢٧	الخميس		٢٦	١٩	١٢	٥	
	٢٠	١٣	٦	٢٨	الجمعة		٢٧	٢٠	١٣	٦	

(جمادى الثانية : ٨ يناير)

* رأس السنة الميلادية

Writing

In Unit 11 we met the letter **jiim**. The same shape, but with the dot above rather than below it, is the letter **xaa**, which sounds like the Scottish pronunciation of the 'ch' at the end of 'Loch' (see *Hints on Pronunciation*). It is written in exactly the same way as **jiim**.
On its own:

At the beginning:

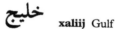 **xaliij** Gulf

In the middle, joined to a preceding letter:

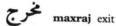 **maxraj** exit

At the end, joined to a preceding letter:

شيخ **shayx** sheikh (lit. old man)

In Unit 8 we met **daal**, which sounds similar to an English 'd'. Remember that it looks like this: د

and joins only onto preceding letters (where the preceding letter allows) but never onto following ones. The same shape, but with a dot above it, is called **dhaal** and sounds like the English 'th' in words like 'that' or 'father':

ذ

Examples: ذلك **dhaalika** that

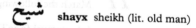 **baydhinjaan** aubergine

Remeber that this sound, in some words, is sometimes replaced by speakers from Jordan, Palestine and other areas by a 'd' and sometimes by a 'z' (see *Hints on Pronunciation*).

Writing

Our third letter in this Unit is called **DHaa** and is a difficult one to pronounce. Like **dhaal**, it has variant pronunciations (see *Hints on Pronunciation*) It is the same shape, and is written in exactly the same way as **Taa**, which we met in Unit 10, but it has a dot written above it: ظ

It always joins onto a following letter. Here are some examples of it:

ظن   **DHann** (or **Zann**) thought

موظف   **muwaDHDHaf** (or **muwaZZaf**) official

حظ   **HaDHDH** (or **HaZZ**) luck

11   Match the following transcriptions to the Arabic street signs below:

(a) **xuruuj faqaT**   exit only
(b) **duxuul faqaT**   entry only
(c) **mamnuu9 il-wuquuf**   no parking
(d) **mamnuu9 it-tadxiin**   no smoking
(e) **mamnuu9 il-muruur**   no entry
(f) **madxal karaaj**   garage entrance

١   مدخل كراج
٢   دخول فقط
٣   ممنوع التدخين
٤   خروج فقط
٥   ممنوع الوقوف
٦   ممنوع المرور

You will learn

- to ask for tourist information
- to give instructions and understand prohibitions
- to ask about opening and closing times and membership of clubs

Study guide

Dialogue 1 + Practise what you have learned
Dialogue 2 + Practise what you have learned
Dialogue 3 + Practise what you have learned
Key words and phrases
Grammar
Your turn to speak
Did you know?
Writing

Dialogues

1 *Rahma feels like a day-trip to Ma'in...*

Rahma	SabaaH il-xeer.
Assistant	SabaaH in-nuur, ahleen.
Rahma	ma9leesh t'uulii lii iza biddi aruuH 9a ma9iin it-tazkara bi 'addeesh?
Assistant	it-tazkara 9indik bi dinaar u nuSS.
Rahma	haay bitkuun rooHa raj9a Tab9an?
Assistant	rooHa raj9a.
Rahma	ah, Tab mumtaaz... u ayy saa9a biyruuH il-baaS?
Assistant	fii baaS iS-SubuH is-saa9a sab9a u nuSS bituuSal la ma9iin Hawaali s-saa9a 9ashra u nuSS, u aaxir baaS min ma9iin is-saa9a arba9a.
Rahma	9a l-arba9a.. u 'abl il-arba9a maa fii gheeruh?
Assistant	laa.
Rahma	Tab... kull yoom nafs is-saa9a?
Assistant	kull yoom nafs ish-shii maa 9ada yoom il-jum9a.
Rahma	maa 9ada yoom il-jum9a... shukran.

tazkara rooHa raj9a return ticket
mumtaaz excellent
aaxir baaS the last bus
maa 9ada except for

> ◆ **ma9leesh t'uulii lii...** would you mind telling me...? **ma9leesh** means 'never mind' normally. This is an idiomatic use.
>
> ◆ **biddi aruuH 9a...** I want to go to... The verb **raaH/yruuH** (to go) is normally followed by **9a** or **9ala** (to) in Jordan.
>
> ◆ **it-tazkara bi 'addeesh** how much is the ticket? (lit. the ticket for how much?).
>
> ◆ **9a l-arba9a** at four (o'clock)...
>
> ◆ **maa fii gheeruh?** aren't there any others? (lit. not there is other than it?). **gheer** means '(something/someone) other than'. Pronouns can be added to the end of it, as here.
>
> ◆ **nafs is-saa9a** at the same time. **nafs** put in front of a definite noun means 'the same': **nafs ish-shii** the same thing; **nafs il-funduq** the same hotel.

Practise what you have learned

1   On the recording you will hear some replies to the questions and comments below, but not in the same order. Indicate which item goes with which by putting the number of the appropriate reply in the right box below. (Answers p.184)

New word: **tarak/yutruk** to leave

(a) ayy saa9a byutruk baaS irbid? ☐

(b) maa fii baaS ba9d is-saa9a tamaanya? ☐

(c) haada l-baaS byaaxud wa't ktiir fi T-Tariiq. ☐

(d) biddak tazkara rooHa raj9a? ☐

(e) il-baaS byutruk bi nafs is-saa9a kull yoom? ☐

2   You want to make a phone call while in central Amman. Listen to George finding out how to go about it, by asking a man in the street. Answer the following questions: (Answers p.184)

(a) Where should George go to make a phone call?
(b) Why can't he make one from a public phone?

New words: **ista9mal/yista9mil** to use;
   ittaSal/yittaSil (bi) to call or ring (someone) up, get in touch
Remember also: **SaaHib maHall** storekeeper

3   Your turn to speak. You want to make an international phone call. You would like some more information, so you take a taxi to the post office and ask the taxi driver on the way:

(a) Do they speak English at the post office?
(b) Can you pay in Sterling or Dollars or must you pay in Dinars? Which is cheaper?
(c) Can you send a telegram from there?

Using the words below, work out how to ask one question at a time, then listen to Nadira's version. See if you can understand the taxidriver's answers as well.

New words: **il-istirliini** £ sterling
   tiligraam telegram
   danaaniir urduni Jordanian Dinar(s)
   dafa9/yidfa9 to pay

Dialogues

2 *Nadira wants some information about an interesting museum...*

Nadira	SabaaH il-xeer.
Assistant	ahleen, SabaaH in-nuur.
Nadira	ayy saa9a biysakkir il-matHaf ballah?
Assistant	il-matHaf il-yoom biysakkir 9ala xamsa u nuSS.
Nadira	ba'dar aaxud Suwar?
Assistant	laa, ma9a l-'asaf it-taSwiir mamnuu9.
Nadira	shu fii fi l-matHaf?
Assistant	huwwa l-matHaf... il-matHaf ish-sha9bi la l-Hily wa l-azyaa', Tab9an azyaa' urduniyya, badawiyya, filasTiiniyya, heek u heek shaghlaat.
Nadira	'addeesh tadhkirat id-duxuul?
Assistant	tadhkirat id-duxuul bi xams u 9ishriin 'irsh.
Nadira	shukran.
Assistant	9afwan.

matHaf museum
ma9a l-'asaf unfortunately
taSwiir photography
mamnuu9 prohibited
sha9bi popular, belonging to the people
azyaa' fashions, costumes
shaghlaat things
duxuul entrance

♦ **ba'dar aaxud Suwar?** may I take photographs?

il-matHaf ish-sha9bi la l-Hily wa l-azyaa' the Jordanian Museum of Popular Traditions (lit. the popular museum for the jewellery and costumes).

♦ **heek u heek shaghlaat** you get things like that (lit. like that and like that things).

tadhkirit id-duxuul entrance ticket. **tadhkira** is the more 'correct' way of pronouncing **tazkira**

JORDAN MUSEUM OF POPULAR TRADITIONS	المتحف الشعبي للحلي والأزياء
THE ROMAN THEATRE	المدرج الروماني
Amman – Jordan	عمان ــ الاردن
ADMISSION TICKET	بطاقة دخول
250 Fils	٢٥٠ فلس
NO PHOTOGRAPHY PLEASE DO NOT TOUCH	الرجاء عــدم التصوير واللمس
٤٢٩٣٨ رقم	

Practise what you have learned

4 You will hear Mary going up to an official outside the amphitheatre in Amman. What time can she visit the amphitheatre, and what other instructions does the official give her? (Answers p.184)

New words: **juwwa** inside

        jaab/yjiib to bring

        fataH/yiftaH to open

        byirja9 yiftaH it will re-open

5 Your turn to speak. Now it is your turn to find out about telephoning. This time you go into a store and want to make a local telephone call. Apart from asking for the necessary information you will need to check you have understood the storekeeper correctly.

Dialogues

3 A student is enquiring about joining a library. First of all, how much does it cost to join?

Student   biddi a9mal ishtiraak fi l-maktaba... 'addeesh rusuum il-ishtiraak bi n-nisba ili?

Librarian   er... OK. bti'dari ti9mali l-ishtiraak fi l-maktaba u btidfa9i r-rusuum illi hunna xams danaaniir – er – bi s-sana ... er – bti'dari min xilaalha taHSuli 9ala arba9 kutub... muddit il-isti9aara 9indna talaat asaabii9...

Student   ana ka Taaliba ba'dar adfa9 talaat danaaniir, ya9ni?

Librarian   na9am.

Student   u iza kunt gheer Taaliba?

Librarian   btidfa9i xams danaaniir bi s-sana.

Student   er – btuTlubu minni ithbaat inni Taaliba?

Librarian   na9am... tjiibu huwiyya shaxSiyya... daftar 9eela aw jawaaz safar aw ruxSit swaa'a.

ishtiraak subscription, membership (of a club, library, etc.)	
maktaba library	**rusuum** fees
btidfa9i you (f. sing.) pay	**hunna** they (f. pl.)
min xilaal by means of	**taHSuli 9ala** you (f. sing.) get
kutub books	**isti9aara** borrowing
ka as	**Taaliba** student (f.)
tuTlubu you (pl.) demand, ask for	**ithbaat** proof
tjiibu you (pl.) bring	
huwiyya shaxSiyya personal identification	
daftar 9eela family card (Jordanian document)	
ruxSit swaa'a driving licence	

◆ **biddi a9mal ishtiraak**   I'd like to become a member (lit. I want to make subscription).

bi n-nisba ili   in my case (lit. in relation to me). We have already met this phrase in the form **bi n-nisba la**. This is a variant of it, using **il-**, a variant of **la**, also meaning 'to'. here **il** has the **-i** suffix (me) attached to it.

ir-rusuum illi hunna xams danaaniir   the fees, which are five dinars. **hunna** is a feminine plural pronoun 'borrowed' incorrectly by the speaker from written Arabic, who is apparently trying to speak in a more 'correct' way than she would normally. In more casual speech, we would expect **hiyya** (feminine singular) to agree with the non-human plural noun **rusuum**.

◆ **ana ka Taaliba...**   I as a student... **ka** means 'as' in the sense of 'in the capacity of', and can be used with any noun: **ana ka ingliizi...** I as an Englishman...

◆ **iza kunt gheer Taaliba...**   if I were not a student... (lit. if I was other than student).

◆ **btuTlubu minni ithbaat inni Taaliba?**   do you require from me proof that I'm a student? (lit. you require from me proof that I student?).

tjiibu   you (pl.) bring. The librarian seems to be addressing subscribers in general through the student, and so uses a plural verb.

Practise what you have learned

6 George wants to go swimming and he has heard that there is a good pool at a club (**naadi**). Listen to him talking to the receptionist, then mark whether the following statements are true or false. (Answers p.184)

(a) George has to join the club to use the pool.
(b) He will have to pay a year's membership fees.
(c) He wants to join for a year.
(d) He needs to pay six dinars.

7 George returns later to the club with a Jordanian friend. You will hear him telling George what to do. Mark off which of the following words and phrases he uses in his explanation: (Answers p.184)

1 (a) **tfaDDal** please come!
  (b) **ta9aala** come!

2 (a) **ghayyir** change!
  (b) **bitghayyir** you change

3 (a) **iTla9** go up!
  (b) **utruk** leave!
  (c) **uTlub** ask!

4 (a) **ta9Ti** you give
  (b) **a9Ti** give!
  (c) **bta9Ti** you give

5 (a) **taaxud** you take
  (b) **btaaxud** you take
  (c) **xud** take!

6 (a) **utruk** leave!
  (b) **btiTla9** you go up
  (c) **iTla9** go up!

7 (a) **laa'i** find!
  (b) **bitlaa'i** you find
  (c) **tlaa'i** you find

8 (a) **maa btinzilsh** you don't go down!
  (b) **maa tinzilsh** don't go down!

8 Your turn to speak. You are going to buy a ticket to use the pool at an international hotel, and you need to find out from the receptionist how it is organized. Nadira will guide you through the conversation as usual.

Key words and phrases

To learn

nafs is-saa9a	the same time (lit. hour)
ish-shahar il-jaay	next month
la usbuu9een	for two weeks
tazkara rooHa raj9a	return ticket, round trip ticket
matHaf (pl. mataaHif)	museum
mithil	like
mathalan	for example
raaH/yruuH 9a (or 9ala)	to go to
sakkar/ysakkir	to shut
fataH/yiftaH	to open
bada/yibda	to begin
a9Ta/ya9Ti	to give
xalaS/yixlaS	to end
simi9/yisma9	to hear, listen
dafa9/yidfa9	to pay
fluus	money
jaab/yjiib	to bring
tarak/yutruk	to leave
ista9mal/yista9mil	to use

To understand

akil	food
ittaSal/yittaSil (bi)	to ring or call (up), contact
it-taSwiir mamnuu9	taking photos is forbidden
xud gheeruh	take a different one

Grammar

The command form

This is the form of the verb you use to give orders, and you have seen Arabic examples like **xud** (take!) and **utruk** (leave!). It is formed for almost all verbs by taking the appropriate 'you' form of the non-past tense and chopping off the first **t**. So:

truuH	you go	**ruuH**	go!
tista9mili	you (f.) use	**ista9mili**	use! (to a woman)
tisma9u	you (pl.) listen	**isma9u**	listen! (to more than one person)

One of the commonest imperatives is odd: **ta9aal** or **ta9aala** (f. **ta9aali**, pl. **ta9aalu**) come! (but **ija/yiiji** to come). Note also **haat** (f. **haati**, pl. **haatu**) bring! give me! as an alternative to **jiib** (f. **jiibi**, pl. **jiibu**) from **jaab/yjiib** to bring. **xud** take! (from **axad/yaaxud**) and **kul** eat! (from **akal/yaakul**) are also slightly irregular.

The negative command is just the 'you' form without the **b(i)** prefix and with the usual negative: **maa truuHsh** don't go!; **maa taakulsh** don't eat!; **maa tisma9sh** don't listen! etc. It is less impolite to use commands in Arabic than the English equivalent, so do not be offended when it is used to you apparently abruptly. But do not over use it yourself. So in general it is more important to understand than to be able to use it.

9 On the recording you will hear five sentences. Write down the imperative in each one with its meaning and whether it is being said to a man, a woman or to more than one person. Then translate the sentences. (Answers p.184)

Verbal nouns

These are words like **sbaaHa** swimming; **duxuul** entrance, going in; **ishtiraak** membership. They are nouns denoting the action of a verb: the examples given come from **sabaH/yisbaH** to swim, **daxal/yudxul** to enter, and **ishtarak/yishtirik** to participate, respectively. They always have the same root as the verb from which they come, but the relation between the form of the verb and the verbal noun is complex and sometimes unpredictable, so verbal nouns are listed in the glossary for each verb. Again, it is more important to be able to recognize them than to use them, so it is worth knowing that some other patterns are: **taCCiiC** (for example, **taSwiir** taking photographs), **muCaaCaCa** (for example, **muHaawala** attempt) and **iCCaaC** (for example, **islaam**, from **aslam/yislim** to be or become a Muslim).

10 In the following sentences underline the verbal nouns and see if you can guess what they mean from their roots. Translate the sentences. (Answers p.184)

(a) maa baHibbsh lu9ub il-gulf.
(b) baHki ma9ak taani ba9d il-mu'aabla ma9a l-mudiir.
(c) tark is-sinama xilaal il-filim mamnuu9.
(d) Hajiz il-maHallaat bi l-baaS mish mumkin.
(e) id-dafi9 biykuun 'abil ir-riHla bi yoomeen.

Your turn to speak

11 Suppose you have just arrived in a town in Jordan and want to find out what there is to see. Think of five questions you might want to ask someone in a store or café, then listen to Nadira doing the same on the tape.

Answers

Practise what you have learned	Exercise 1 (a) 4 (b) 2 (c) 3 (d) 1 (e) 5
	Exercise 2 (a) a shop (b) there are no public call boxes
	Exercise 4 She can visit it between 8.00 a.m. and 6.00 p.m., but she mustn't bring a camera
	Exercise 6 (a) T (b) F (c) F (d) T
	Exercise 7 1. (b) 2. (b) 3. (b) 4. (a) 5. (a) 6. (c) 7. (b) 8. (b)
Grammar	Exercise 9 (a) inzilu - go down (pl.)! (b) 'uul - say (m.)! (c) isma9i - listen (f)! (d) maa tjiish - don't come ([m.] or [f.])!, ta9aali - come (f.)! (e) udxul - come in (m.)!
	Exercise 10 (a) lu9ub - playing (b) mu'aabla - meeting (with someone) (c) tark - leaving (d) Hajiz - reserving (e) dafi9 - payment Translation: (a) I don't like playing golf. (b) I'll speak to you again after the meeting with the boss. (c) Leaving the cinema during the film is prohibited. (d) Reserving seats on the bus is not possible. (e) Payment is made (lit. is) two days before the journey.
Writing	Exercise 12 1. Hafiz al-Asad 2. Saddam Hussein 3. Husni Mubarak 4. Yasir Arafat 5. Mu'ammar al-Gaddafi 6. Jamal Abdulnasser

Did you know?

Driving

It is worthwhile knowing at least the basic Arabic vocabulary associated with driving and servicing cars since mechanics, especially in the rural areas where cars have a nasty habit of breaking down, are unlikely to speak English very well. The vocabulary does differ a little from country to country, and the forms presented here are those which are in active use in the Levant (Jordan, Syria, Palestine and Lebanon), but which would nonetheless be understood in a wider area than this.

First of all some basic vocabulary:

diriksyoon	steering wheel
ghaTa	bonnet/hood
Sanduu'	boot/trunk
mootoor/muHarrik	engine
koontaak	ignition
radyatoor	radiator
fraam	brake(s)
dibrayaaj	clutch
banziin	accelerator
fiitees	gears
duulaab (pl. **dawaliib**)/	
kawshuuk (pl. **kawaashiik**)	tyre
risarv/iHtiyaaTi	spare tyre

If some piece of equipment is not working, the phrase is **maa byishtighil**, for example, **il-fraam maa byishtighil** the brakes aren't working. If something needs adjusting, the phrase is **bidduh** (or **biddha**) **ta9diil**, for example, **id-dibrayaaj bidduh ta9diil** the clutch needs adjusting. Or you could say **fii shii fi d-dibrayaaj** there's something wrong with the clutch. If the car has simply broken down, and you do not know the cause, the verb to use is **ta9aTTal/yit9aTTal**, for example, **mumkin tsaa9idni 9alashaan sayyaarti ta9aTTalat?** can you help me, because my car has broken down? The word for puncture, like many of the words associated with driving, is a borrowing from a European language, in this case English: **banshar** (pl. **bansharaat**), for example, **Saar ma9na banshar** we've got a puncture (lit. there has become with us a puncture). Or perhaps you have run out of petrol: **banziinna xilaS** (from the verb **xalaS/yixlaS** to end, finish).

Did you know?

Mechanics are called **miikaaniki: fii miikaaniki hoon mumkin ysaa9idna ballah?** is there a mechanic here who could help us? The verb 'to repair' is **SallaH/ySalliH**, as in **biddna waaHad yi9raf ySalliH bansharaat** we need someone who knows how to repair punctures. The 'servicing' of cars is called **xidma**, as in **has-sayyaara biddha xidma** this car needs servicing.

A petrol station is called **maHaTTit banziin** or (in Jordan) **kaaziyya**. If you want the attendant to fill your car up, the verb is **9abba/y9abbi** (which we met in Unit 4 in connection with filling in a hotel arrival card): **9abbi l-xazzaan, i9mal ma9ruuf** do me a favour and fill up the tank (lit. fill the tank, do a favour). You might also want the tyre pressure checking: **9ayyir lii d-duulaab kamaan, min faDlak** (lit. check for me the tyre as well, please), and perhaps the oil level: **ifHaS lii z-zeet** (lit. check for me the oil).

Writing

The letter **Haa**, which we have symbolized in our transcription system as **H**, and which sounds like a very breathy, panting 'h' (see *Hints on Pronunciation*) is the same shape as **jiim** and **xaa**, but without any dots, and is written in the same way. On its own it looks like this:

ح

And joined with other letters in words it looks like this:

ملح   بحر   حجز

milH salt   **baHr** sea   **Hajz** reservation

There is another kind of 'soft' h which sounds like its English equivalent called **haa** and which we have symbolized in the transcription as **h**. By itself, this letter is the same as the feminine ending ة but without the dots:

ه

At the beginning of a word it looks like this:

هو

huwa (colloquial **huwwa**) he

In the middle, when printed, it looks like this:

مها

mahaa Maha (girl's name)

And at the end, when joined to the letter before, it again looks like the feminine ending without the dots:

نبيه

nabiih Nabih (man's name)

The next letter, called **Saad**, which sounds like a dull, heavy 's' (see *Hints on Pronunciation*) looks like this by itself:

ص

When joined onto a following letter, it loses its 'tail':

باص   نصف   صحيح

baaS bus   **niSf** (colloquial **nuSS**) half   **SaHiiH** true

In written Arabic, there are some words ending in a long **-aa** vowel, in which this final **-aa** is written not as an **alif**, the normal way, but with a 'y' (**yaa**) without the dots underneath it:

معنى   ذكرى

ma9naa (colloquial **ma9na**) meaning   **dhikraa** commemoration

Writing

12 Recognizing personal names. The ability to read Arabic names on the doors
of offices, visiting cards or other printed matter is particularly useful and
does not require a full knowledge of written Arabic grammar or vocabulary.
See if you can read the following personal names of Arab politicians who
are, or were, frequently in the news and in newspaper headlines:

١   حافظ الاسد

٢   صدام حسين

٣   حسني مبارك

٤   ياسر عرفات

٥   معمر القذافي

٦   جمال عبد الناصر

You will learn

- to talk about your future plans
- to talk about things you would like to do
- to invite people
- to ask and reply to questions in the future

Study guide

Dialogue 1 + Practise what you have learned
Dialogue 2 + Practise what you have learned
Dialogue 3 + Practise what you have learned
Dialogue 4 + Practise what you have learned
Key words and phrases
Grammar
Your turn to speak
Did you know?
Writing

Dialogues

1 Ahmad would like to invite Iman out for the evening. What about a film?

Ahmad	faaDya l-leela ishii? 9aamla shii l-yoom?
Iman	mashghuula l-leela, 9indi draasa.
Ahmad	Tab... eemta bitkuuni faaDya inshaallaah?
Iman	yimkin bukra.
Ahmad	Tab bitHibbi... fii filim Hilw fi s-sinama, bitHibbi truuHi 9aleeh?
Iman	ayy filim?
Ahmad	mish mitzakkir ismuh bas ba9raf innuh Hilw!
Iman	li'annuh kull il-aflaam HiDirthum!

> **faaDya** (f.) free, not busy
> **il-leela** tonight
> **9aamla** (f.) doing
> **mashghuula** (f.) busy
> **draasa** study
> **filim** (pl. **aflaam**) film, movie
> **mitzakkir** remembering, bringing to mind
> **HiDirthum** I've been to them

♦ **faaDya l-leela shii?** would you be free at all tonight? The use of **shii** is a way of asking hopefully whether there is any possibility at all of the question being answered positively. Similarly **9indak maay shii?** would you have any water at all?

♦ **mish mitzakkir ismuh** I don't remember its name... **mitzakkir** is an active participle from the verb **tzakkar/yitzakkar** to remember.

♦ **li'annuh kull il-aflaam HiDirthum** because I've been to see all the films (lit. because all the films, I've attended them). It is often the case that when you wish to emphasize a particular part of the sentence in Arabic, you shift it to the beginning, as here.

Notice throughout this dialogue that neither Iman nor Ahmad use the independent pronouns **ana** (I) and **inta/inti** (you). These are unnecessary because the verb forms and the context make it clear who the subject of each sentence is.

Practise what you have learned

1   Samira is trying to find out what Maha is doing tonight. Listen to the tape and answer the following questions by ticking the correct answer. (Answers p.198)

(a) What is Maha doing tonight?
- going to the cinema
- staying at home
- going with Samira

(b) Who is going to the cinema?
- Sahar
- Hanadi
- Maha
- Samira

(c) Who is visiting Hanadi?
- Maha
- Samira
- Sahar

2   Listen to the conversation between Ahmad and Samir and decide whether the following statements are true or false. (Answers p.198)
New words: **mit'axxir** late; **mista9jil** in a hurry

(a) Ahmad was at the cinema?

(b) The film was very nice and Ahmad liked it.

(c) Ahmad accepts the invitation for coffee.

(d) Ahmad says that he is going to see a friend of his.

(e) Ahmad says that he is late and in a hurry.

3   Your turn to speak. You want to invite your friend out, but you want to find out whether she is free or not first. Nadira will prompt you as usual.

Dialogues

2 *Then what about dinner instead?...*

Ahmad	ah. Tab ween bitHibbi truuHi?
Iman	maa fii maHall mu9ayyan.
Ahmad	OK, Tab shu ra'yik ann a9izmik 9a l-9asha bukra inshaallaah, bukra s-saa9a sitta?
Iman	bukra s-saa9a sitta? Tayyib maashi... la ghaayit is-saa9a tamaanya.
Ahmad	OK.
Iman	binshuufak bukra.
Ahmad	ahleen yaa hala.

maHall	place	**mu9ayyan**	specific, particular
maashi	OK	**9asha**	dinner
binshuufak	we'll see you	**la ghaayit**	up until

♦ **shu ra'yik a9izmik...** what do you say I invite you... (lit. what your opinion I invite you...) **shu ra'y** + pronoun is a very common way of inviting someone to do something.

a9izmik is from the verb **9azam/yi9zim** to invite. We would expect the form **a9zimik** but in the case of some speakers, with some verbs, the vowelling at the beginning of the word is 'rearranged'. Similarly **a9arfak** (I know you) instead of **a9rafak**. This is something you need to be able to recognize, rather than imitate yourself.

♦ **9asha** is 'dinner', and we have the corresponding verb **ta9ashsha/yit9ashsha** (to have dinner). 'Lunch' is **ghada** which corresponds to the verb **taghadda/yitghadda** (to have lunch) which we met in Unit 10.

♦ **binshuufak** we'll see you... It is not at all uncommon for a person to refer to him/herself by using the 'we' rather than the 'I' form. This phrase is used exactly like the British English 'See you!' when leaving someone.

3 *Karim has invited Yousif to dinner at a certain restaurant next Tuesday evening, but Yousif isn't keen...*

Yousif	wallaahi yaa axi ana a9tidhir yoom ith-thalaatha 9ala maT9am 'il'baasha' bi dh-dhaat.
Karim	leesh 9aad?
Yousif	li'annuh la sababeen... li'annuh yoom ith-thalaatha 9indi shughul... ithneen, maT9am il-baasha maa baHibb ajii 9aleeh li'annuh ghaali jiddan ya9ni...

a9tadhir I excuse myself (i.e. say no to an invitation)
bi dh-dhaat in particular
leesh 9aad but why?
sabab reason

♦ **a9tadhir** means 'I apologise' (for example, for having done something wrong) as well as being used (as in this case) to say no to an invitation, idiomatically equivalent to the English 'Sorry but I can't'.

li'annuh la sababeen because it's for two reasons

Practise what you have learned

4 Rearrange the following to form a dialogue. Then listen to check your answer.

leesh laa. ayy saa9a?
maashi, izan bashuufak bukra s-saa9a tamaanya.
marHaba saamir.
eemta?
il-Hamdu lillaah. shu ra'yak ya saamir nit9ashsha sawa.
inshaallaah.
bukra.
ahlan, ahlan 9abid. kiif il-Haal?
is-saa9a tamaanya.

5 Listen to 'Umar telephones Samir to issue an invitation. Tick the correct answer to the following questions. (Answers p.198)

(a) What has 'Umar invited Samir for?
● breakfast
● dinner
● lunch

(b) What day did 'Umar suggest?
● Friday
● Sunday
● Saturday

(c) Which day is more suitable for Samir?
● Sunday
● Friday
● Thursday

(d) What time is the invitation for?
● seven
● seven-thirty
● six-thirty

6 Your turn to speak. You are in Jordan. An acquaintance of yours sees you and wants to invite you out. Respond to his enquiries. Nadira will prompt you. Remember the verb **bi'i/yib'a** to remain, stay.

7 Fill in the blanks from the box below to make a sensible conversation. Then check your answer on page 198.

```
waHda   nitghadda   faaDi   9indi shughul   is-sabt   fikra kwaysa   bukra
```

Ahmad   shu 9aamil ＿＿＿＿＿＿ D-Duhur?

Marwan   bukra D-Duhur ＿＿＿＿＿ .

Ahmad   Tab ba9d bukra ＿＿＿＿＿ ?

Marwan   is-sabt, wala shii, ＿＿＿＿＿ .

Ahmad   shu ra'yak ＿＿＿＿＿ sawa fi maT9am ish-sharq?

Marwan   ＿＿＿＿＿ , leesh laa, ayy saa9a?

Ahmad   is-saa9a ＿＿＿＿＿ .

Marwan   maashi.

8 Your turn to speak. You would like to invite your friend, Nabil, to dinner tomorrow. Nadira will prompt you.

Dialogues

4 'Ayda is talking to Samira about her holiday plans for the summer...

Samira ba9d talaat tashhur 'ariib ijaazit iS-Seef... eesh nawyiin ti9maluuh?

'Ayda mfakkriin bti9rafi naaxud il-iwlaad u nruuH 9a 'ubruS li'annuh byinbisTu ktiir... bti9rafi fii baHar byisbaHu ba9deen bni'dar nruuH 9a jbaal 'Troodos'... taghyiir Ta's biykuun Hilw ktiir bi 'Troodos'.

Samira bas biyjuuz ykuun shoob ktiir!

'Ayda shoob bas lamman yu'9udu kull il-wa't bi l-baHar, bi l-birka u heeka, biykayfu, byinbisTu u bi l-leel binruuH mishwaar, byit9ashshu heek byirja9u biynaamu... yam maa byitHarrakuush!

'ariib near (here in a time sense)	**ijaaza** holiday, vacation, leave
Seef summer	**nawyiin** (pl.) intending
mfakkiriin (pl.) thinking	**'ubruS** Cyprus
byinbisTu they have a good time	**baHar** sea
byisbaHu they swim	**jbaal 'Troodos'** the Troodos
taghyiir Ta's change of air	mountains (central Cyprus)
biyjuuz it's possible, maybe	**shoob** hot (of weather)
lamman when (alternative to **lamma**)	**yu'9udu** they sit
birka swimming pool	**biykayfu** they enjoy themselves
mishwaar walk, outing	**byit9ashshu** they have dinner
byirja9u they come back	**biynaamu** they sleep
yam at all, completely	**maa byitHarrakuush** they
	don't move a muscle

Note that throughout this dialogue 'Ayda uses the B-prefix to indicate habitual action. She has been to Cyprus before, and describes what her children usually do and how they usually behave there.

- **ba9d talaat tashhur 'ariib ijaazit iS-Seef** in three month's time, it'll soon be the summer vacation (lit after three months...).

- **eesh nawyiin ti9maluuh?** what are you (pl.) planning to do? (lit. what planning you do it?). **nawyiin** is the plural form of the active participle **naawi** (f. **nawya**) from the verb **nawa/yinwi** to plan, intend.

- **mfakkiriin** we're thinking of... This is also a plural active participle, from the verb **fakkar/yfakkir** to think.

- **bas biyjuuz ykuun shoob ktiir** but it might be very hot. **shoob** is used for hot weather. Heat in liquids, etc. is **suxun**: **haada sh-shaay suxun ktiir** this tea is very (or too) hot.

- **il-birka u heeka** ... the swimming pool and that. **heek** (or **heeka**) (like that) is commonly used with the same vague sense as English phrases like 'and that', 'and so on', 'and such like'.

- **binruuH mishwaar** we go for an outing. **mishwaar** also commonly means 'errand'.

yam maa byitHarrakuush they (the children) don't move a muscle. The verb is **taHarrak/yitHarrak** to move. This is the negative (with **maa...sh**) of the 'they' form of the non-past tense.

Practise what you have learned

9 Najla and Hind are talking about their next summer holidays. Listen to their dialogue and then answer the questions by marking off the correct answer. (Answers p.198)
New word: **il-yunaan** Greece

(a) Where are Najla and her family going for their holidays this summer?
- Cyprus
- Greece
- They are staying in Amman
- Bahrain

(b) Where are Hind and her family going for their holidays this summer?
- Cyprus
- Greece
- They are staying in Amman
- Bahrain

(c) Where are Hind's sister and children coming from?
- Cyprus
- Greece
- Amman
- Bahrain

(d) When are Najla and her family going to Cyprus or when did they go there?
- They are going this summer.
- They went two years ago.
- They went last year.
- They have never been to Cyprus.

10 Ahmad and his wife are planning to give a party on Friday, so Ahmad has been phoning his friends to find out whether they can make it or not. Listen and match the people with what they are doing at the weekend. (Answers p.198)
New words: **9uzuuma** invitation; **iZ-Zaahir** it appears

(i) Samir and family	**a** invited for dinner
(ii) Nabil and family	**b** going to Irbid
(iii) Ramzi and family	**c** going to Akaba

Key words and phrases

To learn

shu 9aamil (f. 9aamla) …?	what are you doing…?
faaDi (f. faaDya) il-leela?	are you free tonight? (lit. free tonight)
eemta bitkuun faaDi? (f. bitkuuni faaDya)?	when are you free?
shu ra'yak (f. ra'yik) nit9ashsha/nitghadda sawa?	how about having dinner/lunch together?
eesh naawi ti9mal…? (f. nawya ti9mali…?)	what are you planning to do?
ijaaza	holiday, vacation
maT9am	restaurant
shoob	hot
yimkin	maybe
Seef	summer
shita	winter
baHar	sea
lamma	when (as in **lamma shuftuh…** when I saw him)

To understand

9aamil (f. 9aamla) ishii…?	are you doing anything?
biyjuuz	maybe
mfakkiriin…	thinking…
riji9/yirja9	to return
taghyiir Ta's	change of air (lit. change of weather)
inbasaT/yinbisiT	to have a good time

Grammar

Expressing the future

The word **raH** is used before a non-past tense verb to indicate future intention:

eemta raH tiiji?	when are you (m.) going to come?
shu raH ti9mali?	what are you (f.) going to do?
ween raH truuHu?	where are you (pl.) going to go?
eemta raH ysaafir?	when is he going to leave (the country)?

Note that **raH** always stays the same, and that the non-past verb which follows it indicates he, she, you etc.

The active participle of verbs of motion can also be used by themselves with a future sense:

eemta raayiH?	When are you (m.) (or when is he) going? (lit. when going?)
samiir jaay ba9d usbuu9	Samir is coming in a week.
hum msaafriin bukra	They are leaving tomorrow.

Negating the future

You have met negation in earlier units. To negate **raH** or a participle use the word **mish**.

mish raH yiiji ba9d usbuu9	he is not coming in a week
mish raH aruuH bukra	I am not going tomorrow
mish raH tsaafir ba9d usbuu9	she is not leaving in a week

11 Use the correct form of the verbs in the parentheses to translate the English and complete the sentences. (Answers p.198)

(a) samiir _(is going to go)_ 9ala london bukra. (**raaH**)

(b) _(is going to come)_ samiira min amriika ba9d usbuu9. (**ija**)

(c) _(are you going to write)_ yaa 9ali maktuub la aHmad? (**katab**)

(d) _(is going to work)_ samiira fi sharika jdiida ba9d shahar. (**ishtaghal**)

(e) _(I am going to visit)_ uxti fi l-urdun fi S-Seef. (**zaar**)

Your turn to speak

12 It is your turn to invite a friend of yours to dinner. Find out when he is free and arrange a day and time and place for your dinner. Tell him about your holiday plans and find out what his plans are. Then listen to the model version.

Answers

Did you know?

The etiquette of invitations

Arab hospitality is justly renowned, but it is as well to understand the etiquette and meaning of different kinds of invitations since, as in the West, there is a good deal of invitation which is merely 'for form's sake' and is not necessarily expected to be accepted, even though in theory it could be.

If you are introduced to someone socially, or simply meet them accidentally through third parties, it is quite likely that you will be invited there and then, or perhaps at a subsequent chance meeting, to have tea or coffee at their house or in some nearby café, even if it is obvious from the circumstances that the person who is inviting you is really in the middle of doing something else. If you accept, he will take you to have tea/coffee even if it keeps him from his prior engagement. This illustrates the strength of the social obligation to 'play host' in Arab society. It would be terribly bad manners in such circumstances for your acquaintance not to invite you; but of course, with experience, it becomes obvious when a tactful refusal is really the desired response. You can use the phrase used in Dialogue 3, for example, **a9tadhir shukran, 9indi shughul shwayy** Sorry I can't, thank you, I have a little work to do. After a few protestations, the invitation will be dropped.

In rural areas, it is quite common for invitations to lunch or dinner to be given in the same unplanned way at the end of a chance conversation: **yallah tfaDDal 9indna la l-ghada, sharrif il-beet** come on, please have lunch with us, honour our house! Of course, if you accept, the (possibly really reluctant) host will indeed provide you with lunch. But you can quite politely refuse by saying something like **gheer marra, inshaallaah, ana ma9zuum 9ind naas** another time, God willing, I'm invited to someone else's, or say that you have work still to do, as suggested earlier, and honour will have been satisfied on both sides. If the invitation is really genuine it will be more insistent, and repeated, and if it relates to the future a definite time will usually be mentioned.

Did you know?

The 'mañana' tendency in Arab society to put things off (in Arabic the word
is **bukra** tomorrow), and the elastic view of time is proverbial. At one time,
in some parts of the Arab world, western time-keeping (usually GMT plus
2 or 3 hours) competed with Muslim Sun Time, according to which
midnight was the time of sunset each day. The confusion which arose was
unnecessary anyway, it was alleged, since the only kind of time by which
people really lived was **'Ma9leesh'** time, ma9leesh meaning literally 'never
mind, it doesn't matter'! This tendency to place little store by exactitude in
matters of time is recognized and joked about by Arabs themselves, who
have been known to ask, when an appointment has been made, whether it is
maw9id 9arabi willa maw9id ingliizi is it an Arab appointment or an
English one?

Writing

One of the more difficult letters for the English speaker is that which we have symbolized as **D** (see *Hints on Pronunciation*), called **Daad** in Arabic. It is written in exactly the same way as **Saad** which we encountered in Unit 13, except that it has a dot written on top of it. So, on its own it looks like this:

الرياض

ar-riyaaD Riyadh (capital of Saudi Arabia)

And at the beginning, middle and end of a word when joined to the following letter:

مريض   نضال   ضريبة

mariiD ill   **niDaal** Nidal (man's name)   **Dariiba** tax

Finally, we have the letter **thaa**, which in Jordan is sometimes pronounced like the English 'th' in 'thin' or 'path', but more often like 't' in English 'tin' or 'pat'. In a few words, however, **thaa** is replaced in speech by a sound like an English 's'. **thaa** is written exactly like the letters **taa** and **baa** which we met in Units 2 and 3 of this course, except that it has <u>three</u> dots, in a pyramid shape, written above it. Thus in initial and final position, when joined, it looks like this:

ثلث

thulth (colloquial **tult**) third (part)

In medial position:

مثل

mithil (colloquial **mitil**) like

In final position on its own:

ثلاث

thalaath (colloquial **talaat**) three

There remain one or two spelling conventions to be dealt with. There is a so-called 'glottal stop' or 'catch' (see *Hints on Pronunciation*) which is often missing in colloquial Arabic but occurs frequently in writing. This is called **hamza**, which, when it does occur in our transcription, is symbolized '. In most cases **hamza** is not written on its own like other letters but either on top of, or below, one of the letters **alif**, **waaw** or **yaa** (without its dots). Some examples commonly seen:

On top of **alif**:

أسعار   مسألة

'as9aar (colloquial **as9aar**) prices   **mas'ala** question, issue

Below **alif**:

إقامة   إدارة

'iqaama residence (permit)   **'idaara** management, administration

On top of **waaw**:

سؤال   شؤون

su'aal question   **shu'uun** affairs, matters

Writing

On top of **yaa** without its dots:

مسئول

mas'uul responsible (person); official

On its own (often at the end of a word):

عشاء   مساء

9ashaa' (colloquial **9asha**) dinner   **masaa'** (colloquial **masa**) evening

Finally, there is the not very common sign of a horizontal line above an **alif**, which signifies a **hamza** followed by a long **aa** sound:

آثار   آمال

'aathaar (colloquial **aasaar**) ruins, relics   **'aamal** Amaal (girl's name)

13   Match the Arabic street signs on the right hand side of the page with the transcriptions on the left. From the clues given below, can you work out the meaning of the Arabic signs?

(a)	madrasat al-urdun ath-thaanawiyya	١ مدرسة الاردن الثانوية
(b)	sharikat al-yarmuuk li t-ta'miin	٢ خروج فقط
(c)	ittijaah waaHid	٣ الجمعية الاردنية التعاونية
(d)	al-jam9iyya l-urduniyya t-ta9aawuniyya	٤ خطر أمامك دوّار
(e)	xuruuj faqaT	٥ شركة اليرموك للتأمين
(f)	xaTar 'amaamak duwwaar	٦ اتجاه واحد

Clues

madrasa	school
jam9iyya	society
faqaT	only
'amaam	in front of
ta9aawun	co-operation
xaTar	danger
thaanawi	secondary
ta'miin	insurance
ittijaah	direction

You will learn

- to answer questions about your past experiences
- to talk about excursions you have been on
- to talk about what happened in the past

Study guide

Dialogue 1 + Practise what you have learned
Dialogue 2 + Practise what you have learned
Dialogue 3 + Practise what you have learned
Key words and phrases
Grammar
Your turn to speak
Did you know?
Writing

Dialogues

1 *At a tea party, Samya asks 'Ayda what she did last weekend...*

Samya   il-usbuu9 il-maaDi... il-jum9a l-maaDya ween ruHtu? maa
             kuntuush fi l-beet.
'Ayda   ah, ti9rafi ruHna 9a jarash... kaan iT-Ta's ktiir ktiir Hilw... ruHna
             axadna l-iwlaad u taghaddeena hnaak fi maT9am 'yaa hala'... kulluh
             shallaalaat, maay, ktiir Hilwa.
Samya   inbasaTu l-iwlaad?
'Ayda   inbasaTu ktiir, li9bu... kaan fii baTT u maay shallaalaat naazla
             heek, ktiir kayyafu ktiir.

il-usbuu9 il-maaDi last week
fi l-beet at home
shallaal waterfall
li9bu they played
baTT ducks
naazil falling
kayyafu they enjoyed themselves

♦ **jum9a** As well as meaning 'Friday', this word can also be used to
designate the whole of a week, for example, **shuftuh 'abil jum9iteen** I
saw him two weeks ago (lit. I saw him before two Fridays).

♦ **ruHna axadna...** we went and took... (lit. we went we took). There is
no need for a word equivalent to 'and' when verbs are put together like
these. Similarly **ruuH jiib...** go (and) get... See *Grammar* this Unit.

kulluh shallaalaat it was all waterfalls (lit. all of it waterfalls).

♦ **kaan fii baTT** there were ducks. The past tense of 'there is' is simply
formed by putting **kaan** ([it] was) in front of **fii** (there is).

Practise what you have learned

1 You will hear Samya talking to Abd il-Aziz about her trip to Egypt (**miSir**). Abd il-Aziz's questions have been left off the recording, although the place for them is indicated. They are given below in a jumbled order. Complete the conversation by writing the appropriate question number in the box opposite each question. (Answers p.212)

New word: **il-qaahira** Cairo

Remember: **bi'i/yib'a** to stay, remain; **zwaaj** wedding

(a) fi l-qaahira nafisha? ☐

(b) la miSir! leesh? ☐

(c) zurtu maHallaat ktiira bi l-qaahira? ☐

(d) kiif saafartu 9ala hunaak? ☐

(e) 'addeesh bi'iitu? ☐

(f) ween niziltu? ☐

2 You will hear Atiyya telling of his trip to the Jerash festival. Below is the programme of the trip. Mark off the things on it that he did do and put a cross against the ones he did not do. Can you understand what he did instead? (Answers p.212)

	Jerash Festival Trip	
10.00	Bus leaves Amman	(a)
12.00	Lunch at Al-Rayyis restaurant	(b)
1.00–3.00	Visit waterfalls	(c)
7.30	Folk dancing	(d)
10.00	Bus returns to Amman	(e)

3 Your turn to speak. You are in a busy café when a man comes up to your table. Nadira will guide you through a conversation with him.

New word: **ta9allam/yit9allam** to learn

Dialogues

2 *Muhammad asks Naza what she did on the same lovely weekend...*

Muhammad	marHaba naaza.
Naza	ahleen muHammad.
Muhammad	shu sawweetu l-usbuu9 il-maaDi?
Naza	ana mbaariH ruHit zurit Hammaamaat ma9iin.
Muhammad	Hammaamaat ma9iin, laa? kwayyis!
Naza	akalit hunaak laHma mashwiyya...
Muhammad	mumtaaz.
Naza	u sabaHit fi l-birka.
Muhammad	il-maaya suxna?
Naza	il-maaya suxna u kaanat riHla Hilwa ktiir u riji9it ta'riiban is-saa9a sab9a il-masa.
Muhammad	eemta riji9tu, is-saa9a sab9a?
Naza	u taHammamit u nimit.
Muhammad	ayy saa9a Tili9tu min 9ammaan?
Naza	Tili9na s-saa9a sab9a iS-SubuH u axadat iT-Tarii' ma9ana saa9a illa rubu9... wiSilna hnaak u...
Muhammad	bi l – er – sayyaara? bi s-sayyaara aw fi l-baaS?
Naza	laa fi l-baaS... u haay riHla byi9maluuha sharikit il-'jett' u kaanat riHla Hilwa ktiir inbasaTna.
Muhammad	mumtaaz.
Naza	kull ishii kaan Tabii9i, Hilw ktiir...

sawweetu you (pl.) did	**mbaariH** yesterday
Hammaamaat ma9iin Ma'in hot springs (south of Amman)	**mumtaaz** excellent
birka swimming pool	**sabaHit** I swam
riji9it I returned	**riHla** trip
nimit I went to bed	**taHammamit** I took a bath
Tabii9i natural	**Tili9tu min** you (pl.) went out from, you left

♦ **shu sawweetu...?** what did you do...? The verb **sawwa/ysawwi** is an alternative used by some speakers for **9imil/yi9mal** with the same meaning.

♦ **ruHit zurit...** I went and visited (lit. I went I visited). See the note on **ruHna axadna** in the previous dialogue.

Naza consistently uses an **-it** suffix for the 'I' form of the past tense: **ruHit, zurit, akalit, sabaHit, riji9it, taHammamit, nimit** instead of simple **-t** as in **ruHt, zurt, akalt, sabaHt**, etc. This is a frequently heard variant of the 'I' (and 'you (m)') in Jordan and Iraq.

♦ **Hammaam** also means 'toilet', 'bathroom'.

il-maaya suxna? was the water warm?

♦ **axadat iT-Tarii' ma9ana saa9a illa rubu9** the trip took us three quarters of an hour (lit. took the road with us hour except a quarter).

sharikit il-'jett' the Jett company. This is a large Jordanian bus company.

Practise what you have learned

4 Listen to Sa'da talking about her weekend, then fill in the blanks in the summary below about what she did. So if she says **ruHt** you would fill in the blank with **raaHat**. In some cases, more than one word is required. (Answers p.212)

sa9da **(a)** _____ ijaaza u **(b)** _____ riHla la Hammaamaat

ma9iin. **(c)** _____ fi funduq jamb il-maHaTTa u **(d)** _____

hunaak talaat tiyyaam. kull yoom **(e)** _____ il-Hammaamaat.

(f) _____ fi maT9am fi l-balad u ba9d iD-Duhur **(g)** _____ ,

(h) _____ 9ala 9ammaan mbaariH. **(i)** _____ min ir-riHla ktiir.

5 Your turn to speak. You are in Amman on holiday and are talking to a Jordanian acquaintance about what you have been doing. Below are the relevant extracts from your diary for the last couple of days, on which to base your part in the conversation. Nadira will not prompt you this time, but after the pauses she will give you a version of what you could have said. Try to do more than just give the briefest possible answers, but you do not have to include <u>all</u> the information.

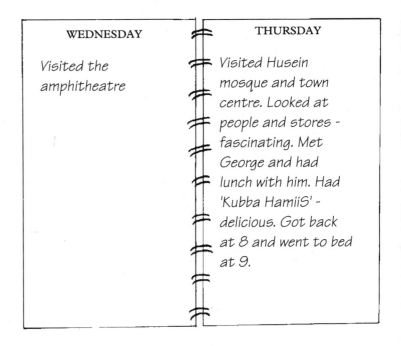

WEDNESDAY	THURSDAY
Visited the amphitheatre	Visited Husein mosque and town centre. Looked at people and stores - fascinating. Met George and had lunch with him. Had 'Kubba HamiiS' - delicious. Got back at 8 and went to bed at 9.

Dialogues

3 *Shahir is talking to Muhammad about his early student days in Britain, and particularly his problems with English food. Eventually, he got used to it...*

Shahir bas ba9dmaa maDa ya9ni Hawaali... faSil bas, 'Christmas Term', intaha l-faSil il-awwal haadha, badeet ana atkayyaf shwayy shwayy u ba9deen lamma maDu l-arba9 sanawaat la l-bakaluuryis kunt ana mughram bi l-akil il-ingliizi u Sirt aHibbuh aktar min il-akil il-9arabi, ah wallah! li'annuh kunt sha9art innuh bartaaH 9aleeh jiddan, mi9dati mitrayHa, ya9ni maa fii hal-bhaaraat, maa fii hal-falaafil, yaa mHammad, il-muHriqa haadhi!!

maDa (it) passed, elapsed
Hawaali approximately
faSil term, semester
intaha (it) ended
atkayyaf I accustom myself to
shwayy shwayy gradually
bakaluuryis Bachelor's degree, BA
mughram bi in love with, very fond of
Sirt I began to
sha9art I felt
bartaaH 9ala I feel happy with, at home with
mi9da stomach
mitrayyiH (f. **mitrayHa**) settled, comfortable
bhaaraat spices
falaafil (hot) pepper
muHriq burning, red-hot

> **bas ba9dmaa maDa ya9ni Hawaali... faSil bas** but after about a term had gone by...
>
> ● **badeet ana atkayyaf...** I began to get used to... (lit. I began I get used to). This is another example of a 'verb string': after the verb **bida** (or **bada**)/**yibda** (to begin) a non-past verb is added directly to make phrases equivalent to English 'to begin to do something'. Other examples: **badeet at9allam 9arabi s-sana l-maaDya** I began to learn Arabic last year (lit. I began I learn...), **byibda yishtaghil halla'** he's beginning to work now (lit. he is beginning he works).
>
> **il arba9 sanawaat la l-bakaluuryis** the four years to the BA.
>
> ● **Sirt aHibbuh...** I'd come to love it (lit. I became I love it). The verb **Saar/ySiir**, followed directly by a non-past verb is structurally exactly like **bida/yibda** + non-past verb and has a similar meaning. It conveys the idea 'to get to the point where', for example, **binti S-Sghiira Saarat timshi** my little daughter has started to walk (in other words, has reached the point where she can walk).
>
> **sha9art innuh bartaaH 9aleeh jiddan** I felt very much at home with it (lit. I felt that I am happy on it very much).

Practise what you have learned

6 Samira has been trying to contact her friend, Maha. Listen to the dialogue and then mark off the answer to each question. (Answers p.212)

(a) Why didn't Maha answer the phone?
- She wasn't feeling well.
- She was at work.
- She was on holiday.

(b) Where did Maha and her family go?
- To Britain.
- To Paris.
- To Beirut.

(c) Decide whether these statement are True or False:
(i) They did not enjoy the trip.
(ii) They do not think Paris is a beautiful city.
(iii) They stayed two weeks.

7 Hind meets her friend Suha and they are exchanging their news, especially about the children. Fill in the blanks with the words/expressions in the box to complete the dialogue. Then check your answer on page 212.
New words: **daras/yudrus** to study

fi	raaHat	badat	byishtaghil	kiif il-Haal	fi
tudrus	ween	hunaak	raaHat	kaanat	

Hind marHaba suha. _____ ? kiif il-iwlaad?

Suha wallah il-Hamdillaah il-kull bixeer.

Hind _____ samiira u nabiil hal-iyyaam?

Suha samiira _____ briTaanya u nabiil _____ l-baHreen.

Hind shu, _____ fi ziyaara 9a briiTaanya?

Suha laa, _____ la draasa. biddha _____ .

Hind kiif inshaallah mabsuuTa _____ ?

Suha wallah, ya9ni mish ktiir. awwalha _____ Sa9ba, bas halla' aHsan _____ titkayyaf.

Hind u shu nabiil 9aamil?

Suha wallah, il-Hamdillaah, _____ , shughluh kwayyis.

Hind allah yixalliihum.

Suha allah yiHfaZik.

Key words and phrases

To learn

il-usbuu9 il-maaDi	last week
sharika (pl. **-aat**)	company
is-sayyid (f. **is-sayyida**)	Mr, Mrs
miin?	who?
maay suxna	hot water
naam/ynaam	to sleep, go to bed
bi'i/yib'a	to stay
ta9allam/yit9allam	to learn

To understand

saafar/ysaafir	to travel
mitrayyiH (f. **mitrayHa**)	comfortable, at ease
maDa/yimDi	to pass (of time)
kayyaf/ykayyif	to enjoy oneself

Grammar

You have encountered a number of 'verb strings'. Examples from this unit are: **ruHna axadna** we went (and) took, **ruHt zurt** I went (and) visited, **badeet atkayyaf** I began to get used to, **Sirt aHibb** I got to like, **kunt sha9art** I had felt. These strings fall into three types, and in all of them the subjects of the two verbs are identical:

1 *Verb (in any tense) of wanting, being able, liking + verb in non-past without b(i)-.* Earlier examples include **baHibb atfarraj...** I like to watch..., **ba'dar awSal** I can get to, **Habbeet ashuufuh** I wanted to see him. The second verb in these cases has a meaning similar to the English infinitive 'to do' or verbal noun 'doing', with no reference to a particular time – the time referred to is set by the tense of the first verb in the string.

Examples of this are:
baHibb atfarraj **9ala t-tilivizyuun kul yoom**. *I like to watch* TV every day.

Habbeet ashuufuh **bas maa 'idirt aaji**. *I wanted to see* him but I wasn't able to come.

2 *kaan + verb in past, non-past with b(i)-, or future, or participle.* These combinations give tenses similar to English 'compound' tenses: **kaan shaaf** he had seen, **kaan raayiH** he was going or had gone, **kaan byruuH** he used to go, **kaan byaakul** he was eating or he used to eat, **kaan raH yruuH** he was going to go.
kunt shuftuh *'abil yoomeen* I had seen him two days before.
Habbeet ashuufuh bas *kaan raayih*. I wanted to see him but *he had gone*.
kunt baakul il-akil il-9arabi kul jum9a. *I used to eat* Arab food every Friday.
lamma shuftuh *kaan raayiH* **9a l-beet**. When I saw him *he was going* home.

3 *Two verbs in the same tense, but the second verb does not take prefixes.* The first verb is often **raaH/yruuH** and the meaning is similar to the English 'he went and saw' – **raaH shaaf** (as opposed to 'he went to see'. – **raaH yshuuf**). For example, **ruHt zurt** I went and visited, **raaHat axadat** she went and took. You will also hear command forms put together without an intervening **wa** (and): **ruuH jiib** go and get!

8 Put the verbs in parentheses into the appropriate forms to match the English translation given. (Answers p.212)

(a) _____ (**bada akal** – she began to eat...) il-fTuur.

(b) _____ (**kaan aja** – I used to come...) hoon ktiir.

(c) maa_____ (**'idir shaaf** – I could not see...) il-mudiir imbaariH.

(d) eemta raH _____-ni (**'idir aja zaar** – you (f.) will be able to come and visit...)?

(e) il-awwal maa _____ (**kaan akal** – I used not to eat...) il-akil il-9arabi, bas halla'_____-uh (**Saar Habb** – I've come to like...) ktiir.

Your turn to speak

9 You are in Jordan and your friend has invited you along with others to a party. You want to speak to one of the guests whom you do not know. Introduce yourself, say where you come from and why you are in Jordan, how long you are staying, and where. Talk about your expereince in Jordan – places you have been to, the food, the people, things you like and things you do not like in Jordan. Talk with this person using as much as you can everything you have learned on this course. Then listen to the recording for a possible version.

Answers

Practise what you have learned

Exercise 1	(a) 3 (b) 1 (c) 6 (d) 5 (e) 4 (f) 2
Exercise 2	(a) ✓ (b) ✗ (he had lunch at 2.00) (c) ✗ (he did this from 12 to 2, not 1 to 3) (d) ✓ (e) ✗ (he missed it because dancing finished at 10.30 not 10.00)
Exercise 4	(a) axadat (b) raaHat (c) nizlat (d) bi'yat (e) kaanat tzuur/truuH (f) taghaddat (g) kaanat tnaam (h) rij9at (i) inbasaTat
Exercise 5	1. ✓ He got the newspaper. 2. ✗ The cinema was closed, so he didn't get the tickets. 3. ✓ He put some things in the post. Additional message: Someone called John Brown came wanting to see him. Mr Brown said he'd come back at 8.00.
Exercise 6	(a) she was on holiday (b) Paris (c) (i) F (ii) F (iii) F
Exercise 7	kiif il-Haal; ween; fi; fi; raaHat; raaHat; tudrus; hunaak; kaanat; badat; byishtaghil

Grammar

Exercise 8	(a) badat taakul (b) kunt aaji (c) maa 'idirt ashuuf (d) ti'darii tiiji tzuuriini (e) kunt baakul, Sirt aHibbuh

Writing

Exercise 10	(a) shaari9 'umayya	Ummaya Street
	(b) kuudaak studyuu shaahiin	Kodak, Shahin Studio
	(c) thallaajaat	refrigerators
	ghassaalaat	washing machines
	jallaayaat	vacuum cleaners
	tilifizyuunaat	televisions
	afraan ghaaz	gas ovens
	mukayyifaat hawaa'	air-conditioners
	far9 la S-Siyaana	maintenance branch (lit. branch for the maintenance)
	(d) maxaazin lil-'iijaar al-muraaja9a 621077	shops for lease. Call 621077
	(e) mamnuu9 al-muruur	no entry
	(f) ja9farsnaak xidma Hatta th-thaalitha SabaaHan	Jaffarsnack... Service until 3.00 a.m.

Did you know?

Medical matters

It is a useful thing to know at least a few basic words and phrases associated with illness and medical treatment should you need to explain simple ailments or symptoms in Arabic. A hospital in Arabic is **mustashfa**, so if you wanted to tell a taxi driver to take you to the University Hospital, you might instruct him **waddiini mustashfa l-jaam9a min faDlak**. Most probably, however, you would go with a minor ailment to a doctor's clinic, in Arabic **9iyaada**, for example, **9iyaadit id-duktuur Hasan** Dr Hasan's clinic.

The profession of doctor is **Tabiib** (or more colloquially **Hakiim**). A dentist is **Tabiib asnaan** (lit. doctor of teeth). So if you wanted to tell a receptionist that you wanted to see a doctor or dentist, the polite phrase would be **biddi ashuuf Tabiib** (or **Tabiib asnaan**) **iza mukin**. If you wanted to make an appointment, the phrase is the same as we encountered in Unit 12 in connection with business appointemts: **biddi aaxud maw9id** I want to make (lit. take) an appointment.

How do you explain what is wrong? If you have a headache, the phrase is **9indi waja9 raas** (lit. with me pain (of) head). **waja9** means pain in general so can be applied to any part of the body, for example, **9indi waja9 Sadar** I have a chest pain, **9indi waja9 Zahr** I have a back pain. A 'fever' is **sxuuna**, for example, **9indi sxuuna** I have a fever, and the adjective is **saxnaan**, so **binti saxnaana** would be 'my daughter feels feverish'. Structurally similar adjectives to **saxnaan** are **ta9baan** (tired), **bardaan** (cold), **na9saan** (drowsy or sleepy). If you have a cold you are **mrashshaH**, and if you have a head-cold the word to use is **muzakkam**. The general word for 'ill' is **mariiD**.

Medicine (the stuff you take, not the profession) is called **dawa**, as in instructions like **xud had-dawa talaat marraat kull yoom** take this medicine three times a day. Pills are called **Hubuub** (sing. **Habba**). The verb 'to prescribe' is the same as the one for 'describe': **waSaf/yuuSif** and a 'prescription' is **waSfa**, so **mumkin ta9Tiini waSfa la...?** would be the phrase to use for 'can you give me a prescription for...?' followed by what you need, for example, **Hubuub man9 il-Hamal** contraceptive pills (lit. pills (for) prevention (of) conception). The pharmacy is **Saydaliyya** in Arabic and so to ask where the nearest pharmacy is you would ask **ween a'rab Saydaliyya, min faDlak?**

Did you know?

If you ever have occasion to visit anyone in hospital, or who is ill, there are a number of possible courtesy expressions which can be used. You can simply say **salaamtak** (your health!) to which the reply from the invalid is **allah yisalmak!** (may God give you health!). Alternatively, the visitor can say **allah yishfiik** (may God heal you!), to which the ill person replies **allah yiHfaZak** or **allah yxalliik** (may God preserve you!). On taking leave of someone ill, a suitable expression might be **allah yishfiik u t'uum bi s-salaama** may God heal you and may you get up well! As for most social occasions, there are expected formulas in Arabic and expected set responses.

Writing

So far, we have covered the Arabic alphabet and its spelling conventions as they appear in normal print. The art of calligraphy, however, is one of the great glories of Arabic civilization, and there are a large number of script styles and sub-styles which you are likely to encounter even in street signs, shop signs and other 'public' writing. In a book like this, we can only give a few examples of some of the commonest types; with time and practice, and especially since many Arabic signs appear alongside an English translation for the benefit of the non-Arabist, you will acquire skill in deciphering and translating them. By way of example, look at the standard printed version of the phrase **al-majlis ath-thaqaafi l-briiTaani** the British Council:

المجلس الثقافي البريطاني

In some of the most commonly encountered script styles, the same phrase would look like this:

(a) copybook **nasx**: المجلس الثقافي البريطاني

(b) ruq9a (the most common cursive handwriting style, often imitated in posters, etc.): المجلس الثقافي البريطاني

(c) ta9liiq style (also common in Persian): المجلس الثقافى البريطاني

(d) kuufi ('Kufic') style, commonly used when a portentous or grandiose effect is desired: المجلس الثقافي البريطاني

Perhaps the most useful of these with which to become familiar is **ruq9a**. An excellent manual exists in T.F. Mitchell's *Writing Arabic* (O.U.P.).

10 Here and on p.216 are some examples of simple street signs and other writing in a variety of scripts. See if you can decipher them and rewrite them in the transcription system we have been using in this book, and then translate them (Answers p.212)

(a)

(b)

(c)

Writing

(d)

(e)

(f)

The final example below shows the intricacy of the caligrapher's art, and is taken from the cover of an aide-memoire which tells fasters when to begin and end their fast day-by-day during Ramadan. In standard printed (and in this case vowelled) Arabic, the words read:

$$ \text{اِمسَاكِيّة شَهر رَمَضانْ} $$

'imsaakiyya shahr ramaDaan month of Ramadan fasting times

See if you can match the printed letters with the delicate interweaving of the shapes in the calligraphed version.

This kind of ornateness is very common on inscriptions in mosques and other religious buildings, in which the depiction of material objects and the human form is not permitted.

Grammar summary

Below is a very brief summary of some of the more important grammatical and structural points. It is not a complete description of the grammar of spoken Jordanian Arabic.

Nouns

definite/indefinite:

funduq	(a) hotel	**sharika**	(a) company
il-funduq	the hotel	**ish-sharika**	the company

singular/plural:

type 1	**mudarris**	**- mudarrisiin**	teacher(s)	
type 2	**Taaliba**	**- Taalibaat**	female student(s)	
	sharika	**- sharikaat**	company(ies)	
	baaS	**- baaSaat**	bus(es)	
type 3	(various patterns), e.g.			
	si9ir	**- as9aar**	price(s)	
	ghurfa	**- ghuraf**	room(s)	
	maktab	**- makaatib**	office(s)	

(type 1 for certain human nouns only; type 2 for certain female human nouns, feminine nouns ending in **-a**, and most foreign borrowings; type 3 the 'broken' plurals, which occur in various patterns, and are the commonest type)

gender:

masculine (most):		**funduq**	hotel
feminine:	by meaning:	**bint**	girl
	by ending **-a**:	**sharika**	company
	by convention:	**suu'**	market

Adjectives

- follow nouns and agree with them in gender and definiteness:

funduq kbiir	a big hotel
il-funduq il-kbiir	the big hotel
sharika kbiira	a big company
ish-sharika il-kbiira	the big company

(if you say **il-funduq kbiir**, it means 'the hotel is big')

- are plural if they follow a 'human' plural noun, feminine after non-human plurals:

fanaadiq kbiira	big hotels
il-fanaadiq il-kbiira	the big hotels
banaat kbaar	big girls
il-banaat il kbaar	the big girls

(if you say **il-banaat kbaar**, it means 'the girls are big')

Comparison

- comparative adjectives are of the general pattern **aCCaC**, where the **C**s represent the consonants of the ordinary adjective: so **rxiiS** cheap, **arxaS** cheaper. 'Than' is **min**. So **il-baaS arxaS min is-sarfiis** means 'the bus is cheaper than a service taxi'.

The superlative is formed by putting the comparative adjective in front of the noun: **arxaS funduq** the cheapest hotel, or by treating the comparative like an ordinary adjective: **il-funduq il-arxaS**.

There is/are

use **fii**, negative **maa fiih**:

(maa) fii naas fi l-ghurfa there are (no) people in the room

Possession	- for 'my', 'your' etc. add the following to the noun

-i	my	**-na**	our
-ak	your (m.)	**-kum**	your (pl.)
-ik	your (f.)		
-uh	his/its	**-hum**	their
-ha	her/its		

(so **beeti** my house, **beeti il-kbiir** my big house. **beeti kbiir** means 'my house is big')

- between two nouns:

method 1: put the 'possessor' noun after the 'possessed':

kitaab aHmad   Ahmed's book

nouns ending in **-a** (e.g. **sayyaara** car), change to **i** and add a **t** when they are the 'possessed' noun:

sayyaarit aHmad   Ahmed's car

the 'possessor' noun can be definite (with **il-**) or indefinite, but in either case the 'possessed' noun doesn't have **il-**:

miftaaH il-sayyaara   the car key
miftaaH sayyaara   a car key

method 2: as an alternative you can use **taba9**:

il-miftaaH taba9 is-sayyaara   the car key
miftaaH taba9 sayyaara   a car key

- 'to have': there is no verb 'to have' in Arabic. Use **9ind** (with) + the endings for 'my', 'your' listed above: **9indi fluus** I have money. The negative is formed using **maa**: **maa 9induh sayyaara** he doesn't have a car.

Verbs	*past tense*	endings are added to the past tense stem (= the 'he' form). Simple verb stems are of five types. Type 1 stems end in **-aC** or **-iC** (where **C** is any consonant); type 2 end in **-aCC**; types 3 and 4 end in a vowel; and type 5 stems end in **aaC**, which always changes to **-uC**, **-aC**, or **-iC** (depending on the verb) before 'I', 'you' and 'we' forms.

Stem Type:	1	2	3	4	5
example:	**Hajaz**	**Habb**	**Haka**	**nisi**	**shaaf**
I	Hajaz-t	Habb-eet	Hak-eet	nis-eet	shuf-t
you (m.)	Hajaz-t	Habb-eet	Hak-eet	nis-eet	shuf-t
you (f.)	Hajaz-ti	Habb-eeti	Hak-eeti	nis-eeti	shuf-ti
he/it	Hajaz	Habb	Haka	nisi	shaaf
she/it	Hajaz-at	Habb-at	Hak-at	nisy-at	shaaf-at
we	Hajaz-na	Habb-eena	Hak-eena	nis-eena	shuf-na
you (pl.)	Hajaz-tu	Habb-eetu	Hak-eetu	nis-eetu	shuf-tu
they	Hajaz-u	Habb-u	Hak-u	nisy-u	shaaf-u

Derived verbs also follow these patterns:

1: **xallaS, Haawal, takallam, ishtaghal**
2: none
3: **xalla, laa'a**
4: none
5: **istafaad** (short vowel **a**), **iHtaaj** (short vowel **i**)

prefixes and endings are added to the non-past stem:

Stem Type:	1	2	3	4	5
example:	**-Hjiz-**	**-Hibb-**	**-Hki-**	**-nsa-**	**-shuuf-**
I	a-Hjiz	a-Hibb	a-Hki	a-nsa	a-shuuf
you (m.)	ti-Hjiz	t-Hibb	ti-Hki	ti-nsa	t-shuuf
you (f.)	ti-Hjiz-i	t-Hibb-i	ti-Hki	ti-ns-i	t-shuuf-i
he/it	yi-Hjiz	y-Hibb	yi-Hki	yi-nsa	y-shuuf
she/it	ti-Hjiz	t-Hibb	ti-Hki	ti-nsa	t-shuuf
we	ni-Hjiz	n-Hibb	ni-Hki	ni-nsa	n-shuuf
you (pl.)	ti-Hjiz-u	t-Hibb-u	ti-Hk-u	ti-ns-u	t-shuuf-u
they	yi-Hjiz-u	y-Hibb-u	yi-Hk-u	yi-ns-u	y-shuuf-u

The vowel of the stem types 1 and 2 may be **a**, **i**, or **u** and **aa** or **ii** or **uu** in the case of type 5 - this has to be learnt with each verb.

Two common exceptions are the verbs 'to take' and 'to eat' which have **aa-**, **taa-**, **yaa-** and **naa-** prefixes rather than **a-**, **ti**, **yi-**, **ni-**: **yaaxud** he takes, **naakul** we eat.

Verbs, the first letter of whose stem is w, are partially exceptional, for example **-wSal-** to arrive. 'I arrive' is **awSal**, as expected. But the other forms of the verb have **yuu-**, **tuu-**, **nuu-** as prefix, e.g. **yuuSal** he arrives.

Derived verbs also follow the patterns exemplified above:

1: **-xalliS-**, **-Haawil-**, **-tkallam-**, **-shtaghil-**
2: none
3: **-xalli-**, **-laa'i-**
4: **-stanna-**
5: **-stafiid-**, **-Htaaj-**

Non-past verbs expressing present time or a general truth normally have a **b-** prefix: **baHki 9arabi** I speak Arabic/I'm speaking Arabic.

To make the command form, first remove the prefix from the non-past verb. If the result starts with two consonants, prefix **i-**. If not, add nothing, e.g.

	masculine	*feminine*	*plural*	
type 1	i-Hjiz	i-Hjizi	i-Hjizu	(reserve!)
type 3	i-Hki	i-Hki	i-Hku	(talk!)
type 5	ruuH	ruuHi	ruuHu	(go!)
type 3 (der.)	Salli	Salli	Sallu	(pray!)

Negative commands are the same as the ordinary verb preceded by **maa** not and followed by **-sh**: **maa taakulsh haada** Don't eat that!

must/have to/had to: **laazim** + past or non-past verb

laazim yruuH	he must/has to go
laazim raaH	he must have gone
kaan laazim yruuH	he should have gone/had to go

may/might: **yumkin** or **mumkin** + verb

mumkin yruuH	maybe he'll go
mumkin raaH	maybe he went
kaan mumkin yruuH	he could've gone (but e.g. didn't)

want/need to: **bidd** + possessive ending + non-past verb

bidduh yruuH he wants to go/needs to go

can/could: **'adar** + non-past verb

byi'dar yruuH he can go
'idir yruuH he was able to go/could go

Non-past verbs which follow any of the expressions for 'must', 'can', etc. listed above, or which are the object of another verb do not have the **b**-prefix: e.g. **baHibb asbaH ktiir** I like swimming a lot (NOT **baHibb basbaH...**).

Participles	active participle

This is roughly equivalent to English '...ing/having ...ed' or 'a person or thing which ...s'

examples:

type 1:	**9aarif**	knowing/have known
type 2:	**maarr**	passing by/having passed by/passer-by
type 3:	**maashi**	going/having gone (= O.K.)
type 4:	**naasi**	forgetting/having forgotten
type 5:	**shaayif**	seeing/having seen

To form the active participles of derived forms simply put **m-** or **mi-** in front of the non-past stem, e.g. **m-xalliS** finishing/having finished, **mi-stafiid** benefitting/having benefitted/beneficiary etc. The only slight exception to this are stems like **-tzawwaj-** which always change the last **a** to an **i**: **mitzawwij** marrying/having married/married person.

passive participle

These are often equivalent ot English 'is/was ...ed':

type 1:	**ma9ruuf**	known
type 2:	**maHbuub**	liked, loved (hence: popular)
type 3 & 4:	**maHshi**	stuffed (e.g. vegetables)
type 5:	**mabyuu9**	sold

To form the passive participles of derived verbs change the final **i** or **ii** of the active partciple to **a** or **aa**; if it is already **aa**, it stays the same: **mxallaS** finished, completed, **miHtaaj** needed.

Subject Pronouns	The subject pronouns are as follows:

ana	I	**niHna** (or **iHna**)	we
inta	you (m.)	**intu**	you (pl.)
inti	you (f.)		
huwwa	he/it	**humma**	they
hiyya	she/it		

These pronouns are not usually used with verbs except for emphasis, e.g. compare **ruHt is-suu'** I went to the market, with **ana ruHt is-suu', mish huwwa** I went to the market, not him. However, in verbless sentences, these pronouns are normally used: **huwwa mish mawjuud** he isn't here.

Object Pronouns	- for 'me', 'him', etc. add the same endings to the verb as are added to the noun to indicate possession, except that 'me' is **-ni**, not **-i**: **shaafni** he saw me, **aHibbuh** I like him. When these endings are added to a verb form which ends in a vowel, lengthen the vowel: **a9Tiini l-kitaab** give me the book!, **xallaani aruuH** he let me go. When **-uh** (him) is added to a verb ending in a vowel, the **u** is dropped: **xalliih yruuH** let him go!

Verbs and Tenses	To say things like 'I am English', 'she is here', 'they are businessmen' you don't need a verb in Arabic. Simply say 'I English' (**ana ingliizi**) etc.

For describing past actions, use the past tense. For the present and 'timeless' statements ('I like ice-cream.') use the non-past. For intentions and future actions use **raH** + non-past verb: **raH asaafir bukra** I'm leaving tomorrow. For past-in-the-past ('The bus had gone when I arrived.') use **kaan** + active participle (**il-baaS kaan raayiH lamma waSalt**). For past continuous ('I was talking when he entered.') use **kaan** + non-past (**kunt baHki lamma daxal**). The same combination is used for 'used to': **kunt bal9ab tanis ktiir ayyaam il-madrasa** I used to play tennis a lot at school. To say 'been ...ing for ...' and similar expressions use the expression **Saar la ...**, e.g.

'addeesh Saar lak hoon?	How long have you been here?
ana Saar li saa9a bastanna	I've been waiting an hour
huwwa Saar luh sana fi 9ammaan	He's been in Amman a year

Negation	with verbs: use **maa ... (i)sh**. The **(i)sh** element is optional:

maa baHibb or **maa baHibbish**	I don't like
maa Habbeet or **maa Habbeetish**	I didn't like
maa tiHkiish!	Don't speak!

with **bidd-**, **9ind-** and **fii**: as with verbs:

maa biddi aruuH	I don't want to go
maa 9indha 9amal	she doesn't have a job

with nouns, pronouns, adjectives, participles, and prepositions: use **mish** (or **mu**):

ana mish mudarris	I'm not a teacher
inta, mish ana!	you, not me!
ana mish faaDi il-leela	I'm not free tonight
hiyya mish fi l-ghurfa	she isn't in the room
mish laazim yiiji	he doesn't have to come
mish mumkin yiiji	he can't come

Vocabulary

This is a complete list of all the Arabic words which appear anywhere in this course. Alphabetical order here is in English except that: capital letters follow their small equivalents; **sh, th** etc. are treated as single letters and follow **S** and **t** respectively; initial **'** is treated as equivalent to **q. 9** comes last.

Some words have various pronunciations. In particular the short vowels **a, i** and **u** are sometimes dropped, or inserted, so if you cannot find a word here it may be worth checking any possible alternative spelling. Where two variants of a word are common they are listed together, with a comma between. Verbs are listed in past tense/non-past tense form. Verbal nouns are given after the past/non-past forms, if in common use. The 'I' form of the past tense of a hollow verb is given in square brackets after it. For nouns and adjectives plurals are given where appropriate, except in the case of relative adjectives and nouns (see Unit 9 *Grammar*).

Abbreviations

(B)	Bedouin or non-urban usage
(F)	formal usage
part.	participle

aab August
aadhaar March
aali automated, automatic
aan: il-aan (F) now
aanisa Miss
aathaar (pl.) (F), asaar ruins
aaxir: aaxir ... the last ...
9a l-aaxir extremely
ab, (pl.) abaa' father
abu father of
abadan: mish ... abadan not at all
abriil April
abyaD, f. beeDa, pl. biiD white
aDaaf/yDiif, iDaafa [aDaft] (9ala) to add (to)
aghustus August
ah yes
ahil family, relatives
ahlan hello
ahlan wa sahlan, ahla u sahla welcome
ahleen hello, you're welcome
aHad: (yoom) il-aHad Sunday
aHmar, f. Hamra, pl. Humur red
aHsan better, best
aHsan shii preferable
aja (see ija) to come
ajaar fare, hire fee
ajnabi, pl. ajaanib foreign, foreigner
akal/yaakul, akil to eat
akiid certain(ly)

akil food
aktar more, most
aktar shii the most
akthar (F), aktar more most
alf, pl. (t)alaaf 1,000
allah God
almaanya Germany
amaam (F) in front of
amaana municipality
amaanit il-9aaSima City Hall
amar: taHt amrak at your service
amriika America
amriiki, pl. amriikaan American
ams yesterday
ana I
aqall, a'all less
a'rab: a'rab ... the nearest ...
arba9a four
arba9iin 40
arba9miyya 400
arba9ta9sh 14
arxaS cheaper
asaar (pl.) ruins
asaf: ma9a l-asaf unfortunately
aswad, f. sooda, pl. suud black
aSfar, f. Safra, pl. Sufur yellow
aSlan originally
aw (F) or
awwal first
awwalmaa as soon as
ax, pl. ixwa brother

axud/yaaxud, axd, part. maaxid to take

axDar, f. xaDra, pl. xuDur green

axiiran at last, finally

ayaar May

ayluul September

aywa yes

ayy(a) which, any

a9jab/yi9jib, i9jaab to please

azra', f. zar'a, pl. zuru' blue

azyaa' (pl.) fashions, costumes

a9Ta/ya9Ti, i9Taa' to give

baab, pl. abwaab door, gate

baal mind

    ija 9ala baali it occurred to me

baar, pl. -aat bar

baarid cold, cold drinks

baaS, pl. -aat bus

baa9/ybii9, bee9 [bi9t] to sell

baba ghannuuj eggplant/ aubergine puree

bada/yibda, bidaaya to begin

badawi, pl. badu Bedouin

badinjaan aubergine, eggplant

bagha/yibgha (B) to want

baHar sea

baHath/yibHath, baHth (F) to discuss

bakaluuryis Bachelor's degree

bakeet, pl. -aat packet

bakkiir early (in the morning)

balaash: balaash at9ibak I don't want to trouble you

    bi balaash free, for nothing

balad, pl. blaad village, town, country

baladiyya municipality

ballah, ballaahi please

banduura tomato(es)

bank, pl. bunuuk bank

banTaloon, pl. -aat (pair of) trousers

baraka, pl. -aat blessing

bardaan, pl. bardaniin (feeling) cold

barDuh also

bariid mail, post

    (maktab) bariid post office

barnaamij, pl. baraamij programme

bas only, just; but

basiiTa no problem, that's OK

baTaaTis potatoes

    baTaaTis maqli French fries

baTTa, pl. baTT ducks

baxshiish tip, tips

bayaan, pl. -aat announcement

ba9at/yib9at, ba9t to send

ba9d after

ba9deen sfterwards, then

ba9dmaa (+ verb) after

ba9D each other

ba9iid (9an) far (from)

beeDa, pl. beeD egg

been between

beet, pl. byuut house

    fi l-beet at home

bi in, with, by

bida see **bada** to begin

bidaaya beginning

biddi, biddak, etc. I want, you want, etc.

biduun without

biira beer

binni, f. -iyya, pl. binni brown

bint, pl. banaat girl, daughter

bi'i/yib'a, baqaa' to stay

birka, pl. -aat swimming pool

biskoot biscuit

biyjuuz (see **jaaz**) it's possible, maybe

bi9tha, pl. -aat scholarship abroad

bluuza, pl. -aat blouse

bukra tomorrow

    ba9d bukra the day after tomorrow

bulbul nightingale

briiTaanya Britain

briiTaani British

burtu'aana, pl. burtu'aan orange (fruit)

buufee buffet

daaxiliyya: id-daaxiliyya the Interior Ministry

dafa9/yidfa9, dafi9 to pay

daftar 9eela family card

dahab gold

dajaaj chicken

daliil, pl. dalaayil guide, directory

dall/ydill, dalaala (9ala) to show or guide s.o. (to)

da'ii'a, pl. da'aayi' minute

daraj stairs, steps

daras/yudrus, draasa to study

dawa medicine

dawaam: (wa't) id-dawaam working hours

dawla, pl. duwal state, country

daxal/yudxul, duxuul to enter

daxxan/ydaxxin, tadxiin to smoke

dayman always
diisambar December
dimashq Damascus
dinaar, pl. dananiir dinar
door, pl. adwaar storey; role
dughri straight ahead, straightforward
duktuur, pl. dakatra doctor
dulaab, pl. dawaliib cupboard; tyre
duush, pl. -aat shower
duuz (slang) straight ahead
duwali international
duwwaar, pl. -aat roundabout, circle
duxuul entrance

Dall/yDall, Dall to keep on
Dariiba, pl. Daraayib tax
Diffa: iD-Diffa l-gharbiyya the West Bank
Duhur: iD-Duhur noon
ba9d iD-Duhur in the afternoon

dhaat: bi dh-dhaat in particular
dhikraa commemoration

DHabT: bi DH-DHabT exactly
DHall/yDHall, DHall (F) = Dall to keep on (doing something)

eemta when?
eesh what?
ey, aywa yes

fa so, and then, and
faahim, pl. faahmiin (I, you, he, she) understand(s) pl. (we, you, they) understand
faaDi, pl. faaDyiin free, not busy
faDDal/yfaDDil to prefer
faDil: min faDlak, f. faDlik please
fakkar/yfakkir, tafkiir (fi) to think (about)
falaafil falafel, bean rissoles; hot pepper
faqaT (F) only
farawla strawberry
farraj/yfarrij ... (9ala) to show ... (something)
faSil, pl. fuSuul term, semester
fataH/yiftaH, fatH to open
fatHa, pl. -aat opening; unit on a meter
fatra, pl. fataraat period of time
fatta dip with bread

fattaaHa, pl. -aat tin opener
faTar/yifTar, fTuur to have breakfast
fi in
fibraayir February
fiDDa silver
fihim/yifham, faham to understand
fii there is
fikra, pl. fikar idea
filasTiini Palestinian
filfil pepper
filim, pl. aflaam film
fils, pl. fluus a 100th of a dinar
finjaan, pl. fanajiin cup
fi9lan really, actually
fluus (pl.) money
foo', foog (B) upstairs, above
fTuur, fTaar breakfast
funduq, pl. fanaadiq hotel
fustaan, pl. fasatiin dress
fuul beans
fuuTa, pl. fuwaT towel

ghaali, pl. ghaalyiin expensive, dear
ghaaya: la ghaayit ... up till ..., until ...
ghada lunch
ghadda/yghaddi, taghdiya to give s.o. lunch
ghalaba a nuisance, pain in the neck
ghalaT, pl. aghlaaT wrong; mistake
gharbi Western
ghayyar/yghayyir, taghyiir to change (sth.)
gheer apart from, except; non-
gheer marra again
gheeruh another one
ghurfa, pl. ghuraf room

ha l- ... this ...
haada, f. haadi, pl. hadool(a) this
haadha (F), haada this
haat, f. -i, pl. -u bring!
haay this, these
haayil, pl. haayliin wonderful
hala or yaa hala welcome, reply to a greeting
halla' now
haram pyramid(s)
heek, heeka like that
mish heek? isn't it? aren't you? didn't they? etc.
hidiyya, pl. hadaaya gift

hiwaaya, pl. -aat hobby
hiyya she, it
hoon here
huduum (pl.) clothes
humma they
huna (F), hoon here
hunaak, hnaak there
hunna (F) they (f.)
huwiyya shaxSiyya personal
  identification
huwwa he, it

HaaDir yes, Sir
Haal (m. or f.) pl. aHwaal state
  bi Haali by myself
  kiif Haalak/Haalik/il-Haal?
  How are you?
Haali present (time)
Haawal/yHaawil, muHaawla
  to try
Habb/yHibb, Hubb to like, love
Habiibi, f. Habiibti my dear,
  darling
Hadiiqa, pl. Hadaa'iq park,
  garden
HaDirtak, f. HaDirtik you
  (polite)
HafaZ/yiHfaZ: allah yiHfaZak
  God preserve you
Hafla, pl. -aat party
  Hafla muusiqiyya concert
Hajaz/yiHjiz, Hajiz to reserve
Hajiz reservation
Hajj pilgrimage to Mecca
Haka/yiHki, Haki to speak, to
  speak to
Hakiim, pl. Hukama doctor
Haliib milk
Hamd: il-Hamdulillah, il-
  Hamdillah Praise be to God
  Hamdillah 9a s-salaama
  Thank God for your well-being
  (esp. after a journey)
Hammaam, pl. -aat bathroom,
  toilet, hot spring
  Hammaam sbaaHa
  swimming pool
Harr hot (weather)
HaSal/yiHSal, HuSuul 9ala to
  obtain
Hatta even, until
HaTT/yHuTT, HaTT to put
Hawa/yiHwi 9ala to contain
Hawaali approximately, about
Hayy, pl. aHyaa' quarter (of a
  city)
Hayya: Hayyaak allah God give
  you life (see Unit 9)

Haziraan June
HaZZ luck
HiDir/yuHDur, HuDuur to go
  to, attend
Hilw, pl. -iin nice, sweet
Hily jewellery
Hisaab, pl. -aat bill, account
  'addeesh il-Hisaab How
  much does it come to?
HSaan, pl. HuSun horse
Hukuuma, pl. -aat government
HummuS houmous

ida, iza, idha (F) if
iftakar/yiftikir, fikr (innuh) to
  think (that)
iHda9sh eleven
iHna we
iHtaaj/yiHtaaj, iHtiyaaj [iHtajt]
  (la) to need (something)
iid (f.), pl. ayaadi hand
ija/yiiji, majii', [(i)jiit] to come
  part. jaay
ijaaza, pl. -aat holiday, leave
ijtimaa9, pl. -aat meeting
illa except
  tinteen illa rubu9 quarter to
  two
illi which, who (see Unit 10
  Grammar)
iluh, ilak, etc. to him, to you,
  etc.
imkaaniyya, pl. -aat possibility
inbasaT/yinbasiT, inbisaaT to
  have a good time, enjoy oneself
ingiltera England
ingliizi, pl. ingliiz English;
  English person
innuh that (eg. after to know,
  say, believe)
inshaallah if God wills
inta you (m.)
intaaj production
intaha/yintihi, intihaa' (F)
  to end
intaqal/yintiqil, intiqaal to
  transfer, move
inti you (f.)
intu you (pl.)
iqtiraaH, pl. -aat proposal,
  suggestion
irtaaH/yirtaaH, irtiyaaH (9ala)
  to feel happy (with), at home
  (with)
isim, pl. asmaa' name
ishaara, pl. -aat traffic light,
  signal
ishii anything, something

ishtaghal/yishtaghil, shughul
to work
ishtara/yishtiri, shiraa' to buy
ishtarak/yishtirik, ishtiraak (fi)
to participate (in)
ishtiraak membership,
subscription
islaam: il-islaam Islam
issa at the moment
istafaad/yistafiid, istifaada
[istafadt] (min) to benefit
(from), use profitably
istanna/yistanna to wait
ista'jar/yista'jir, isti'jaar to hire
istaraaH/yistariiH, istiraaHa
[istaraHt] to rest, relax, sit
down
ista9add/yista9idd, isti9daad
to get ready
ista9jal/yista9jil, isti9jaal to be
in a hurry, urgent
ista9mal/yista9mil, isti9maal
to use
istiqdaam summoning
istirliini pound sterling
isti9aara borrowing
isti9laamaat: maktab il-
isti9laamaat enquiry office
ithbaat proof
itna9sh twelve
itneen, f. tinteen two
(yoom) it-tneen Monday
ittaSal/yittaSil bi to ring up s.o.,
get in touch with
ittijaah, pl. -aat direction
iTaali Italian
iTaalya Italy
iza if
iza mumkin please
iza samaHt, f. -i please, if you
wouldn't mind
izan (F) so, therefore
i9tadhar/yi9tadhir, i9tidhaar
(9an) to excuse oneself (from)

jaab/yjiib [jibt] to bring
jaahiz, pl. jaahziin ready
jaami9, pl. jawaami9 large
mosque
jaam9a, pl. -aat university
jaanib (bi jaanib (F)) next to
jaay coming, next
jaaz/yjuuz to be possible
jabal, pl. jbaal mountain, hill
jadiid, pl. judad new
jakeet, pl. -aat jacket
jalaaltak Your Majesty
jamal, pl. jmaal camel

jamb next to
jamiil beautiful
jamii9: il-jamii9 (F) everyone
jam9a a gathering
jam9iyya, pl. -aat society
januub south
jariida, pl. jaraayid newspaper
jaw weather
jawaab, pl. -aat reply
jawaaz (safar), pl. jawaazaat
passport
jayyid (F) good
jdiid, jadiid new
jibna cheese
jiddan (F) very
jiit (see ija) I/you came
jisir, pl. jusuur bridge, flyover
jum9a week; Friday
(yoom) il-jum9a Friday
juwwa inside
ju9aan, pl. -iin hungry

ka as
kaamil, pl. kaamliin complete
kaan/ykuun, koon [kunt] to be
kaanuun il-awwal December
kaanuun ith-thaani January
kabaab kebab, meatballs
kaffa/ykaffi ... to be enough
(for ...)
kakau cocoa
kalaam talk, chat
kalima, pl. -aat (F), kilma word
kallaf/ykallif, takliif to cost
kam how many, how much?
kamaan also, another, more
kamera camera
kaniisa, pl. kanaayis church
karaaj, pl. -aat garage
kariim, pl. kurama noble,
generous
kart, pl. kruut card, postcard
kassar/ykassir, taksiir to break,
smash
katab/yiktib, kitaaba to write
kathiir (F), ktiir much, many
kayyaf/ykayyif, takyiif to enjoy
oneself
kbiir, pl. kbaar big
kiif, keef how
kiifak f. kiifik pl. kiifkum
how are you?
kiilo kilogram, kilometre
kiilomitir, pl. kiilomitraat
kilometre
kilma, pl. -aat or kalaam word
kishka cracked wheat dish
kitaab, pl. kutub book

ktiir many, much, too much
kubba meatballs
   kubba HamiiS deep-fried meatballs
   kubba nayya raw meatballs
kufta kofta, meatballs
kull all, every, each
   il-kull everyone
   kull shii everything
kunaafa sweet pastry with nuts
kundara, pl. -aat pair of shoes
kwayyis, f. kwaysa, pl. -iin good
kweet: il-kweet Kuwait

la to, for
laa no
laakin but
laa'a/ylaa'i to find
laazim necessary, must
laff/yliff, laff to wrap, turn
laHma meat
   laHmit ba'ar beef
   laHmit dajaaj chicken
   laHmit xaruuf lamb
laHza, pl. laHaZaat moment
lakaan so, then
lamma, lamman when (not in questions)
landan London
law if, were it to be the case that ...
   law samaHt, f. -i please, if you permit
laysa (F) it isn't
leel night
leela, pl. layaali a night
   il-leela tonight
leesh why?
li'annuh because
liira, pl. -aat pound, lira
lissa not yet
li9ba, pl. al9aab game
li9ib/yil9ab, lu9ub to play
loon, pl. alwaan colour
   shu loon ... What colour is...?
lubnaan Lebanon
luTuf: haada min luTfak, f. luTfik It's very kind of you

maa not; what
   maa lak, f. lik What's wrong with you?
maaDi: il-usbuu9 il-maaDi last week
maars March
maashaallah what God has willed (see Unit 1, Dia. 4)
maashi OK
   maashi l-Haal OK, fine
maaxid taking (see **axad**)

maay (f.), maaya water
   maay ma9daniyya mineral water
maayu May
mabna (m.), pl. mabaani building
mabruuk Congratulations!
mabsuuT, pl. -iin happy, well
madaalya, pl. -aat medallion, medal
madiina, pl. mudun city
madrasa, pl. madaaris school
madxal, pl. madaaxil entrance
maDa/yimDi to pass, elapse
maftuuH open
mahrajaan, pl. -aat festival
maHall, pl. -aat shop, place
maHalli local
maHaTTa, pl. -aat bus-stop, station
maHlabiyya a milk pudding
maHshi stuffed vegetables
majlis, pl. majaalis council, reception room
   il-majlis ith-thaqaafi l-briiTaani the British Council
makaan, pl. amaakin place
maktab, pl. makaatib office
maktaba, pl. -aat library, bookshop
maktuub, pl. -aat letter
malfuuf cabbage
mamarr, pl. -aat corridor
mamnuu9 prohibited, forbidden
   mamnuu9 it-tadxiin no smoking
   mamnuu9 il-wuquuf no parking
mana9/yimna9, mana9 to forbid, prevent
manga mango
manTiqa, pl. manaaTiq area, region
manZar, pl. manaaZir sight, view
ma'aas, pl. -aat size (clothes etc.)
maqli fried
maq9ad, pl. maqaa9id (F) seat
marag stew
marHaba hello
mariiD, pl. marDa ill
markab, pl. maraakib ship
marra, pl. -aat a time, once
   kamaan marra again
   maa ... bi l-marra not ... at all

masa evening, late afternoon
   masa l-xeer good afternoon,
   good evening
masaafa, pl. -aat distance
mas'uul, pl. -iin (9an)
   responsible (for)
masraH, pl. masaariH theatre
masraHiyya, pl. -aat play
mashghuul, pl. -iin busy,
   occupied
mashkuur thank you
mashwi, pl. mashaawi roast;
   roast or grilled meats
mashy: raaH/yruuH mashy to
   go on foot
masluu' boiled
maSaari (pl.) money
matalan, mathalan for example
matHaf, pl. mataaHif museum
maT9am, pl. maTaa9im
   restaurant
mawjuud, pl. -iin present, here
maw'if, pl. mawaa'if bus or taxi
   station
maw9id, pl. mawaa9id
   appointment, time when
   something is due
maxadda, pl. -aat cushion
maxbaz, pl. maxaabiz bakery
maxluuTa a variety of dishes
maxraj, pl. maxaarij exit
mayuneez mayonnaise
maZbuuT true, correct, exact
ma9a, ma9 with, together with
ma9leesh never mind, that's OK
ma9luumaat information
ma9na (m.) pl. ma9aani
   meaning
ma9'uul, ma9quul reasonable
   mish ma9'uul incredible!
ma9ruuf: i9mal, f. -i ma9ruuf
   do me a favour
ma9zuum, pl. -iin invited
mbaariH yesterday
mbayyin it seems
mfakkir, pl. -iin (fi) thinking (of)
mHammaS toasted
miHtaaj, pl. -iin (la) in need (of)
miin who?
miiteen 200
milH salt
min from, of, than
   min saniteen two years ago
mineen from where?
minyu menu
mirtabiT, pl. mirtabTiin (fi)
   connected (to)
misaafir, pl. misaafriin
   traveller, travelling

mista9jil, pl. -iin urgent, in a
   hurry
miSir Egypt
mish not
mishi/yimshi, mashy to go, go
   away
mishmish apricots
mishwaar, pl. mashawiir walk,
   outing, errand
mitDaayi', pl. mitDay'iin
   irritated
mitil, mithil like
mitir metre
mit'assif, pl. mit'asfiin sorry
mit'axxir, pl. mit'axriin late
mitrayyiH, pl. -iin settled,
   comfortable
mitshakkir, pl. -iin thankful
mitzakkir, pl. -iin remembering
mitzawwij, pl. -iin married
mithil (F), mitil like
miyya (construct from miit) 100
   bi l-miyya percent
mi9da stomach
mi9jib ... pleasing (to ...)
mniiH, pl. mnaaH good
mrashshaH, pl. -iin having a
   cold
msabbaHa chick pea dip with
   spices
mtabbal puree of roasted
   aubergine/eggplant
mTarraZ embroidered
mu (B), mish not
mubaashir direct
mu'assasa, pl. -aat institution
   mu'assasit in-naql il-9aamm
   the Public Transport Company
mudarraj amphitheatre
mudarris, pl. -iin teacher
mudda, pl. -aat period of time
mudiir, pl. mudara manager,
   director
mufrad, pl. -iin single
muftaaH, pl. mafatiiH key
mughram, pl. -iin (bi) in love
   (with), very fond (of)
muhandis, pl. -iin engineer
muHriq burning hot
mujaddara lentil and rice dish
mujawharaat jewels
mukaalma, pl. -aat
   conversation
mulawwan coloured
mulk property
mumaththil, pl. -iin
   representative
mumkin possible
mumtaaz, pl. -iin excellent

munaasba, pl. -aat occasion
muqaabil (F) opposite
muqaamara gambling
muqabbilaat hors d'oeuvres
muruur passing; traffic
  shurTit il-muruur traffic
  police
musaa9id, pl. musaa9diin
  assistant
muslim, pl. -iin Muslim
mustashfa (m.), pl. -yaat
  hospital
mustawrad imported
musta9idd, pl. -iin ready, willing
mushakkal varied, mixed
mutabbal puree of roasted
  eggplant/aubergine
muxaabraat: il-muxaabraat
  il-9aamma General
  Intelligence Organisation
muxtalif, pl. muxtalfiin (9an)
  different (from)
mu9ayyan, pl. -iin specific,
  particular
mwaafiq, pl. mwafqiin (ma9a)
  in agreement (with)

naas (f. or m. pl.) people
naazil, pl. naazliin (fi) staying
  (at) (eg. a hotel)
naa9im smooth, soft
naadi, pl. nawaadi club
naam/ynaam, noom [nimt]
  to sleep
naasab/ynaasib to be convenient
  to, suit
naawi, pl. nawyiin intending
nabaat, pl. -aat plant
nabaati vegetarian
nabiid wine
nafs: nafsuh, nafsi etc. himself,
  myself, etc.
  nafs il- ... the same ...
naql: in-naql il-9aamm public
  transport
nawa/yinwi, niyya to plan, intend
na9am yes; yes?
na9saan, pl. -iin drowsy
neskafe instant coffee
nhaar daytime
nihaaya end
niHna we
niil: in-niil the Nile
niisaan April
nisba: bi n-nisba la with regard
  to
nizil/yinzil, nuzuul to go down;
  stay (eg. at a hotel)
noo9, pl. anwaa9 kind, sort

nuSS half
  nuSS 9a n-nuSS, nuSS u
  nuSS so so, not bad
nuufambar November

'aabal/y'aabil, mu'aabla to meet
qaahira: il-qaahira Cairo
'aal/y'uul ['ult] to say, tell
qaa'ima menu
'abil before, ago
'abilla, 'abilmaa (+ verb) before
qaddam/yqaddim, taqdiim to
  serve, offer, put forward
'addeesh how much
  'addeesh si9ruh? How much
  does it cost?
'adiim, pl. 'udama old, ancient
'ahwa coffee
  'ahwa 9arabi Turkish coffee
'alam, pl. i'laam pen
'amiiS, pl. 'umSaan shirt
'ariib min ... near ...
qarya, pl. qura (F) village
'aSar, qaSr, pl. 'uSuur palace,
  fort
'aTaayif (pl.) pancakes
'aTa9/yi'Ta9, 'aTa9 to cut, pick
'azaaza, pl. -aat bottle
'a9ad/yi'9ud to sit down
'a9da sitting area
'idir/yi'dar, qudra to be able to
'irsh, pl. 'uruush a piastre,
  100th of a dinar
'ubruS Cyprus
'uddaam in front of
quds: il-quds, il-'uds
  Jerusalem

raabi9, f. raab9a fourth
raaH/yruuH [ruHt] to go (to)
raas, pl. ruus head
raayiH going
radd, pl. ruduud answer, reply
rafa9/yirfa9, rafa9 to lift up
raH + non-past verb going to
  (future)
raHma mercy
rajul, pl. rijaal (F) man
  rajul a9maal businessman
rakaD jogging, running
ra'a/yara (F) to see
raqam, pl. arqaam number
ra'aS shar'i belly dancing
ra'iis, pl. ru'asa president, head
  (eg. of department)
ra'y, pl. aaraa' opinion, view
  shu ra'yak, f. ra'yik (fi) ... ?
  what d'you think (of) ... ?
raxiiS, rxiiS cheap

raza'/yirza', rizi' to give sustenance to

riHla, pl. -aat trip, outing, journey

riif countryside

riji9/yirja9, rujuu9 to go back
  riji9 yi9mal to do again, redo

rijjaal, pl. rijjaala man

rikib/yirkab, rukuub to ride, get into or take (bus, car, bicycle etc.)

riyaaDa sport

rooHa: tazkara rooHa raj9a return ticket
  tazkara rooHa bas one way ticket

rubu9, pl. arbaa9 quarter

rusuum (pl.) fees

ruumaani Roman

ruusi Russian

ruxSa: ruxSit swaa'a driving licence

ruzz rice

saabi9, f. saab9a seventh

saada plain, without sugar

saadis, f. saadsa sixth

saafar/ysaafir, safar to travel, go away

saakin, pl. saakniin fi living in

saakin, pl. sukkaan inhabitant

saa9a, pl. -aat hour; watch; clock
  'addeesh is-saa9a? What time is it?

saa9ad/ysaa9id, musaa9da to help

sabab, pl. asbaab reason, cause

sabaH/yisbaH, sbaaHa to swim

saba9miyya 700

saba9ta9sh 17

sabt: (yoom) is-sabt Saturday

sabtambar September

sab9a seven

sab9iin 70

safariyyaat travel agency, ticket office

sahra muusiqiyya musical evening

sahhal/ysahhil: rabbina ysahhil May God make it easy

sahil easy

sajjal/ysajjil, tasjiil to record, register

sakan/yuskun, sakan (fi) to live (in)

sakkar/ysakkir to close

salaam: is-salaam 9aleekum Peace be upon you (greeting)

salaama: ma9a s-salaama goodbye

salaamtak Your health! (to ill person)

salaTa, pl. -aat salad

sallam/ysallim: allah ysalmak God give you peace

samak fish

sambuusak meat pastry

samma/ysammi, tasmiya to name, call

sammaa9a telephone receiver

sana, pl. sniin, sanawaat year

sandawitsh, pl. -aat sandwich

sa'al/yis'al, su'aal (9an) to ask (a question) (about)

sarii9 quick, express

sawa together

sawa/yiswi to be worth

sawwa/ ysawwi to do

saxnaan, pl. -iin feverish

sayyaara, pl. -aat car

sayyid gentleman
  is-sayyid ... Mr. ...
  is-sayyida ... Mrs. ...

sa9aadtak Your Excellency

sa9uudiyya: is-sa9uudiyya Saudi Arabia

sbaaHa swimming

sibaaq il-xeel horse-racing

sifaara, pl. -aat embassy

sigaara, pl. sagaayir cigarette

siidi: yaa siidi 'sir' (term of address)

siinama cinema

sikriteera, pl. -aat secretary (f.)

simi9/yisma9, sama9 to hear, listen

sirviis 'service' taxi

sitt (f.), pl. -aat woman

sitta six

sitta9sh 16

sittiin 60

si9ir, pl. as9aar price

steek steak

sukkar sugar
  sukkar 'aliil medium sugar (coffee)

su'aal, pl. as'ila question

sur9a: bi sur9a quickly

suubarmarkit, pl. -aat supermarket

suu', suuq (f.), pl. aswaa' market

suurya Syria

suxun hot (tea, etc.)

sxuuna fever

SaaHib, pl. aSHaab friend, owner
SaaHbi my friend
Saar/ySiir [Sirt] to become, begin
Saar lii sana hoon I've been here a year
SabaaH il-xeer Good morning
SabaaH in-nuur Good morning (reply)
Sadaf sea-shell
Sadar chest
SaHiiH true, correct
SaHra desert
SallaH/ySalliH, taSliiH to repair
SaraaHa: bi SaraaHa frankly
Saydaliyya chemist's shop, pharmacy
Sa9b difficult
Seef summer
Sghiir, pl. Sghaar small, young
SiHHa health
SubuH morning
Suura, pl. Suwar picture

shaaf/yshuuf [shuft] to see
shaami Syrian
shaari9, pl. shawaari9 street
shaay tea
shab9aan, pl. -iin full up, satiated (after a meal)
shafa/yishfi: allah yishfiik May God heal you! (to an ill person)
shaghghal/yshaghghil, tashghiil to operate, set going
shaghla, pl. -aat thing
shahar, pl. shuhuur, ashhur month
shallaal, pl. -aat waterfall
shams (f.) sun
sha'n, pl. shu'uun matter, affair
bi sha'n about, on the subject of
sharaab drink, squash
sharHa, pl. -aat slice
sharika, pl. -aat company, firm
sharq east
ish-sharq il awsaT the Middle East
sharqi eastern
sharraf/ysharrif: sharraftuuna You've honoured us (host to guest)
shaxS, pl. ashxaaS person
shayx (F), sheex old man, sheikh
sha9ar/yush9ur, shu9uur (bi ...) to feel (...)
sha9bi popular, folk

shii, pl. ashya, ashyaa' thing, something
ay shii anything, which thing?
fii shii fi ... there's something wrong with ...
shiik, pl. -aat cheque
shiish tawuk roast chicken on a spit
shimaal north, left
shirib/yishrab, shurba to drink
shismuh, shismah what's-his-name, thingummybob
shita winter, rain
shmaal north, left
shoob hot (weather)
shu? what?
shubaaT February
shugfa, pl. shugaf chunk (eg. of meat)
shughul work, occupation
shukalaaTa chocolate
shukran thank you
shukran jaziilan (F) thank you very much
shu'uun (pl. of sha'n) affairs
shurba soup, drinking
shuwarma doner kebab
shwayy, shwayya a little
shwayy shwayy slowly, gradually

taalit, f. taalta third
taamin, f. taamna eighth
taani, f. taanya, pl. taanyiin second, other
taariix, pl. tawariix date (calendar)
taasi9, f. taas9a ninth
taba9 belonging to
tabbuula salad made with cracked wheat
tadxiin smoking
tadhkira (F), tazkara ticket
tafarraj/yitfarraj, furja (9ala) to watch
tafSiil, pl. tafaSiil detail
taghadda/yitghadda to have lunch
taghyiir, pl. -aat change
taHammam/yitHammam to have a bath or shower
taHarrak/yitHarrak, Haraka to move
taHat under, below, downstairs
takayyaf/yitkayyaf, takayyuf to get used to
taksi, pl. taksiyyaat, takaasi taxi

talaaf (see **alf**) thousands
talaata three
  (yoom) it-talaata Tuesday
talaatiin 30
talaatmiyya 300
talaatta9sh 13
tamaam excellent; OK
tamaaniin 80
tamaanmiyya 800
tamaanta9sh 18
tamaanya eight
tammuuz July
tamra, pl. tamar date (fruit)
tana' 'al/yitna' 'al, tana' 'ul
  to move around
tanis tennis
tannuura, pl. tananiir skirt
ta'miin insurance
ta'riiban about, almost
tarak/yutruk, tark to leave
taSawwar/yitSawwar, taSawwur
  to imagine
taSwiir photography
tasharraf/yitsharraf: tasharraft
  I'm honoured (guest to host)
tashkiila variety, selection
tatbiila spicy dressing
taTriiz embroidery
tawaaliit, pl. -aat toilet
tawakkal/yitwakkal 9ala llah
  to put one's trust in God (see
  Unit 9)
tawqii9, pl. -aat signature
tazawwaj/yitzawwaj, zawaaj
  to get married
tazakkar/yitzakkar to remember
tazkara, pl. tazaakir ticket
ta9aala, f. ta9aali, pl. ta9aalu
  come!
ta9aawun co-operation
ta9allam/yit9allam, ta9allum
  to learn
ta9ashsha/yit9ashsha to have
  dinner or supper
ta9aTTal/yit9aTTal to break
  down
ta9baan, pl. -iin tired, not very
  well
tfaDDal, f. -i, pl. -u Be so kind.
  Come in. Please sit down. etc.
tibigh tobacco
tiina, pl. tiin fig
tikram, f. -i, pl. -u You're too
  kind
tilifoon, pl. -aat telephone
tilighraam, pl. -aat telegram
tinteen (f.) two
tisa9miyya 900
tisa9ta9sh 19

tismaH, f. -ii, pl. -uu lii Would
  you permit me?
tis9a nine
tis9iin 90
tishriin il-awwal October
  tishrin ith-thaani November
tneen, itneen two
tuffaaHa, pl. tuffaaH apple
tult a third (fraction)
turki Turkish

thaalith (F), taalit third (first,
  second, ...)
thaani (F) or (B), taani second,
  other
thalaatha (F) or (B), talaata
  three

Taabi9, pl. Tawaabi9 stamp
Taalib, pl. Tullaab, Talaba
  student
Taawla, pl. -aat table
Tab, Tayyib well, OK
Tabiib, pl. aTibbaa' (F) doctor
  Tabiib asnaan dentist
Tabii9i natural
Tab9an of course
Talab, pl. -aat order (in
  restaurant); application
Talab/yiTlub, Talab (min ...)
  to ask (...) for, order
Ta's weather, climate
Tarii', Tariiq (m. or f.), pl.
  Turu' road
Tawiil, pl. Twaal long, tall
Tayyaara, pl. -aat plane
Tayyib well, OK; kind, good-
  hearted
Tili9/yiTla9, Tuluu9 to go up,
  go out, set out, get into (bus),
  come out as
Tuul: 9ala Tuul immediately,
  straight on

u, wa (F) and
ujra fare
uktuubar October
umm, pl. ummahaat mother
  umm 9ali a sweet heavy
  pudding
urdun: il-urdun Jordan
urduni Jordanian
usbuu9, pl. asabii9 week
utiil, pl. -aat hotel
uxt, pl. ixwaat sister

wa (F), u and
waaHad, f. waHda one

waafa'/ywaafi', muwaaf'a (9ala)
to agree (to)
wadda/ywaddi to lead, take
waja9 pain
wala shii nothing
   wala maHall nowhere
walad, pl. iwlaad boy, child
wallah, wallaahi by God
wa' 'af/ywa' 'if to stop
wa't, waqt, pl. aw'aat time
wara' 9inab vine leaves
wasT centre, middle
   wasT il-balad the centre of
   town
waSSal/ywaSSil, tawSiil (9a)
to take someone to a place, give
someone a lift
waziir, pl. wuzara minister
(government)
ween where?
   ween inta? Where've you been
   (all this time)?
wi and
widd- (B), bidd- want
willa or
wiSil/yuuSal, wuSuul (la 9ind)
to arrive (at)
wizaara, pl. -aat ministry
wuquuf (F) parking

xaaf/yxaaf, xoof, [xuft] to fear,
be afraid of
xaaliS pure; completely
xaamis, f. xaamsa fifth
xaarij outside
xaaSS special
**xaaTrak: min shan xaaTrak, f.
-ik** for your sake
xabiir, pl. xubara expert
xalaaS OK, that's it
xalaS/yixlaS to finish, end
xaliij: il-xaliij the Gulf
xalla/yxalli to leave
   xalla ... yi9mal to let or make
   ... do
   allah yxalliik God preserve
   you
xallaS/yxalliS to finish something
xamasmiyya 500
xamasta9sh 15
xamiis: (yoom) il-xamiis
   Thursday
xamsa five
xamsiin 50
xaraj/yixruj, xuruuj to go out
xarrab/yxarrib, taxriib to ruin
xarTa, pl. xaraayiT map
xass lettuce
xashab wood

xaTa', pl. axTaa' mistake
xaTar danger
xaTT, pl. xuTuuT line
xeer: bi xeer (F) well
xidaama: ayy xidaama Can I
help you?
xidma service (charge)
xilaal during
   min xilaal by means of
xishin rough
xubiz bread
xud, f. -i, pl. -u (see **axad**) take!
xuDra, xuDaar vegetables
xuSuuS: bi xuSuuS concerning,
about
xuSuuSi private

yaa ... ...! (addressing someone)
yallah let's go! off you go! come
on!
yam at all, completely
yamiin right (opp. of left)
yanaayir January
ya9ni it means; 'I mean' or 'you
know'
yimkin perhaps
yoom, pl. (t)iyyaam day
   il-yoom today
yunaan: il-yunaan Greece
yuulyu July
yyaa- See Unit 8 *Grammar*

zaaki delicious
zaar/yzuur [zurt], ziyaara to
visit
zaayid plus
zaayir, pl. zuwwaar visitor
zamaan time, a long time ago
zayy like
za9laan, pl. -iin upset, annoyed
za99al/yza99il to upset, annoy
zeen (B), mniiH, kwayyis
   good, OK
zeet oil
ziina decoration
ziyaara, pl. -aat visit
zooj husband
zooja, pl. -aat wife
zrii9a plants
zwaaj, pl. ziijaat wedding

Zaahir: iZ-Zaahir it appears,
apparently
Zahar (person's) back
Zann: 9aZunni I think

9aad: leesh 9aad But why?
9aada, pl. -aat custom

9aadi ordinary, normal

9aam: kull 9aam wa antum bi xeer Happy Eid, Happy Birthday, etc.

9aamil, pl. 9ummaal worker
shu 9aamil? What are you doing?

9aamm general, public

9aarif, pl. 9aarfiin (I, you, he, she) know(s), pl. (we, you, they) know

9aashir, f. 9aashra tenth

9abba/y9abbi, ta9biya to fill in (form), fill up (tank)

9ada: maa 9ada except for

9adas lentils

9add/y9idd, 9add to count, list

9addaad, pl. -aat meter (eg. in taxi)

9afwan, il-9afu You're welcome (reply to shukran)

9ala on, against, to etc.

9alashaan because, for

9am See Unit 11, Dialogue 5

9amal, pl. a9maal work
rajul a9maal businessman

9amm, pl. a9maam uncle on father's side
yaa 9amm informal way of addressing older man

9ammaan Amman

9arabi, pl. 9arab Arab, Arabic

9arD display, showing (of film)

9asha dinner, supper

9ashaan because, for, in order to

9ashra ten

9ashsha/y9ashshi to give dinner or supper to

9aSiir fruit juice

9aSir afternoon

9aTni give me (see a9Ta)

9aTshaan, pl. -iin thirsty

9azam/yi9zim, 9uzuuma to invite

9aZiim, pl. 9uZama great

9ibaara 9an in other words, consists of

9idda: 9iddit a number of, several

9iid, pl. a9yaad festival
9iid il-fiTir festival at the end of Ramadan
9iid il-aDHa festival at the end of the pilgrimage
9iid mubaarak Happy Eid

9ilba, pl. 9ilab can, box, packet

9imil/yi9mal, 9amal to do, make

9ind with, at, at the house of

9iraaq: il-9iraaq Iraq

9irif/yi9raf, ma9rifa to know, come to know

9ishriin 20

9iyaada, pl. -aat clinic, surgery

9umaan Oman

9umur, pl. a9maar age, length of life
9umri maa shuft ... I've never seen ...

9unwaan, pl. 9anawiin address

9u'ud pl. 9u'uuda necklace

9uTul, 9uTla, pl. -aat holiday, day off
9uTlit il-usbuu9 weekend

9uTur perfume

9uzuuma, pl. -aat invitation

English–Arabic Glossary

This glossary contains the words which appear in the *Key Words and Phrases* sections of each unit, plus some items which have been added on grounds of general usefulness. Nouns are given in the singular and plural. Adjectives are given in the masculine form, and feminine and plural only if not predictable. Irregular past tenses in English, like 'went', should be looked up under the present tense (in this case 'go'). The Arabic verbs are listed with past tense form first, followed by non-past without the **b-** prefix. Phrases like 'Do you mind if...' are listed under the key word in the phrase (here 'mind').

able, (to be - to) **'idir/yi'dar**
about (= approx.) **Hawaali**
(= concerning) **bixsuSuuS**
what's the meeting about?
bixuSuuS eesh il-ijtimaa9?
above **foo'**
address **9unwaan pl. 9anaawiin**
aeroplane **Taa'ira pl. Taa'iraat**
after **ba9d + noun; ba9d maa + verb**
after breakfast **ba9d il-fTuur**
after a couple of days **ba9d yoomeen**
after he'd gone... **ba9d maa raaH...**
afternoon **ba9d iD-Duhur, il-9aSir**
afterwards **ba9deen**
again **kamaan marra**
ago **'abil, min**
a couple of days ago **'abil yoomeen, min yoomeen**
agree (to) **waafaq/ywaafiq (9ala)**
I don't agree to that **ana mish mwaafiq 9ala haada**
airport **maTaar pl. maTaaraat**
all **kull**
also **kamaan, barDuh**
always **dayman**
America **amriika**
answer **jawaab, radd**
anything **ay shii (or ay ishii)**
anything else? **shii taani?**
and **u, wa**
apple **tuffaaH**
appointment **maw9id pl. mawaa9id**
do you have an appointment?
9indak maw9id?
I'd like to make an appointment with... **biddi aaxud maw9id ma9a...**
approximately **Hawaali, ta'riiban**
April **abriil**
Arab, Arabic **9arabi**
ask (a question) **sa'al/yis'al**
I'd like to ask if... **biddi as'al iza...**

ask for **Talab/yuTlub**
as soon as **awwal maa**
as soon as he comes... **awwal maa yiiji...**
as well **kamaan**
at **fi, bi, 9ind**
he isn't at home **huwwa mish fi l-beet**
at all **bi l-marra**
I don't like it at all **maa byi9jibni bi l-marra**
attempt **Haawal/yHaawil**
August **aghustos**

bank **bank pl. bunuuk**
bad **mish kwayyis, mish mniiH**
not bad **mish baTTaal**
bath (to take a -) **taHammam/yitHammam**
bathroom **Hammaam pl. Hammaamaat**
be **kaan/ykuun**
beans **fuul**
beautiful **jamiil**
because **9alashaan**
become **Saar/ySiir**
beef **laHmit baqar**
been:
how long have you been...?
'addeesh Saar lak...
before **'abil + noun; 'abil maa + verb**
before the meeting **'abil il-ijtmaa9**
before he comes... **'abil maa yiiji...**
beforehand **min 'abil**
begin **bada/yibda; Saar/ySiir + non-past verb**
I began work today **badeet il-9amal il-yoom**
I began to like it **Sirt aHibbuh**
behind **wara**
below **taHat**
beside (= next to) **(bi) jaanib**
best **aHsan, il-aHsan**
the best one **aHsan waaHad**
the best thing **aHsan shii**

better (than) **aHsan min**
big **kbiir pl. kbaar**
bill **Hisaab**
   the bill, please **a9Tiini l-Hisaab min faDlak**
biscuit(s) **biskoot**
black **aswad, f. sooda, pl. suud**
blouse **bluuza pl. bluuzaat**
blue **azra', f. zar'a, pl. zuru'**
boiled **masluu'**
book **ktaab pl. kutub**
boss **mudiir pl. mudaraa**
bottle **'azaaza pl. 'azaazaat**
box (chocolate, etc.) **9ilba pl. 9ilab**
boy **walad pl. iwlaad**
bread **xubiz**
breakfast **fTuur**
bring **jaab/yjiib**
   bring! **haat, haati (f.)**
Britain **briiTaanya**
brown **binni**
bus **baaS pl. baaSaat**
   by bus **bi l-baaS**
   bus station/stop **maHaTTit il-baaS**
business (commerce) **a9maal**
busy **mashghuul**
but **bas, laakin**
buy **ishtara/yishtiri**

call (telephone) **ittaSal/yittaSil bi**
camel **jamal pl. jmaal**
can (verb) **mumkin; 'idir/yi'dar + non-past verb**
   can you say it slowly? **mumkin shwayy shwayy?**
   can you direct me to... **mumkin tdillni 9ala...?**
   how can I get to...? **kiif ba'dar awSal la 9ind...?**
can (container) **9ilba pl. 9ilab**
car **sayyaara pl. sayyaaraat**
chair **kursi pl. karaasi**
change (buses, money, etc.) **ghayyar/yghayyir**
cheap **raxiiS**
   is there anything cheaper? **fii ishii arxaS?**
check (= bill) **Hisaab**
chemist's shop **Saydaliyya pl. Saydaliyyaat**
chicken **dajaaj**
   roast chicken **dajaaj mHammar**
child **walad pl. iwlaad**
cigarette **sigaara pl. sagaayir**
   pack of cigarettes **9ilbit sagaayir**

chocolate **shukalaaTa**
   box of chocolates **9ilbit shukalaaTa**
church **kaniisa pl. kanaa'is**
cinema **siinama pl. siinamaat**
city **madiina pl. mudun**
   city centre **wasT il-balad**
close **sakkar/ysakkir**
closed **musakkar**
coffee (Arab) **'ahwa**
coffee (instant) **niskafee**
come (to) **aja/yiiji (9ala)**
   come on! **yallah!**
comfortable (= at ease) **mitrayyiH**
company (= business) **sharika pl. sharikaat**
cold (weather, etc.) **baarid**
   would you like a cold drink? **biddak tishrab baarid?**
complete (verb) **kammal/ykammil**
complete **kaamil**
concerning **bi n-nisba la**
congratulations! **mabruuk!**
contact **ittaSal/yittaSil bi**
convenient **munaasib**

day **yoom pl. (t)iyyaam**
   half-day (working) **nuSS in-nhaar**
December **diisambar**
dentist **Tabiib asnaan**
desk **maktab pl. makaatib**
details **tafaSiil**
diary **muzakkira pl. muzakkiraat**
different (from) **muxtalif (9an), gheer**
   take a different one **xud gheeruh**
difficult (for) **Sa9b (9ala)**
dine **ta9ashsha/yit9ashsha**
dinner **9asha**
direct (to a place) **dall/ydill (9ala)**
director **mudiir pl. mudaraa**
discuss **baHath/yibHath**
distance **masaafa**
   what's the distance from...? **kam il-masaafa min...?**
do **9imil/yi9mal**
   what are you doing? **shu 9aamil, f. 9aamila?**
doctor (medical) **Tabiib pl. aTibbaa**
door **baab pl. abwaab**
down, downstairs **taHat**
downtown **wasT il-balad**

left (opposite to right) **shmaal**
  on the left **9a sh-shmaal**
  take a left **xud shmaalak**
let **xalla/yxalli**
  let's go for a trip! **xalliina
nruuH riHla**
  don't let him do that! **maa
txalliihsh yi9mal heek**
lift (to give a - to) **waSSal/
ywaSSil**
like (= have a liking for) **Habb/
yHibb, a9jab/yi9jib**
  do you like swimming? **bitHibb
is-sibaaHa?**
  do you like Jordan? **bti9jibak
il-urdun?**
like (= want) **bidd + pronoun**
  would you like tea? **biddak
shaay?**
like (= similar to) **mitil or mithil**
  like this/that **heek**
listen **simi9/yisma9**
litre **litir pl. litraat**
little (amount) **'aliil or qaliil,
shwayya**
  a little milk **shwayyit Haliib**
live **sakan/yuskun**
  where d'you live? **ween saakin/
saakna (f.)?**
look (at) **tafarraj/yitfarraj 9ala**
  look! **shuuf, f. -i, pl. -u**
long **Tawiil**
(a) lot **ktiir**
  I like it a lot **baHibbuh ktiir**
  a lot of people **ktiir min
in-naas**
lunch **ghada**
lunch (verb) **taghadda/yitghadda**

mail **bariid**
make **9imil/yi9mal**
manager **mudiir pl. mudaraa**
man **rijjaal pl. rjaal**
  businessman **rajul a9maal pl.
rjaal a9maal**
many **ktiir**
map **xarTa pl. xarTaat**
March **maars**
market **suu' or suuq pl. aswaaq**
  vegetable market **suu' il-xuDra**
  meat market **suu' il-laHm**
married **mitzawwij**
May **maayuu**
maybe **biyjuuz, yumkin**
  maybe he'll come **biyjuuz yiiji**
mean:
  what does... mean ? **shu
ya9ni...?**
meat **laHma**

mechanic **miikaniiki**
meeting (business, etc.) **ijtimaa9
pl. ijtimaa9aat**
middle **wasT**
milk **Haliib**
mind:
  d'you mind if...? **tismaH, f. -i,
pl. -u**
minister **waziir pl. wuzaraa**
ministry **wizaara pl. wizaaraat**
minute **da'ii'a (or daqiiqa) pl.
da'aayi'**
Miss **il-aanisa**
moment:
  just a moment! **laHZa!**
Monday **(yoom) it-tneen**
money **fluus, maSaari**
month **shahar pl. ashhur**
more **aktar**
  I can't do more than that **maa
ba'darsh a9mal aktar min
heek**
morning **SabaaH or SubuH**
  good morning!
**SabaaH il-xeer!
SabaaH in-nuur! (reply)**
  in the morning **iS-SubuH**
mosque **masjid pl. masaajid**
  Friday (large) mosque
(masjid) jaami9
most **aktar shii**
  I like swimming most **baHibb
is-sibaaHa aktar shii**
movie **filim pl. aflaam**
movie-house **siinama pl.
siinamaat**
Mr. **is-sayyid**
Mrs. **is-sayyida**
much **ktiir**
museum **matHaf pl. mataaHif**
must:
  you must go **laazim truuH**

name **isim pl. asaami**
  your name (polite)? **il-isim
il-kariim**
near (to) **'ariib (min)**
  the nearest... **'a'rab...**
necessary **laazim**
need **iHtaaj/yiHtaaj ila, bidd +
pronoun**
  d'you need money? **biddak
fluus? tiHtaaj ila fluus?**
newspaper **jariida pl. jaraayid**
never **abadan**
never mind **ma9leesh**
next **jaay**
  the next time **il-marra l-jaaya**
  next year **is-sana l-jaaya**

nice **mniiH**
night **leel, leela**
  at night **bi l-leel**
  every night **kull leela**
  good night! **tiSbaH 9ala xeer!**
nine **tis9a**
nineteen **tisa9ta9sh**
ninety **tis9iin**
no **laa**
  no parking **mamuu9 il-wuquuf**
  no smoking **mamnuu9 it-tadxiin**
normal (= ordinary) **9aadi**
not **maa...sh, laa or mish**
  I don't know **mish 9aarif, f. 9aarifa**
  don't go! **maa truuHsh!**
November **nuufambar**
now **halla'**
number **raqam pl. arqaam**
  telephone number **raqam it-tilifuun**

obligatory **laazim**
occupied (= busy) **mashghuul**
o'clock:
  it's five o'clock **is-saa9a xamsa**
October **uktuubar**
of course **Tab9an**
office **maktab pl. makaatib**
official (person) **muwaZZaf pl. muwaZZafiin**
oil (for cars, etc.) **zeet**
  check the oil for me please **ifHaS lii z-zeet min faDlak**
OK (= fine!) **Tayyib! or maashi!**
  is that OK? **ma9leesh?**
on (top of) **9ala, foo'**
old (of people) **kbiir pl. kbaar**
  how old are you? **'addeesh 9umrak?**
old (of things) **'adiim or qadiim**
one **waaHad, f. waHda**
once **marra, marra waHda**
  once again **kamaan marra**
only **bas**
open **fataH/ yiftaH**
opposite (= facing) **mu'aabil or muqaabil**
or **willa**
orange **burtu'aan**
order **'amar/yu'mur**
  what's your order? **shu btu'mur?**
ordinary **9aadi**
other **taani**
outside **xaarij, barra**
owner **SaaHib, f. SaaHiba, pl. aSHaab**

pack or packet (cig's) **9ilba pl. 9ilab**
packet (biscuits) **bakeet**
Palestine **filasTiin**
Palestinian **filasTiini**
pants (= trousers) **banTaloon**
paper (piece of -) **wara'a or waraqa pl. awraaq**
pardon? **na9am?**
park (public) **Hadiiqa pl. Hadaayiq**
passport **jawaaz safar**
past:
  it's five past three **is-saa9a talaata u xamsa**
pay **dafa9/yidfa9**
pen **'alam or qalam pl. i'laam or aqlaam**
people **in-naas**
petrol **banziin**
petrol station **maHaTTit banziin**
per cent **bi l-miyya**
  ten per cent **9ashra bi l-miyya**
person **shaxS pl. ashxaaS**
pharmacy **Saydaliyya pl. Saydaliyyaat**
photograph **Suura pl. Suwar**
photography **taSwiir**
picture **Suura pl. Suwar**
place **maHall pl. maHallaat**
plan (verb) **nawa/yinwi**
  what are you planning to do? **eesh naawi ti9mal, f. naawya ti9mali?**
play (verb) **li9ib/yil9ab**
please...! (invitation) **tfaDDal, f. -i, pl. -u**
please...? (request) **iza mumkin or law samaHt, f. -i, min faDlak, f. -ik**
possible **mumkin**
postcard **kart pl. kruut**
post-office **maktab il-bariid**
present (= here) **mawjuud**
present (= gift) **hidiyya pl. hadaaya**
pretty **jamiil**
price **si9ir pl. as9aar**
  what's the price? **'addeesh is-si9ir?**
problem **mushkila pl. mashaakil, ghalaba**
prohibited **mamnuu9**
put **HaTT/yHuTT**

quarter **rubu9 pl. arbaa9**
  three-quarters **talaatt arbaa9**
question **su'aal pl. as'ila**

read **'ara or qara/yi'ra or yiqra**
I can't read Arabic well **maa
ba9rafsh a'ra 9arabi mniiH**
ready **jaahiz; musta9idd**
is the food ready? **il-akil jaahiz?**
are you ready to go? **inta
musta9idd truuH?**
reasonable **ma9'uul**
a reasonable price **si9ir ma9'uul**
red **aHmar, f. Hamra, pl.
Humur**
refridgerator **thallaaja pl.
thallaajaat**
repair **SallaH/ySalliH**
reservation **Hajiz**
reserve **Hajaz/yiHjiz**
restaurant **maT9am pl.
maTaa9im**
return **riji9/yirja9**
rice **ruzz**
ride (horse, bus, cycle) **rikib/
yirkab**
right (opposite to left) **yamiin**
on the right **9a l-yamiin**
take a right **xud yamiinak**
right (= correct) **maZbuuT,
SaHiiH**
road **Tarii' (or Tariiq) pl. Turu'
(or Turuq)**
roasted **mashwi**
room **ghurfa pl. ghuraf**
room (= space) **maHall**
there's no room **maa fii maHall**

salad **salaTa**
salary **raatib**
same **nafs**
the same thing **nafs ish-shii**
at the same time **fi nafs il-waqt**
sandwich **sandawitsh pl.
sandawitshaat**
Saturday **(yoom) is-sabt**
say (to) **'aal (or qaal)/y'uul
(or yiquul)**
school **madrasa pl. madaaris**
sea **baHar**
second (third, fourth...) **taani**
see **shaaf/yshuuf**
can I see...? **mumkin
ashuuf...?**
see what I mean? **shaayif kiif?**
self:
by myself **bi Haali**
by himself, etc. **bi Haaluh**
sell **baa9/ybii9**
send **ba9at/yib9at**
September **sabtambar**
set out (for) **Tili9/yiTla9 (9ala)**
seven **sab9a**

seventeen **saba9ta9sh**
seventy **sab9iin**
she **hiyya**
shirt **'amiiS pl, 'umSaan**
shoes (a pair of) **kundara**
shop **dukkaan pl. dakaakiin**
shower (bathroom) **duush**
silver **fiDDa**
single:
single room **ghurfa la shaxS
waaHad**
sit, sit down **'a9ad/yu'9ud;
istaraaH/yistariiH**
please sit down! **tfaDDal,
istariiH! (f.) -i**
six **sitta**
sixteen **sitta9sh**
sixty **sittiin**
skirt **tannuura pl. tananiir**
sleep (verb) **naam/ynaam**
sleep **noom**
slowly **shwayy shwayy**
small **Sghiir pl. Sghaar**
smoke **daxxan/ydaxxin**
so as to **9alashaan**
so-so **nuSS u nuSS**
sorry **mit'assif, f. mit'asfa**
speak **Haka/yiHki**
do you speak English? **btiHki
ingliizi?**
spend (time) **qaDa/yaqDi**
spend (money) **Saraf/yiSruf**
sports **riyaaDa**
stamp (postage) **Taabi9 pl.
Tawaabi9**
stand up **'aam/y'uum**
station (bus, train) **maHaTTa
pl. maHaTTaat**
stay (in hotel) **nizil/yinzil**
stay (= remain) **bi'i/yib'a**
stop **wa' 'af/ywa' 'if**
store (= shop) **dukkaan pl.
dakaakiin**
straight ahead **dughri or duuz**
go straight on **Dall dughri, f.
Dalli dughri**
street **shaari9 pl. shawaari9**
student **Taalib pl. Tullaab or
Talaba**
sugar **sukkar**
suit **naasab/ynaasib**
when would suit you? **eemta
biynaasibak?**
suit (clothes) **badla pl. badlaat**
summer **Seef**
Sunday **(yoom) il-aHad**
sweet **Hilw**
swim **sabaH/yisbaH**
swimming **sibaaHa**

swimming pool **birka**
Syria **suurya**
Syrian **suuri**

table **Tawla pl. Tawlaat**
take **axad/yaaxud**
  to take a shower **axad duush**
take (s'one s'where) **wadda/ywaddi**
  take me to the office! **waddiini l-maktab!**
tall **Tawiil pl. Twaal**
talk **Haka/yiHki**
taxi (fixed route) **sarviis**
taxi (private) **taksi xuSuuSi or sayyaarit ujra**
tea **shaay**
teach **darras/ydarris**
teacher **mudarris pl. mudarrisiin, f. mudarrisa pl. mudarrisaat**
telephone **tilifuun**
telephone (s'one) **ittaSal/yittaSil (bi...) bi t-tilifuun**
television **tilivizyuun**
tell **'aal/yi'uul la**
  I want to tell you... **biddi a'uul lak...**
ten **9ashra**
thanks **shukran**
there (= over there) **hunaak**
there is **fii**
they, them **humma, hum or hun**
thing **shii pl. ashyaa, shaghla pl. shaghlaat**
  the same thing **nafs ish-shii**
think **iftakar/yiftikir**
think (opinion):
  what d'you think of...? **shu ra'yak fi...? kiif shuft...?**
third (fourth, fifth) **taalit**
third (fraction) **tult**
  two-thirds **tulteen**
thirsty **9aTshaan**
thirteen **talaatta9sh**
thirty **talaatiin**
this/that **haada, f. haadi, pl. haadoola**
thousand **alf pl. aalaaf**
three **talaata**
Thursday **(yoom) il-xamiis**
ticket **tazkara pl. tazaakir**
  return ticket **tazkara rooHa raj9a**
time **wa't or waqt**
  I don't have time **maa 9indi wa't**
  some time ago **'abil fatra**
time (= length of) **mudda**
  a long time **mudda Tawiila**

time (= occasion) **marra pl. marraat**
  this time **hal-marra**
  (the) last time **aaxir marra**
  several times **9iddit marraat**
time (o'clock):
  what time is it? **'addeesh is-saa9a?**
time (to have a good -) **inbasaT/yinbisiT**
  we had a great time **inbasaTna ktiir**
times of opening **awqaat id-dawaam**
tired **ta9baan**
to **la**
  from... to... **min... la...**
  it's five to three **is-saa9a talaata illa xamsa**
today **il-yoom**
together (in each other's company) **sawa**
tomato(es) **banduura**
tomorrow **bukra**
  day after tomorrow **ba9d bukra**
tonight **il-leela**
too:
  that's too much **haada ktiir**
travel **saafar/ysaafir**
travel agency **wakaalit is-safariyyaat**
trip **riHla pl. riHlaat**
trouble:
  I don't want to put you to any trouble **balaash at9ibak**
trousers **banTaloon**
try **Haawal/yHaawil**
Tuesday **(yoom) it-talaata**
twelve **itna9sh**
twenty **9ishriin**
twice **marrateen**
two **itneen**

under **taHt**
understand **fihim/yifham**
  I don't understand **mish faahim, f. faahma**
university **jaami9a pl. jaami9aat**
until **la ghaayit**
unreasonable **mish ma9'uul**
upset **za9laan**
upstairs **foo'**
use **ista9mal/yista9mil**
used to (to get -) **takayyaf/yitkayyaf (9ala)**

visit (verb) **zaar/yzuur**
visit **ziyaara pl. ziyaaraat**

walk **masha/yimshi**
want:
    I want, you want, etc. **biddi,**
    biddak etc.
washing-machine **ghassaala pl.**
    ghassaalaat
watch (wrist) **saa9a pl. saa9aat**
watch **tafarraj/yitfarraj 9ala**
water **maay, maaya**
    mineral water **maay**
    ma9daniyya
we **niHna or iHna**
wear **libis/yilbas**
Wednesday **(yoom) il-arba9a**
week **usbuu9 pl. asaabii9**
    next week **il-usbuu9 il-jaay**
    last week **il-usbuu9 il-maaDi**
weekend **9uTlit il-usbuu9**
weather **jaw**
    The weather's hot **il-jaw Haarr**
welcome! hello! **ahlan wa sahlan;**
    ahlan fiik, f. -i (reply)
welcome: you're welcome! **9afwan**
    (reply to **shukran**)
west **gharb**
western **gharbi**
what? **shu or eesh?**
what is...? **shu...?**
when? **eemta?**
when (= at the time when) **lamma**
    when he comes... **lamma yiiji...**
where? **ween?**
    from where? **mineen?**
    where to? **9ala ween?**
which...? **ayy...?**
which (= that which) **illi**
white **abyaD, f. beeDa, pl. biiD**
who? **miin?**
who/whom (= the person who) **illi**
why? **leesh?**

wife **zooja, pl. zoojaat**
winter **shita**
with **bi, ma9a**
    tea with milk **shaay bi Haliib**
    I came with him **jiit ma9uh**
without **biduun**
woman **sitt pl. sittaat**
wood **xashab**
work **shughul pl. ashghaal or**
    9amal pl. a9maal
work (verb) **ishtaghal/yishtaghil,**
    9imil/yi9mal
    where d'you work? **ween**
    btishtaghil/bti9mal?
    it isn't working right **maa**
    btimshiish maZbuuT
worker **9aamil pl. 9ummaal**
would:
    what would you like? **eesh**
    bitHibb?
wrap **laff/yliff**
    wrap it up for me **liff lii yyaah**
write **katab/yiktib**
wrong **ghalaT**

year **sana pl. sanawaat or sniin**
    next year **is-sana l-jaaya**
    last year **is-sana l-maaDya**
yellow **aSfar, f. Safra, pl. Sufur**
yes **na9am, aywa, ee**
yesterday **mbaariH**
    day before yesterday **awwal**
    mbaariH
yet:
    he hasn't come yet **lissa maa**
    ajaash
you **inta, f. inti, pl. intu**
you (polite) **HaDirtak, f.**
    HaDirtik
young **Sghiir pl. Sghaar**

Breakthrough Language Packs

Complete self-study courses

Each Breakthrough Language Pack is designed as a complete self-study course using audio cassettes and a course book. Each pack contains:

* Three 60- or 90-minute audio cassettes or CDs
* The course book

Breakthrough Language Packs available:

Breakthrough Arabic	ISBN 0–333–56692–0
Breakthrough French	ISBN 0–333–48191–7
Breakthrough German	ISBN 0–333–56730–7
Breakthrough Greek	ISBN 0–333–48714–1
Breakthrough Italian	ISBN 0–333–48179–8
Breakthrough Russian	ISBN 0–333–55726–3
Breakthrough Spanish	ISBN 0–333–57105–3
Breakthrough Further French	ISBN 0–333–48193–3
Breakthrough Further German	ISBN 0–333–48189–5
Breakthrough Further Spanish	ISBN 0–333–48185–2
Breakthrough Business French	ISBN 0–333–54398–X
Breakthrough Business German	ISBN 0–333–54401–3
Breakthrough Business Spanish	ISBN 0–333–54404–8

* CD Packs are also available for

Breakthrough French	ISBN 0–333–58513–5
Breakthrough German	ISBN 0–333–57870–8
Breakthrough Spanish	ISBN 0–333–57874–0